Published by

ATLANTIC

PUBLISHERS & DISTRIBUTORS (P) LTD

7/22, Ansari Road, Darya Ganj, New Delhi-110002
Phones : +91-11-40775252, 40775214, 23273880, 23275880
Fax : +91-11-23285873
Web : www.atlanticbooks.com
E-mail : orders@atlanticbooks.com

Branch Office: Chennai
Phones : +91-44-48531784, 28291383
E-mail : chennai@atlanticbooks.com

Printed & bound in India by Atlantic Print Services

Acknowledgements

It is a matter of great pleasure for me to acknowledge the overarching support received from my family, teachers, colleagues and friends for completing the book. Special thanks are due to my mentors Prof. Pralay Kanungo and Prof. Rahul Mukherji for their consistent guidance and motivation. I was also supported by books and the required reading material by them that were either unavailable in the Indian libraries or inaccessible in the market. I would specially like to thank Mrs. Niraja Tripathi and Dr. Sharad Mani Tripathi without whose intervention fixing interviews with the managers and professionals in the IT firms in Noida, Bengaluru, Gurugram was not possible. On a similar note, I would like to acknowledge the help extended by Mr. Rajiv Ranjan, Spurti Didi and Mrs. Anjoo Tripathi in providing me a series of contact in the IT companies. I am really indebted to all of them for having made the fieldwork a successful exercise.

My colleague and friend Sudhir has extended tremendous help in styling of the document. He has been a great support throughout the exercise. Thanks to all my colleagues Prof. Ripu Sudan Singh, Prof. Sartik Bagh, Dr. S.K. Pandey and Dr. Preety Choudhary who have always stood by me in my efforts and have constantly motivated me in this academic venture. Their valuable inputs from time to time also helped me sharpen my arguments.

My biggest source of inspiration for this entire exercise is none other than my mother Mrs. Chandana Mukherji. Right from the beginning she showed me the right path to achieve this goal. She has been a friend, guide and a guardian in every moment of difficulty, hardship and success of my book-writing. I also feel delighted to acknowledge the consistent support and motivation of my sister Sanyukta and bother-in-law Abhinav all through the process.

Finally, I dedicate this book to my father late Dr. Rajeev Mukherji seeking his blessings for this and my future academic endeavours.

Siddhartha Mukerji

Contents

Abbreviations

ADR	American Depository Receipt
APSWAN	AP State Wide Area Network
BJP	Bhartiya Janata Party
BOP	Balance of Payment
BPO	Business Process Outsourcing
BSNL	Bharat Sanchar Nigam Ltd
CAGR	Compound Annual Growth Rate
CCP	Communist Party of China
CMC	Computer Maintenance Corporation Pvt. Ltd
CPI	Communist Party of India
CST	Central Sale Tax
DGTD	Directorate General of Technical Development
DIT	Department of Information Technology
DoE	Department of Electronics
DoT	Department of Telecommunications
DPCO	Drug Price Control Order
DTA	Domestic Tariff Area
ECIL	Electronics Corporation of India Limited
EOU	Export Oriented Unit
EPCG	Export Promotion Capital Goods

EPZ	Export Processing Zone
EXIM	Export and Import Bank
FDI	Foreign Direct Investment
FERA	Foreign Exchange Regulation Act
FOB	Free on Board
GDR	Global Depository Receipt
ICL	International Computers and Tabulators
ICT	Information and Communication Technology
IIM	Indian Institute of Management
IISc	Indian Institute of Science
IIT	Indian Institute of Technology
IPR	Intellectual Property Rights
ISTDC	Information Security Technology Development Council
ITA	Indian Telegraph Act
ITES	Information Technology Enabled Services
KPO	Knowledge Process Outsourcing
MAT	Minimum Alternate Tax
MIS	Management Information System
MIT	Ministry of Information Technology
MOST	(Ministry of Science and Technology) - China
MRTP	Monopoly Trade Restrictive Practices
MTNL	Mahanagar Telephone Nigam Limited
MGNREGA	Mahatma Gandhi National Rural Employment Guarantee Act
NASSCOM	National Association of Software and Service Companies
NDA	National Democratic Alliance
NeGP	National E-Governance Plan
NPPA	National Pharmaceuticals Pricing Authority

OGL	Open General License
PDS	Public Distribution System
R&D	Research & Development
S&T	Science & Technology
SAP	Structural Adjustment Programme
SEEPZ	Santa Cruz Electronics Export Processing Zone
SEZ	Special Economic Zone
SME	Small and Medium Enterprise
STP	Software Technology Park
STQC	Standard, Testing and Quality Certification
TCS	Tata Consultancy Services
Trg & Dev	Training and Development
TRIPS	Trade Related Intellectual Property Rights
UI	User Interface design
UID	Unique Identity Project
VAT	Value Added Tax
VLSI	Very Large Scale Integration Design
VSNL	Videsh Sanchar Nigam Limited
WAN	Wide Area Network

Introduction

With the growth of information and communication technology it became easy to connect even the remotest corners of the world. The process of globalization was facilitated by the emergence of IT & software worldwide. This helped on several fronts like international business, expansion of service sector, cultural amalgamation, education and banking. The addition of prefix 'e' meaning electronics to a whole range of public activities like e-governance, e-business, e-banking, e-ticketing, e-mail, and so on carried out by the government and the private sector led to a far smoother delivery of public services. With the development of ICT (information and communication technology) it was now possible to deliver services without being present at the client site. IT & software therefore emerged as a highly lucrative and profitable business in the international market.

For any modern economy, it became essential to promote the computer industry as computer technology could enhance productivity and efficiency in a variety of economic activities. The unprecedented breakthrough in microelectronic technology led to the emergence of new products in the market characterized by high levels of efficiency, reliability, and versatility. The convergence of electronics, computing, and telecommunications also referred to as the 'New Industrial Revolution' or the 'Information Technology Revolution' brought significant transformation in the organizational structure of industrial activities. For India, it became important to develop the industry on priority basis, as both Western and the newly industrialized countries in East Asia had already attained high level of efficiency in several technology-driven sectors. However, being a late-industrializing nation, the guidance of state became crucial for the development and promotion of nascent but prospective sectors. In accordance with this belief, the software sector stood alone to receive maximum governmental support for its growth since the mid-1980s. Being an export-oriented industry, the policy incentives were extended to support not only the large firms but also the newcomers in the SME (small and medium enterprises) segment.

As a result of a continuous support extended by the government through its STPI scheme, the decade of 2000s witnessed unprecedented growth of the Indian software services sector in the international market. A NASSCOM report observes that the IT-BPO (business process outsourcing) sector is estimated to generate revenues of $88.1 billion by the end of the FY 2011 with IT and software service sector accounting for nearly $76.1 billion. While its contribution towards national GDP increased from 1.2% in 1998 to 6.4% in 2011, its share in total Indian exports witnessed a steep rise from less than 4% in 1998 to 26% in 2011. Additionally, direct employment in the sector is estimated to be nearly 2.5 million in the current financial year[1] (NASSCOM website). The IT and software sector has therefore been a purely export-driven sector with very little incentive for its expansion in the domestic market. This phenomenon could be gauged through the fact that the revenue generated from the domestic market was barely $14 billion in FY 2009-10[2] (Annual Report 2009-10, Ministry of Information and Communication Technology).

Policy developments in the electronics industry in the early-1970s came to identify the significance of the software component and felt the need to pay special attention to it. But, the political circumstances that favoured the establishment of public-sector monopoly were not conducive for the growth of

1. www.nasscom.in (official website of NASSCOM).
2. *Annual Report 2009-10*, Department of Information Technology, Ministry of Information and Communication Technology, Government of India.

private entrepreneurship in computer and electronics industry. The socialist agenda of the government prioritized public-sector driven industrialization, thereby putting several restrictions on private investment, production and capacity expansion. To begin with, with the passage of Industrial Development and Regulation Act of 1951 the government under the leadership of Nehru took necessary steps for the development of certain basic and key industries, regulating the pattern and direction of industrial development and controlling the activities of industrial undertakings in public interest. The Industrial Policy Resolution of 1956 made a forceful plea for public sector-driven industrialization as it stated that, "The adoption of the socialist pattern of economy as the national objective, as well as the need for planned and rapid development, require that all industries of basic and strategic importance, or the nature of public utility services, should be in the public sector." Currently these Acts are being administered by the Department of Industrial Policy and Promotion in the Ministry of Commerce and Industry.

The industrial policies were modelled on the principles of import-substitution industrialization the fundamental thrust of which was to ensure protection to the public sector from external competition. The ISI strategy also favoured capital-intensive industrialization necessitating heavy investments to develop some of the basic or key industries like iron, steel and coal.

Industrial regulation and control was made even more stringent under the leadership of Indira Gandhi with the advancement of industrial licensing, nationalization of commercial banks and industries, passage of restrictive Acts like MRTP (Monopoly Trade Restrictive Practices) and FERA (Foreign Exchange Regulation Act), heavy taxation, import restrictions, and so on. Also, the industrial policies of the government encumbered the private sector with a spate of restrictions on capacity expansion and investment in new industrial projects. Under nationalization drive during Indira Gandhi's regime public sector companies made inroads and captured areas that were previously open for private sector investment. Overall, the industrial policies during Indira Gandhi's first tenure followed three important trends enlisted below:

1. Public sector dominance vis-à-vis private sector
2. Restriction and regulation of private sector
3. Import-substitution industrialization

The general policy shift towards liberalization and market economy initiated since the mid-1980s was inspired by the achievements of East Asian countries like South Korea, Taiwan, Singapore, Malaysia, Japan, and China (at a later stage) that adopted open door policies to derive the benefits accruing from global integration of their economies. Globalization that involved integration of the economies worldwide encouraged the newly-industrializing nations to embark upon high-tech areas of production and investment like electronics and telecommunications. This provided them with a competitive edge in the international market over advanced industrial economies of the West. Export-led growth thus became the principle strategy for industrial growth in the East Asian Countries. The success of these countries in their electronics sector where the state took multiple initiatives to promote the export-oriented firms not only indicated how newly-industrializing nations could make their presence felt in the technologically-driven global market but also necessitated qualitative intervention of the state in the market by establishing a corporatist pattern of relationship with private business.

In this background, the software industry in India embarked on a developmental path with a solid back-up of the state. As a result, it becomes absolutely pertinent to understand its development trajectory from a political economy perspective in following ways:

1. State support was crucial for the promotion of emerging software firms in India. However, this resulted in a changed political context in which a technocratic leadership along-with a supportive bureaucracy favoured liberalization and private investment in technology-intensive sectors.
2. Global integration and the momentous growth of the software and IT sector after 1991 could well be understood in terms of consistent state support for

the export-oriented software firms and the political collaboration between the Ministry of IT and NASSCOM, the umbrella organization for software and business services industry.

3. Being a globally integrated sector its developments are driven by the prevailing political and economic conditions in the client country. So politics in the client countries becomes relevant to understand the growth prospects of the IT and software industry in the host country.

In India, the necessity of developing the software sector was realized by a technocratic political leadership way back in the 1980s. Although the growing potential of software was well identified and recognized by the policy-makers in the early-1970s, it was not accorded the status of an independent industry until the mid-1980s. Also, the political regime during the mid-1970s prioritized the strengthening of public sector enterprises through import-substitution industrialization. As a result, despite recognizing the export potential of the software sector the government did not provide any special incentive for its promotion in the international market. In fact, software industry being a part of the electronics industry faced the brunt of several regulations and controls.

Therefore, the real story of software development in India began during 1980s. It was identified as an industrial sector having an independent status and a strong export potential, therefore becoming a recipient of special benefits by the government since the mid-1980s. The political environment during the 1980s was generally conducive for the start-up of technology-intensive sectors of the industry like software, telecommunications, biotechnology and electronics hardware as the major focus of the industrial policy was on induction of sophisticated technology that was largely missing in Indian industry. Industrial liberalization thus facilitated rapid proliferation of such sectors. While few of them like telecommunications still faced the brunt of excessive bureaucracy and indiscriminate regulatory checks, others like biotechnology and software flourished in an exhortive political and administrative environment. However during the late-1980s, the opposition parties and the old guards of the Congress party who preferred maintaining status quo did not leave any chance to disparage the liberal policies for the software industry. Liberalization was still politically unacceptable by dint of adherence to the fundamentals of socialism by a large section of leaders in both Congress and opposition parties. Therefore, software policies during the late-1980s were largely driven by the influence of domestic politics that made it difficult to resolve the contradiction between socialism-driven industrial policy and liberalization of trade policies. Policy backtrack imposing checks on import liberalization and reduction of tax benefits is well indicative of this phenomenon.

The advent of globalization alongside liberalization since 1991 necessitated special incentives for the promotion of export-oriented sectors like computer software. The structural changes in the economy that followed in response to the BOP (balance of payment) crisis provided a strong impetus for this. It facilitated the creation of new institutions like STPs (software technology park) that provided new windows of opportunity to prospective export-oriented software firms. The establishment of NASSCOM (National Association of Software and Service Companies) as an umbrella organization for software and services companies strengthened the link between the private industry and the government. NASSCOM has been able to develop wide networks with the government at the Centre and the states, foreign companies, and several other sectors of the domestic industry. It has emerged as a close associate of the Ministry of IT providing continuous information about the requirements, successes and challenges facing the software and services industry. The analysis of the role of NASSCOM and its collaboration with the ministries, concerned Departments and state governments therefore becomes critical to the understanding of policy shifts in the software industry.

The software policies in the post-1991 period entirely focused its attention on global integration of the industry by extending every possible incentive to the export-oriented software firms. But was export promotion which finally resulted in excessive dependence on the US market the right strategy for growth?

Globalization puts limits to the exercise of state autonomy in taking policy decisions. Often the governments led by the requirements of global market tend to frame policies that are dictated by the terms and conditions of the external players and institutions. Policy decisions are therefore not taken independently. Inordinate liberalization to promote private capital undermines regulation and control which are necessary for the sustenance of capitalism itself. However, loss of state autonomy has deleterious repercussions for the economy as a whole. It leads to lob-sided sectoral growth benefitting only certain sections of consumers in the society. The compulsions of global integration act as a deterrent in taking free decisions and the boundaries that the state maintains with social forces tends to get blurred. But, this does not necessarily work to the advantage of local firms. Excessive dependence may produce short-term business advantages but will surely show its ill effects in the longer-run.

Software sector being one of the most globally-integrated sectors of the Indian economy also faced the brunt of global economic crisis. Its dependence on the global market has made it vulnerable to the pressures of the foreign clients located mostly in United States. An attempt is therefore made to understand how global integration or excessive dependence on international trade particularly with United States increases the vulnerability of an industrial sector. Economic downturn in the globally-oriented advanced countries that causes policy instabilities and thus political uncertainties disturbs the business links with the developing counterparts. The situation becomes even more precarious when the state in the developing countries itself succumbs to the pressures of global economy and fails to adopt necessary regulatory and protectionist measures to reduce such vulnerability.

Such dependence has also led to certain predicaments related with innovation, technological capabilities, telecommunication bottlenecks, body shopping, and brain drain. On one side, the private companies seems to have taken little effort in moving up the global value chain, on the other the state has not initiated any policy incentive for retaining its talented engineers and attract those working in US and Europe for a comeback to the home country. There has also been little debate within the state and parliament regarding these bottlenecks that have considerably impeded the attainment of greater innovative capacities by the Indian software firms. An attempt is made to highlight some of these key issues and trace the history of policy developments since mid-1980s to account for the impact of path dependence on the existing policies. In addition, the interplay of interests of state and non-state actors and articulation of such interests in the policy-making process will also help understand the political context of policy shifts in the software industry.

The existing literature on industrial policies of governments in developing countries has primarily focused on the impact of domestic politics on the growth prospects of certain industrial sectors. Its fundamental concern has been to locate the possibilities of industrial growth in the context of varied forms of state-capital alliance. Substantiating their argument on the achievement of the developmental goals through state-private sector collaboration, the Neo-statist advocates cite the developmental achievements of East Asian economies. However, they fail to recognize that state's role takes different forms in the context of globalization. A comparative study of the role of developmental state requires a broader understanding of the external dynamics of the global market, internal political economy dynamics of the developed countries (client country) as well as the internal political economy dynamics of the developing country (offering services). The interplay of these factors determines the trajectory of policy developments.

The benefits of globalization become visible only when the state adopts appropriate regulatory measures particularly for export-oriented sectors of the economy like that of software. Uncontrolled globalization often gives rise to new kinds of predicaments. The Indian economy has been largely driven by global forces since 1991. While the domestic market in certain sectors like automobiles and electronics have been dominated by multinational companies, software entrepreneurs have looked forward to the international market for their growth prospects. However, when the focus of a sector like software which has a significant role to play in meeting the developmental goals as well becomes completely export-oriented to accrue the benefits of globalization its growth story becomes superficial. As Avgerou points out that, "ICT has potentially the capacity to contribute to the improvement of various aspects of life from alleviating poverty to strengthening the democratic polity.... But not ICT research in developing countries explicitly with questions of development as action to transform the socio-economic conditions"[3] (Avgerou 2010: 5). R&D in the globally-oriented software firms remains abysmally low as a result of which only few big companies can celebrate the success on the technological front. Moreover, little effort seems to have been taken by the government and private companies to channel the available technologies for local developmental purposes until very recently. A critical review of the existing scholarly works will help understand the external and internal political economy dynamics of software policies. It will help locate different forms of state action in the context of its relations with the domestic entrepreneurs who are dependent on the global market for the sustainability of their business.

Several questions need to be addressed in order to get a clear understanding about policy developments in the computer software and IT industry and to account for the political basis of policy shifts since 1970s to the present times. Firstly, the marked shift towards policy liberalization in the 1980s requires an analysis of the smoothness with which the bureaucratic interests were transformed within the electronics industry. Concomitantly, the close-knit collaboration between political leadership in the PMO and the DoE facilitated policy shifts without any visible opposition. In connection to this, it becomes relevant to understand how policies favouring export-promotion created groundwork for the future growth of the industry? Also, what led to a slight policy backtrack from incentive-based export promotion in the late-1980s? Why did opposition parties and some Congress members show apprehension towards government policies on import liberalization and tax incentives?

---

3. Chrisanthi Avgerou, "Discourses on ICT and Development", *Information Technology and International Development*, Fall 2010, vol. 6, no. 3, p. 5.

The institutional framework that provided a business-friendly environment during the 1990s raises several questions about political linkages between state-level institutions and business organizations. In this regard, it becomes relevant to understand how Department of Electronics and NASSCOM, the umbrella organization for the software and service companies came together to initiate the STP scheme which was started in the early-1990s? Later, the continuous engagement between NASSCOM and the newly-constituted Ministry of Information and Communication Technology led to significant policy decisions like extension of the term of tax exemption for IT firms operating in STPs. Other than this, how did such institutional collaboration and concomitant pressures over other political bodies facilitated liberalization in the telecom sector that in-turn created possibilities for faster data communication links in STPs at competitive prices?

The next set of questions relate to the impact of an exaggerated export-oriented policy programme for growth prospects of the software firms. Has there been any political disagreement either between political parties or even the respective ministries regarding heavy reliance of the Indian software industry on the US companies for its business? It appears that the state was more sensitive to policies like import liberalization and tax incentive in the late-1980s and the principle of checks and balances was widely employed to see that a balance was maintained between regulation and promotion. Moreover, policies favoring and supporting global integration of the software industry created new kinds of challenges before the domestic software firms. Did it nurture the firms in such a way that they moved up the value-chain in technological innovation? Did lack of R&D and absence of large turnkey projects result in lob-sided growth of the industry? Also, since the IT sector is largely dependent on the US market for its business, how has the recent economic meltdown and political uproar over IT outsourcing affected the prospects of the Indian IT industry? This leads us to a related question: Is re-introduction of regulatory provisions like discontinuing tax exemption and other infrastructural support a response to new global dynamics (a rising wave of protectionism in the West particularly United States)? What is the opinion of our private industry on the government decision of terminating tax benefits within STPs?

The role of state is central to the understanding of policy shifts in the software industry. Since 1980s a corporate relation between the state and private business resulted in institutional innovations like the STPI scheme. But do policies promoting exports without any checks and balances make the state genuinely corporatist? A corporatist state, as it developed in countries like Japan and South Korea, produced a mutually beneficial relation between the state and local capital. While the state provided monopoly of representation to certain prospective electronic and automobile companies by extending tax benefits and subsidies, the state expected overall support and assistance from them in its developmental programmes and projects.

In view of these questions, I make an attempt to locate the possible political linkages between state and the software industry individually and at the organizational level (NASSCOM)—areas of conflict and cooperation—to analyze its impact on policy-making and regulations. Secondly, a comparative study of varied forms of state interventions in India, China and South Korea to promote their ICT sector enables us to understand the Indian state and its economic role in a more systematic manner. I further identify and explain the political context of policy shifts in broadly two phases; the 1970s and the 1980s and rapid developments towards global integration in 1990s and 2000s. The political contexts become critical in the understanding of liberalization in 1980s, policy backtracks in the late-1980s, indiscriminate opening-up since the early 1990s especially after the emergence of NASSCOM and a possible return to protectionism and a development-oriented strategy of e-governance most recently. While locating these shifts I shall look into the success of one of the major innovative schemes of the government, the STPI that undoubtedly was a brainchild of DoE and NASSCOM.

The second phase of policy development, as highlighted, witnessed several challenges confronting the industry as a result of globalization. The emerging problems and concerns could be located in the internal functioning of the software firms and BPOs which left little scope for innovation for the software employees and the externalities associated with the impact of an uncertain and precarious global market on growth and technological upliftment of the Indian firms. I shall explore these predicaments by an analysis of the nature of business and technical services offered by the Indian IT firms and BPOs as this would signify the nature of employment or the position of the Indian software industry in the international division of labor—the story of structural dependence of Indian software and services industry on the US economy. In addition to this, major policies and programmes of the government to ensure rapid development of the industry in the international market and measures to meet the impending challenges coming from the highly competitive global market will be understood critically.

In the last decade, the business prospects of the IT industry came under serious threat not simply because of the global economic downturn but also due to certain political developments in United States, the biggest market for India's IT and BPO companies. Outsourcing to Indian companies especially in the area of white-collar jobs threw up serious concerns over job losses in the local market. The employee's associations held the government responsible for shipping American jobs abroad and clearly cited the failure of government policies in checking unemployment. The issue got seriously politicized when the Democrat Party used outsourcing as a political plank for opposing the anti-people and pro-outsourcing programmes of the government during the Presidential elections. After two Presidential terms of George Bush, when Democrats assumed the charge of the Presidential office under the leadership of Barrack Obama, it promised to live up to its promises of creating employment by restriction outsourcing. Many of its restrictive policies like the Immigration bill, new visa policies and others send shock waves in India. The IT companies and its umbrella organization NASSCOM showed serious apprehensions over rising protectionism in US.

These developments in US politics were also supplemented by attempts of the Indian government to terminate the tax benefits that were extended to the export-oriented firms in STPs. Also, it was during the same time that the government introduced e-governance programmes and other IT-oriented schemes seeking the partnership of private companies for domestic development. Does this also mark a shift in strategy of the government—a shift from export-promotion to indigenous development and a re-orientation of IT policies focusing more on internal progress than external growth? Is it a temporary safeguard to protect the IT companies from the dangers of protectionism in United States? These questions need to be plumbed to see how recent policy shifts, if at all they are policy shifts, provide a haven for the IT companies to explore its business opportunities within the country and reduce its dependence on the American market which is, both economically and politically, a bit too volatile for a stable business.

The central argument is that the state played the role of a 'guardian' in the development of computer industry in the 1980s maintaining a perfect balance between promotion and regulation through its policies. Inordinate import liberalization that was seen to be detrimental for an economy which was already witnessing deterioration in the balance of payment situation was met with stiff political opposition. As a result, regulatory checks and restrictions were re-imposed during the policies of 1980s. With global integration of the Indian software industry accompanied by loss of state autonomy with the state moving away from a balanced-developmental strategy to a lob-sided growth strategy since 1991 has increased the dependence and vulnerability of the software industry. These vulnerabilities can be understood both internally and externally—internally by the inferior nature of jobs performed for the US companies and issues of employee's freedom within the industry; and externally by the impact of global economic downturns and a protectionist political regime in the United States on the growth prospects of the Indian software and IT industry.

Methodology

The book primarily involves the study of policy developments in the software sectors from a historical perspective. It adopts an analytical, historical approach to account for the policy shifts in the software sector. Furthermore, to analyze the nature of state intervention and state autonomy and its implications for the growth of electronics sector, particularly computer sector in India, China and South Korea a comparative method is used.

Reference to Five-year Plans, Annual Reports of Ministry of Information Technology, and Committee Reports have been made to get policy-level data. To acquire political opinions on policy shifts and regulations, Lok Sabha debates on relevant subjects have been looked at. Other than this, reference has been made to NASSCOM Reports, particularly 'Strategic Review', the Annual Report published by NASSCOM to get the perspective of the industry and relevant data on the growth of the IT-BPO sector. It was difficult to secure English translations of several government reports of China and South Korea. Similar difficulty was faced in getting data on growth aspects documented by the concerned industrial organizations in these countries. As a result, the required information and data had to be secured from secondary sources and websites. The secondary sources include relevant books, journal articles and newspaper reports and documentations.

To establish the causal linkage between the role and nature of state-functioning in varying political contexts and the impact on the development trajectory of the IT/software sector and to locate the perspective of the corporate industry on the past and present policies and regulations, the research involved conducting formal interviews of the CEOs (Chief Executive Officer), MDs (Managing Director), and software professionals in various software firms. A questionnaire was prepared to seek opinions on innovative capacities; policy bottlenecks; foreign collaborations; nature of tasks performed for the foreign clients and any change in this regard; future plans for expanding exports to other nations; level of state support for innovative investments and telecommunications; and government schemes like STPs and SEZs, its benefits and shortcomings. The interviews were conducted in some of the major IT destinations of India like Noida, Gurugram, Bengaluru, Pune and New Delhi. It involved either face-to-face interaction or in some cases communication through e-mail. The second mode of communication was adopted as many interviewees preferred to respond through e-mail. The respondents were selected from companies of all levels, i.e. the larger ones, SMEs (small and medium enterprise) located in STPs and SEZs (special economic zone), and also those who were members of NASSCOM. The underlying objective was to seek inputs from different strata of the software industry. Some informal conversations with the software professionals at all levels of companies were conducted to get their opinions on the work culture and the level of satisfaction with management. This was based on non-participant method of observation.

Framework of Chapters

The book has been divided into five chapters. Following the introduction of the research problem, research objectives and other relevant sections in the introductory chapter, the second chapter of the book critically analyzes the dominant theoretical positions on the subject of state and industrialization in developing countries. It also analyzes the developmental trajectories of developed and developing countries as rooted in their historical contexts. To begin with, I cite the works of Neo-classical scholars like Thomas Friedman and Jagdish Bhagwati who make a forceful advocacy for free enterprise at the global level and the need for developing countries to venture into innovative areas of private investment for achieving high growth rates. This theory highlights the success stories of East Asian countries to show how the state supported and encouraged private investment in the emerging electronics sector of these countries and resorted to export-promotion strategy; while others like India and Russia adopted protectionism and supported public-sector monopoly with undesirable consequences for industrialization and economic growth.

An alternative explanation is offered by Neo-statist theorists like Peter Evans, Robert Wade and Alice Amsden who give a different viewpoint about the East Asian story stating that the success was more a result of qualitative control by the state on private business. But this theory also falls short of locating the global economic and political dynamics that interlink with domestic politics to produce varied policy outcomes. In the light of the theories attempting to understand the advantages and constrains of globalization on state's policies, I will offer an explanation of both internal and external political economy dynamics of policy-making in the context of globalization discussing the role and nature of state intervention to strike a balance between regulation and liberalization.

Chapter 3 understands the role of state in promoting electronics particularly computer sector in India, China and South Korea from a comparative perspective. The logic of comparison is that all three Asian countries are now leading players in the global market for electronics and computers (hardware or software). To begin with, the levels of development was much the same during the initial stages but over a period of time South Korean economy excelled much faster than the other two countries. Today, China also provides a stiff competition to India in many sectors. India certainly has an advantage over China in the IT-BPO sector with its pool of skilled-English speaking young professionals. But, today the Chinese state has tried to overcome these disabilities by introducing English-speaking courses for its engineers and software professionals. The state has also attracted its engineers working in United States by providing several incentives for reverse brain drain. India is still less likely to give such attractive packages. These identifiable differences in the strategies and goals of the state for development require systematic comparison which is what the aim of this chapter is.

Chapter 4 traces the policy history of the software industry in India. The decades of 1970s and 1980s have been covered in this chapter. This chapter analyzes the political context in which the software industry emerged as a focal point for policy-makers. It also understands the policy backtracks and regulations during the late-1980s and the political reasons behind it. It explains the guardian role of state in promoting software development by striking a balance between promotion and regulatory checks by controlling excessive liberalization. In addition, the chapter will try to show how a smooth transition in the ideas and interests of bureaucracy combined with the active promotional strategies of a technocratic leadership facilitated the process of liberalization in the software sector.

As the year 1991 signifies an important juncture in the history of Indian economy, it also proves to be a landmark for the future growth of the software industry. In view of this major development, Chapter 5 accounts for the policy and institutional developments since 1991 to the present time and the consequent growth of export-oriented firms during this period. Considering telecom links as one of the major infrastructural requirements of the software and IT sector, the chapter also discusses the genesis of regulatory institutions in the telecom sector. It covers the entire gamut of issues and challenges facing the software sector as a result of globalization and absence of state control over certain areas of critical concern. It shows how a transformative state in the context of globalization provided incentives for export-promotion without any visible attempt to ensure technological innovation, greater investment in in-house R&D, and absence or partial application of IT solutions for local development and good governance till very recently. The chapter will delve into the role of NASSCOM that assumed enough political clout through its engagement at multiple governmental levels for pushing through critical policy changes. The influence of NASSCOM in policy-making on IT promotion and education has become exceedingly high since its inception in the late-1980s. Overall, the chapter provides a comprehensive picture of state support for global integration and how IT sector was singled out to receive maximum institutional support for export-promotion.

Chapter 5, mainly based on the inputs received through an interview-based fieldwork explores the opinions, views and perspectives of the private sector on the impact of globalization, state regulation, policies in general, and the future prospects of growth. Providing a background on how these issues emerge as a challenge before the industry, the Chapter delves into how the private industry thinks about it. Opinions were sought on areas of critical concern like work culture, human resources, IT education, competition from China and other Asian countries, outsourcing, technological capabilities, and R&D. The chapter shows how internationalization of the industry and dependence on the US market particularly for its outsourcing business has increased the vulnerability of the Indian software industry in the international market. This is followed by the conclusion that summarizes the argument by drawing inferences about how policy shifts and checks, and balances has determined the path of development of the Indian software during different periods of time. Accordingly, it points out the major policy trends for the software industry during various stages of its development.

Chapter 1

State and Industrial Transformation: Theories and Criticality

Introduction

The comparative literature that emerged in the recent past has aroused focused attention on the subject matter of state and industrial transformation in the developing world. In view of comparative understanding, the role of state in terms of its relationship with social forces has been redefined. Change in political regimes in response to the changing socio-economic conditions has produced varied forms of economic policy and industrialization strategies. Comparative studies have clearly highlighted such variations where, forms of state intervention have been analyzed in highly restrictive regimes of India and USSR to relatively liberalized governments in East Asian countries like South Korea, Singapore, Taiwan and Malaysia. In contemporary world, most states fall somewhere between the continuum of no intervention to very high intervention. Irrespective of such variations, all government require consistent revision of their policies in responses to the changing dynamics of the global market. Adoption of new strategies and methods to improve economic performance under global competitive pressures is a matter of continuous practise in all political regimes.

The Chapter begins with a comparative analysis of industrial trajectories in developed and developing economies to account for the reasons behind the differences in levels of development and the models of industrial development adopted by them.

Studies on state and industrial transformation have been reviewed critically in the light of contemporary developments in state-capital relationship. Most of the scholarly works cite the case of East Asian countries in accounting for the differences in rates of success. The last part of chapter situates the Indian software industry within the given theoretical frameworks to locate the gaps in the explanations.

Paths of Industrial Development

The developed and developing countries have followed different paths of industrialization. The political and historical contexts in which the industrialization drive started in these countries resulted in different forms of state intervention in the economy. Industrial revolution that was initiated in England in the 16th century became widely established in the rest of Europe in due course of time. The fundamental force behind it was the emerging middle class also referred to as the bourgeoisie class by Marx and his contemporaries. Therefore, industrial modernization that brought tremendous progress in the West European countries was one of the stages in their path of development. In other words, the natural course of development brought in modernization.

Even within the European world the patterns of industrialization have differed and have therefore taken different routes. Alexander Gerschenkron in his famous work 'Economic Backwardness in Historical Perspective' has examined such differences between the early and late-industrializing nations in Western and Eastern Europe. Comparing the patterns of industrialization in Britain, Germany and Russia Gerschenkron observes that, "Early industrializers like Great Britain could attribute their success to the original accumulation of capital by private entrepreneurs, late industrializers like Germany attributed their success to investment banks, and late-late industrializers like Russia found success in state-led industrialization practices"[1] (Gerschenkron 1962: 13).

1. Alexander Gerschenkron (1962), *Economic Backwardness in Historical Perspective*, Harvard University Press, p. 13.

The developing countries have followed a different historical trajectory experiencing colonialism which became a fundamental determinant of their future course of industrialization and modernization. The colonial drive was initiated by Europe and Japan in search for new markets, cheap labour and raw materials that was easily available in resource-rich countries of Asia, Africa and Latin America. In view of this, these countries were brought under colonial rule at different historical junctures. Under colonial rule, their wealth and natural resources were exploited to meet the requirements of the industries back home. Henceforth, as the Dependency theory argues, underdevelopment was artificially created through colonialism. It did not mark a historical phase in the natural course of transition from one pattern of production to the other, as observed in Western countries. As the historical contexts of industrialization were different in developed and developing countries the nature and extent of modernization also followed dissimilar routes.

However, at this juncture the developing countries came in contact with the industrially advanced countries of the world. Colonial exploitation of their natural resources was accompanied by a positive development which was the introduction of modern technology and infrastructure that became absolutely critical for industrialization in the post-colonial period. The nature of colonialism also determined the type of entrepreneurship that developed in different countries of the developing world. In his pioneering study on industrialization in the global periphery, Atul Kohli observes the impact of colonialism on the patterns of industrialization in the post-colonial era in four countries, namely South Korea, India, Brazil and Nigeria. Recognizing the successes of South Korean industry and economy Kohli observes that, "The Japanese colonial influence on Korea, from 1905 to 1945, was important in shaping a modern political economy that later evolved into high growth path to development" (Kohli 2004: 27). The contribution of the colonial masters in the economic success of South Korea can be located on following grounds:

1. Establishment of a highly cohesive and disciplined bureaucratic structure

2. Co-opting the Korean entrepreneurs in the task of industrial development, so that by the end of colonial period we already have an industrial class well equipped with the production and marketing techniques
3. Building up a strong infrastructure as compared to other colonized nations and establishing a highly educated and disciplined labor force.

On the contrary, in India the entrepreneurship that came forth during the colonial period could never get any kind of assistance from the colonial masters. Therefore, they lacked the business spirit and technological skill that the South Korean businessmen learnt from their colonial masters. Second, there was absence of a well-trained educated workforce. In many ways, these social forces collaborated with Congress party in their struggle against the colonial rule. Gandhi's theory of trusteeship served as a moral encouragement for the capitalist class in India to provide whole-hearted support to the freedom movement. The Congress party received adequate financial support from the private entrepreneurs to lead the movement. This collaboration continued for almost two decades after independence until the nationalization drive started by Mrs. Gandhi's regime under emerging political compulsions. The Bombay Plan, a draft depicting the future course of industrialization in India, submitted by eight leading industrialists of that time clearly assigned a larger and interventionist role to the state in industrial transformation. It is rather unique to observe that the entrepreneurs in India realizing their weakness in undertaking big industrial and infrastructural projects expressed their faith on the government to undertake the task of development.

Despite differences in the impacts of colonial rule on the patterns of industrialization, the common strategy adopted by the late-late industrializing, post-colonial nations was state-led industrialization wherein the state played a crucial and pro-active role in the industrial arena. But in order to account for variations in the nature and pattern of state intervention in developing countries, I would proceed to review some of the popular theoretical interventions in this domain.

The recent scholarly contributions towards comparative political economy have aroused substantial attention towards the developmental or welfarist role of state in developing countries. It has led to a revision of conventional understandings about the relationship between state and market. The question of state autonomy has been revisited not only in light of diverse patterns of state interventions in the developing world but also in terms of strategies that the state along with market forces of developing countries like India, China or Philippines adopt to engage with developed countries on the business front. New terms like developmental state, predatory state, guardian state or welfare state have been coined by comparative analysts to project or highlight varied forms of economic interventions.

The corporatist association between state and private entrepreneurs have been further strengthened in response to greater integration of the economies worldwide. In other words, the impact of globalization has led to substantial modifications in domestic industrial policies and developmental strategies of state actors across the globe. The emerging political context in which state actors take keen interest in promoting private business has produced a conducive investment climate and even involving keys players of the business community in economic decision-making and governance.

The emergence of technology-intensive industries like biotechnology, information technology and pharmaceuticals necessitated the adoption of innovative strategies by the governments in collaboration with the domestic and global entrepreneurs to achieve salience in these respective fields and accrue the opportunities emerging in global and local markets. Government involvement in the promotion of technology-driven and knowledge-based service sector in developing nations has been crucial for their integration into the global market. As Shin and Ho observe that, "In most developing countries, government intervention is necessary because market uncertainties, a limited and unstable capital supply, inadequate understanding of technological requirements, and an unstable political environment disturb investors for making continuous investments to upgrade an industry"[2] (Shin and Ho 1997: 238).

The competitive pressure in the global market for goods and services is far-reaching. Countries like China and Philippines have made inroads in the market for new technologies and information and communication services. State support for technocratic entrepreneurship and their innovative business ventures in these countries is well recognized. To this observation, Peter Evans rightly remarks that, "Without the state, markets, the other master institution of modern society, cannot function"[3] (Evans 1995: 3). Today, private capital needs the state as much as the state requires private partners for its economic and developmental projects.

The legitimacy of the state in modern times is largely based on its economic role and its potential to adjust with fast-changing international market. This is mainly to do with rapidly changing technologies that require substantial skill, innovation and creativity on the part of producers. In order to achieve this, the state assists innovative private entrepreneurs in their ventures who can devise new business strategies to reach out to client companies based in developed countries. The state helps the private companies not only by removing unnecessary controls and checks and facilitating clearance of different investment projects but also through necessary infrastructural and financial support to the prospective firms and companies.

The relationship between state and private entrepreneurship an important subject to understand the nature of industrial policy has been shaped by the political and institutional conditions in the respective countries. Therefore, in order to understand the changing nature of industrial policies it is important to account for the domestic and international political circumstances that have provided a certain direction to these policies. The economic logic of industrial reforms is therefore insufficient to

2. Roy W. Shin and Alfred Ho, "The Role of Science and Technology in Creating Korea's Electronics Industry", *Asian Affairs*, Winter 1997, vol. 23, no. 4, p. 238.
3. Peter Evans (1995), *Embedded Autonomy: States and Industrial Transformation*, New Jersey: Princeton University Press, p. 3.

provide a holistic picture of the reasons behind transformation in industrial policies. A comprehensive understanding of industrial transformation in the developing world requires an integrated approach; an analysis of the interplay of political and economic factors. Overemphasis on the role of market leads to economic determinism which diminishes the significance of state intervention as a causal factor to understand economic growth and industrialization in developing countries.

The nature of industrial policy-making clearly depicts the quality of state intervention in economy in terms of strategies it adopts for industrialization and the institutional framework it creates to support the new business ventures. Elaborating on this account, Evans states that most of the literature that focuses on state's role in industrialization is confined to the understanding of the degree of state intervention rather than the nature of involvement in policy-making. In his comparative study of South Korea, Brazil and India he shows how different patterns of regulatory or promotional institutional mechanisms produced differential levels of growth in the electronics and software industry. Evans makes a distinction between predatory and developmental states. Predatory states are the ones that lack the ability to prevent individuals from pursuing particularistic goals. In predatory states, there exists a nexus between the state and patrimonial elements of the society. The state policies are largely dictated by the dominant groups within the society and the state-society relation that emerges in a predatory state is one that is typically found in feudal societies.

A developmental state is primarily concerned with common welfare of the people and society at large. It is directed towards the goal of collective good. The state is directly involved in building the industrial base along with the assistance of economic players like the private entrepreneurs and labor. In a developmental state, there is an attempt on the part of the state to establish coherent corporate institutions that denounces personal or paternalistic ties between the state and societal actors. The state possesses a substantial degree of autonomy vis-à-vis the private players of the economy. The bureaucratic agencies, which are responsible for systematic implementation of policies, resemble Weberian model of ideal bureaucracy which is based on meritocracy and is dispassionate in its official functioning.

The emerging areas of comparative enquiry takes cognizance of the state selection of firms qualifying to receive incentives based on their performance in the global market. Selective promotion ensures quality checks and regulatory standards to be maintained at all levels of enquiry. Most of the scholarly works on political economy of state regulation carry out a systematic analysis of state autonomy and state networking with market forces to understand growth trajectories. An empirical analysis of diverse strategies adopted by the states in the developing world has furnished new ideas about institutional mechanisms for regulation and facilitation of market institutions. For example, in order to secure intellectual property rights, which is now a global concern; governments in different countries have attempted to enact legislations that ensure protection of intellectual property rights, particularly in the fields of information technology and pharmaceuticals where the security concerns are grave and serious.

Broadly, three streams of ideas can be accounted for while explaining industrial transformation in developing countries. These are as follows:

1. The Neoclassical Theory
2. Neostatism
3. The Globalization Argument.

The commonality between all three theoretical positions is that they follow a comparative approach in carrying out their studies on the nature of state intervention and the possible impact on the pattern of industrialization. The studies involve a comparison of East Asian countries with other emerging economies of the developing world like India, China and Brazil. The reason behind selecting East Asian countries is to understand the unique patterns of state-business relations that emerged in these states, the historical roots of which could be traced back to colonial times. The relevance of studying them also lies in the fact that they were able to achieve technological progress in a short course of time. Localized patterns of development assuming global significance in such countries have been exemplary.

Additionally, all three theoretical strands selected India as one of their case studies because of the stability of its democratic institutions. Indian case also stands different in view of combining liberal democracy with a socialist pattern of economy in its constitution. However, it is an irony that while democracy has succeeded irrespective of all its shortcomings it has not translated into equitable distribution of wealth and social egalitarianism. Heightening political participation and mass-scale involvement in political activities has not been complimented by desirable improvements in the economic conditions of people. I shall come to this point more clearly in the last chapter where I discuss the objectives of good governance in the context of newly-emerging technological infrastructure.

The Neoclassical Theory—Antithetical to Regulation

The basic theoretical assumption that the neoclassical theory holds is that the private entrepreneurs must have sufficient autonomy from the state in the management of economic affairs. The government's task should remain confined to the creation of a suitable environment for the private entrepreneurs, to function freely. Thus, according to it an important precondition for a competitive economy is minimal intervention of state in the economic arena. Economy thus appears as an exclusive domain of the market. The idea of state regulation is strictly denounced by the neoclassical theory. The market is seen as an institution that provides an alternative to state as the direct producer in an economy. In this framework, the state's role is simply confined to providing the most basic infrastructural facilities, protection of private property and maintaining law and order for a conducive entrepreneurial environment.

The Neoclassical theory is inspired by the Classical liberal theory of Adam Smith and David Ricardo who advocated the idea of a 'free man'. Men by nature are considered to be rational and self-oriented. When self-interested individuals tend to maximize their interests and utilities particularly economic ones, it automatically leads to social progress and common good. Therefore, according to this theory, the state must protect economic freedom of enterprising and creative individuals in the society. Economic freedom includes free enterprise, creation of private property and freedom to trade. Furthermore, they believe that market is an arena of free interaction between enterprising individuals. Therefore, their advocacy is that the state must not interfere with a freely functioning market as this would mean undermining individual freedom. Accordingly, market autonomy presides over state autonomy in the classical liberal framework.

Thus, the Classical liberal theory laid the foundation for the emergence of neoclassical theory that modified the former in the light of new developments in the fields of international trade, technology and industrialization. Embracing the idea of globalization, it advocated greater integration of the economies. This position was substantiated by the fact that globalization offers new avenues to private players in the economy to explore innovative strategies for industrialization. Entry of multinational companies leads to knowledge and technology transfer which benefits the domestic industry and the economy as a whole. Therefore, in order to accrue the benefits of globalization, the state is required to provide a level playing field to domestic entrepreneurs and multinational companies and accordingly must remove all forms of bureaucratic restrictions that seek to block the process of globalization and interfere with the freedom of enterprise. A new legal and institutional framework is therefore required to support liberalization and privatization of economy.

The neoclassical theory lays emphasis on providing a suitable investment climate for the private sector. It also believes that the private sector creates ample employment opportunities to people and thus contribute to their social well-being. Private firms are considered as the forerunners of innovative investments. On the other hand, they denounce excessive state intervention in industrialization on the ground that it leads to clientalistic ties between the state and vested interests in the society. It increases the possibilities of corruption and mismanagement of public resources.

The neoclassical theory may be further classified into two approaches, namely the free-market approach and the simulated-market approach. These approaches differ with regard to their positions on the degree of state intervention in the economy and industry.

Free-market Approach

The free-market approach is thoroughly inspired by the Classical liberal theory. The main proponents of this approach are Milton Friedman and Rose Friedman. The basic assumption here is that the domestic industry can prosper only under the condition of market freedom. Resultantly, the state must interfere least in the market and extend substantial degree of autonomy to the market forces. The two scholars trace the relevance of liberty in a historical context. They observe that, "The combination of economic and political freedom produced a Golden Age in both Great Britain and United States in the 19th century. The United States prospered even more than Britain" (Friedman 1980: 3).

The free-market approach advocates that the government's action must remain confined to providing a favorable environment to the private entrepreneurs so that they can function freely. It completely rejects the model of centralized planning as it restricts private investment and technological innovations. Centralized planning, according to this approach, also leads to undue empowerment of bureaucratic agencies that has serious implications for industrial development. Excessive power corrupts authorities and causes mismanagement or wastage of public resources. Further, it is believed that the politicians and the bureaucrats lack the requisite entrepreneurial capacities and must seek the assistance of private business while taking key policy decisions on the assumption that big businessmen have greater experience and capacity in the arena of commerce and trade. In view of their experience and expertise in business management, marketing, and fields of technology they are far superior to politicians and bureaucrats in undertaking developmental projects in industry and infrastructure-building.

The free-market approach suggest an outward-oriented industrialization as they believe that in a globalized economy, remaining insulated from the international market is harmful for domestic growth. In view of this assumption, it advocates that the state must remove restrictions on international trade by minimizing taxes and duties on imports. The free-market proponents espouse free flow of capital, labour and technology globally because they believe that the process of economic globalization is mutually beneficial for all countries.

While accounting for different levels of success in developing economies, Milton Friedman argues that the East Asian countries like South Korea, Singapore, Taiwan and Japan which relied heavily on private business for their industrialization without state controls are thriving. In contrast, India, Indonesia and Communist China following centralized planning and protectionism experienced high levels of economic stagnation[4] (Friedman 1980: 57). Thus, in his view, it was precisely the differential roles of states in East Asia and other developing economies of Asia that led to variations in the levels of industrial development. While in East Asian countries the market forces were given complete freedom to pursue their industrial activities, governments in other countries advanced restrictive industrial policies according primacy to public sector over private business. The initiatives of the private business were stifled in India, China and Indonesia. Ironically, in India import-substitution industrialization embodying restrictive policies like industrial licensing exhorted rent-seeking tendencies in bureaucracy and safeguarded the interests of dominant classes. According to Bardhan, such propertied classes form a dominant coalition and derive the advantages of a locked-in economy. Referring to the position of business in the dominant coalition, Bardhan observes that,

> The industrial capitalist class, mainly under the leadership of some of the top business families from western India, was reasonably strong at the time of independence. It supported the government policy of encouraging import substitution industrialization, quantitative trade restrictions providing automatically protected domestic

4. Milton Friedman (1980), *Free to Choose*, Mariner Books, p. 57.

> markets, and of running a large public sector providing capital goods, intermediate products and infrastructural facilities for private industry, often at artificially low prices. (Bardhan 2013: 6)

Interestingly, China despite being a communist state initiated its industrial reforms much before the Indian state did. India pursued a socialist pattern of industrialization till the mid-1970s punctuated by partial liberalization (Rahul Mukherji, *Pacific Affairs*) in the devaluation episode of 1966.

Conceptually, free-market proponents equate outward-orientation or export-oriented industrialization with lack of state intervention which becomes empirically refutable when the patterns of state-led industrialization are understood in case of developmental states of East Asia, India, and some of the Latin American countries like Brazil and Argentina that have witnessed high levels of industrialization in past few decades. In case of the East Asian states, outward-oriented industrialization has coexisted with state intervention in the market. In fact, in the contemporary world almost all the countries, ranging from capitalist states like United States and Britain to a socialist state like China have found state intervention necessary for the growth of trade and commerce. What is however important is to account for the nature of state intervention i.e. specific strategies devised jointly by the state and private companies for industrialization. The government plays the dual role of a regulator and facilitator while creating condition for the growth of private enterprise. So, state retains its power and autonomy and appears as the chief player in an economy where private capital flourishes.

The free market approach falls short of capturing the critical role of state in the developmental process and the significant degree of autonomy it exercises while taking key economic decisions. A state can play a positive role as an interventionist institution by being a facilitator as well as a guardian to the emerging entrepreneurs. The dual role is played by providing necessary assistance to prospective market players for investment and exports and turning punitive in its actions if such supports are not translated into desired denouements.

In addition, the political context under which state regulation or promotion plays its part is not addressed by this approach. There are interests involved in creating conditions for the state to act in specific ways or adopt certain strategies to promote industrial sectors. The interests of the actors may clash or converge to influence policy outcomes and giving them a particular direction. Also, political lobbies within different industrial sectors may influence the government in contradictory ways creating difficulties for formulating coherent policies. For instance, the labour appears to be a strong political grouping within the textile and automobile sectors in India. History is laden with examples of strikes by textile mill workers in Bombay and other parts of the country. Also, the recent strike by the Maruti workers at Manesar, Haryana is a case in hand. Clashes between management and labour in such instances affect policy-making in these sectors. Therefore, to understand policy shifts the developmental ensemble formed by state and societal actors requires special attention. But, its imperative to recognize the heterogeneity within the industry to see how the configuration of interests and power differ from sector to sector and how state responds to this variation through its policy decisions.

The neoclassical view would accredit the success of software to minimal intervention by the state, and the innovative strategies adopted by the private sector under the condition of complete freedom from state regulation. But such an explanation becomes plausible mainly on its observation that software sector in India succeeded in achieving high growth rates and the assumption that this was made possible by minimal government interference in investment and trade. In the first case, the theory takes a qualified view of the industry's performance in totality. Assessments made by Sridharan and D'Çosta (2004) about the capabilities of the software and service companies clearly indicate the infirmity of the industry in serving high-end tasks. There has however been a slow process of upgradation from low-end to high-end services in the industry. This point will be elaborated in the fourth chapter. The second assumption concerning minimal state intervention is clearly refutable on the ground that state support for the growth of the industry in the form of direct assistance since 1980s is of critical importance.

The assumption of minimal state intervention in industrial development, as advanced by the neoclassical scholars, is often questioned by the proponents of Neo-statism. Contrarily, they see state intervention as a crucial factor for industrial growth. While accounting for the differential levels of growth in the electronics sector of India, South Korea and Brazil, Peter Evans views state autonomy and its guidance to market players as the driving force behind economic success. A comparative analysis of state's economic role in the context of electronics industry makes him classify states in developing economies. He advances the embedded autonomy thesis to show how developmental states were able to achieve remarkable success in their economic arenas. In Peter Evans' analysis of the development of electronics sector in India, Brazil, and South Korea, India has been placed in the middle of the 'embedded autonomy spectrum', a framework that understands state-capital collaboration from a developmental perspective[5] (Evans 1995: 57). I shall take up these arguments in greater details in the latter part of this chapter.

Simulated Market Approach

The emphasis of the simulated market approach is more on the positive role of state in bringing about industrial transformation. According to this approach, the state provides moderate incentives to the private entrepreneurs for export-promotion. These incentives come very close to the relative prices of the products that exist in a free trade regime. In other words, states must facilitate export-promotion by extending incentives to the private entrepreneurs from time to time.

The main proponent of this approach is Jagdish Bhagwati. Bhagwati compares the levels of industrial development in India and South Korea to justify the superiority of liberal regimes and the dangers associated with protectionism. A comparative analysis of growth trends in the two countries suggested that while South Korea adopted export-oriented industrial policies

5. Peter Evans (1995), *Embedded Autonomy: State and Industrial Transformation*, *op. cit.*

in the 1960s and developed rapidly, Indian industry remained stagnant as a result of its protectionist policies during the same period. The burgeoning of sick industrial units in the public sector by the late-1970s has been cited as an example to justify the claim in support of trade-liberalization. In this context, Bhagwati points out that,

> By far more effective was the demonstration by the trade-liberalizing countries that their superior performance had led to more successful and substantial industrialization than what more protectionist nations had managed. By making external markets at least as attractive as home markets, and even by creating a certain pro-export bias by policy design, these countries made their new industries register rapid growth by breaking out of the confines of smaller domestic markets.[6] (Bhagwati 1993: 93)

Comparing the growth trends in India and South Korea, Bhagwati inferred that South Korea's manufactured exports which was almost negligible as compared to India in the 1962, amounted by 1980 to nearly four times those of India. The statistical analysis of growth figures in a trade-liberalizing and a protectionism regime made Bhagwati suggest that, "The contrast in the levels of industrialization have been so enormous between the trade-liberalizing and the protectionist countries that protectionism as a strategy to promote industrial development has become outmoded"[7] (Bhagwati 1993: 93).

While both free-market and simulated market approaches hold the assumption that industries flourish under the conditions of free trade and free market, they differ in their views with regard to the role of state in the market. While the free market advocates completely obscures state intervention, the simulated market approach emphasizes some degree of state intervention through extension of moderate incentives to private entrepreneurs. However, even the simulated market approach advocates that the government's role must be minimal and

6. Jagdish Bhagwati (1988), *Protectionism*, Cambridge: MIT Press, p. 93.
7. *Ibid.*, p. 93.

seemingly limited in nature. It must act as a facilitator rather than an active player in the economic arena and provide an open space to the market forces. Accordingly, the government's legitimacy lies in its commitment towards maintaining a policy framework corroborating export-oriented industrialization and that it would loose its legitimacy if it drifts away from this strategy and resort to protectionism.

Elaborating further on the comparison between the role of state in newly industrializing nations, Bhagwati observed that the Far-East Asian governments issued prescriptions to their private entrepreneurs, while countries such as India did just the opposite[8] (Bhagwati 1993: 98). Additionally, he states that the government of 'dos' generally produce economic performance superior to that produced by the governments of 'don'ts'.[9] Even if it is considered that the prescriptive governments prescribe as badly as the proscriptive governments, the latter will leave no scope for initiatives to be taken by the private entrepreneurs. On the contrary, prescriptive governments will provide an open ground to the private entrepreneurs for undertaking new initiatives. The prescriptive governments provide ample amount of opportunities to private entrepreneurs for investments in new areas of production and technical change, while proscriptive governments put a whole lot of restrictions on entrepreneurial activities. Proscriptive governments clearly exhibit an adverse relationship with the private capital and attempt to promote public sector enterprises at the cost of private business. Resultantly, proscriptive governments advance industrial policies that involve stringent licensing policies, high taxation, import restrictions, tariffs and restrictions on production capacities. This will cause industrial sickness or endemic industrial stagnation as exemplified by India since the late-1970s.

The Neoclassical theory has come under a critical spotlight while theorizing state-market relations in newly-industrializing nations of the developing world. The assumptions are found

8. *Ibid.*, p. 98.
9. The government of dos refers to liberal regimes and the government of 'don'ts' refer to protectionist regimes.

to be misleading in explaining the industrial trajectories of not only the developing countries but also the developed countries in recent times. Both the approaches of Neoclassical theory fall prey to economic-determinism and society-reductionism. While the simulated approach seems a little more accommodative regarding the role of state, the free market approach completely undermines the state by viewing it as a neutral agency having a limited autonomous existence of its own. State's autonomy in taking coherent policy decisions for economic development is ignored and free play of market forces has been suggested as the only remedy to overcome industrial and economic backwardness.

Regulation does not necessarily imply elimination of private enterprise, as advocated by free-market theory. Rather, government regulation strikes a balance between control and autonomy and is essential for effectiveness, economy and efficiency in the industry. On the contrary, lack of regulation would mean giving free hand to profit-oriented, self-seeking private companies which would be detrimental to overall growth of the economy. It would only reflect short-sightedness and lack of vision and perceptiveness on the part of its stakeholders. Regulatory mechanisms may thus be devised in such a manner that a balanced and sustainable industrial growth is achievable.

Furthermore, the neoclassical theory has also ignored the interplay of internal and external political factors that result in necessary adjustments in industrial policies from time to time. The case of IT/software industry clearly substantiates this hypothesis. Industrial policies do not exist in vacuum. There is a political logic of initiating changes at the policy level. This includes the ideology and interests of the state and societal actors which may be both complimentary and conflicting in nature. The interplay of such political factors is more prominent in case of a democratic country like India where every policy measure comes under public spotlight. The need to change policy orientation for different sectors depends on the level of their contribution towards mass welfare. For instance, IT was a commodity of elites and business class till the late-1990s. But, lately it is seen as an instrument of social development which has led the government shift its policy orientation in this sector towards e-governance. Private companies have also been co-opted in this developmental agenda. Neoclassical theory fails to capture these policy dynamics that result from ideational change within the state and shifts in orientation towards an economic sector.

Neostatism-balance between Promotion and Regulation

Neostatism, as a theory of political economy, assigns a centre stage to the state in industrialization. It emerged in the 1970s as a challenge to the neoclassical, Marxist, and pluralist thought, all of which adopted a society-centric view to explain the political economy of industrial transformation in developing economies. The common assumption that the state and its institutions are considered as instruments of societal groups to advance their interests came to be challenged by the Neostatists. While the pluralist theory viewed state as a mediating agency the task of which was to manage conflicts amidst competing claims, the Marxists stream of thought saw state as an instrument of the dominant class, which was the capitalist or bourgeoisie class in a modern capitalist society.

The main proponents of Neostatism are Theda Skocpol, Peter Evans, Robert Wade, Alice Amsden, Stephan Haggard, Joel Midgal, and Atul Kohli. This new line of thought emerged as a result of the scholarly curiosity to understand the remarkable economic success of East Asian countries like Hong Kong, Japan, Singapore, Taiwan, and South Korea. In their exploration of the causes behind this success they observed that the governments in all these countries played a pro-active role to promote selective companies by providing them special incentives for investment. These incentives were however performance-based implying that the recipients of the incentives were required to achieve export targets pre-fixed by the government itself.

Neostatism could be broadly classified into two approaches which are as follows:

1. The Governed Market Approach
2. State-in-Society Approach

The core assumption of Neo-Statists is that the state agencies must act autonomously in formulating industrial policies and that successful industrialization could be achieved when an outward-oriented strategy of industrialization is followed. They discard the idea of unregulated market as they consider the need for state regulation along with state assistance and guardianship to private business. However, the approaches differ with regard to their understanding of the nature and quality of state intervention and relative autonomy of the state vis-à-vis private entrepreneurs, transnational actors like the multinational companies and the labor. These approaches are also distinct from each other with regard to their emphasis on state-society interface. While the governed market approach lay more emphasis on the creation of corporate state institutions that provide the state a certain degree of autonomy vis-à-vis the societal players, the state-in-society approach delves into the patterns of state-society interactions that produces desirable policies for public welfare and economic progress.

The Governed Market Approach

The governed market approach holds a more radical view about state's position in the management of economic affairs of the nation. This approach found its initiation in the writings of Robert Wade and Alice Amsden. It states that a corporate relationship between state and private capital is a precondition for building a potent industrial structure. Wade describes the developmental virtues of what he calls as 'soft authoritarian states' in East Asia. In his comparative analysis of state-capital relations in East Asia and other countries of the developing world he observes that the presence of centralized bureaucratic agencies along with a centralized system of planning in countries like India and Indonesia could have led to the allocation of resources in proper channels. However, due to mutual hostility between state and private capital in these countries the desired developmental goals of industrialization and technological development could not be achieved. So while centralization is seen as a necessary condition for development it is not sufficient in producing desirable results. Centralization must be complimented by co-option of prospective market players in the developmental process.

Second, the governed market approach emphasizes the necessity of export-oriented industrialization for achieving rapid economic growth. The government's decision in incentivizing and promoting sectors with comparative advantage in the global market is seen to be critical for industrial development. Alice Amsden exemplifies such imperative by citing state support for the electronics industry in South Korea. While advocating export-promotion and outward-orientation, this approach does not completely discard protectionism. It views protectionism only as a temporary arrangement in a situation when the industry is at the initial stages of its growth. It clearly states that the strategy of export-promotion and import-substitution are not mutually exclusive. Both the strategies of industrialization are required for a step-wise industrial progression. Building the supply side of production through import substitution may be a prerequisite for demand side growth of exports. The example of the development of automobile industry in Japan has been cited to illustrate this point. To begin with, import substitution was seen as the right strategy to build the initial base for automobile industry. The economic rationale behind the adoption of import substitution industrialization was the monopolization of the industrial sector by American firms in the international market. Subsequently, the local automobile industry became well equipped to produce high quality cars for the domestic market. Once an optimal level of productivity was achieved an excess capacity was created with the increase in supply of cars for the domestic market. The creation of this excess capacity then helped in exploring avenues for sale in the international market. It is observed that the Japanese state followed a step-wise development strategy for its local automobile industry and took the lead for its global promotion only when the conditions were favourable and local companies had gained comparative advantage.

In governed market theory, the state is considered as the captain of the ship. The steering of the economy is completely in the hands of the state. Accordingly, it suggests that state institutions must develop political and administrative capacities to undertake large developmental projects. For this, it is essential for the state to develop coherent corporate institutions which are not beholden to any particular group within the society. In other words, it is only through the instrument of corporate coherence that the state can formulate policies independently and autonomously or without any influence or pressures of societal actors that includes the private entrepreneurs, labor and the multinational companies. However, it must seek the cooperation of these groups by receiving proper inputs from them time to time. It is implicit in the title 'the governed market theory' that the state must be well equipped to govern the market by creating coherent institutions to coordinate the efforts of the private firms, public sector enterprises and the foreign firms. Elaborating on this account, Robert Wade takes a radical position that the most effective strategy for industrialization would be to create coherent corporate institutions before the political system is democratized. In this context, Wade states that,

> "State effectiveness depends on the coherence of state policies, which is difficult to maintain when important parts of the state are beholden to sectarian, regional and ethnic interests. Effectiveness is therefore a function of the degree of autonomy from the surrounding social structure."[10] (Wade 1990: 375)

The rigour with which the governed market theory makes an advocacy for a strong state indicates that in the newly developing countries administrative discipline along with corporatization may be required for coherent industrial policies. Wade illustrates the efficient functioning of a corporate state in East Asian countries like Japan, South Korea and Taiwan. The state is seen to be playing the part of a guardian that nourishes the private industries in a manner that resembles the nourishment and upbringing of a child by her parents. At the same time, the governing bodies maintain strict vigilance over the performance

---

10. Robert Wade (1990), *Governing the Market: The Economic Theory and the Role of Government in East Asian Industrialization*, New Jersey: Princeton University Press, p. 375.

of private firms and in case of performance failures withdraws support and assistance. At the initial stages of growth, the state provides preliminary support to private entrepreneurs and prefers import-substitution industrialization as a desirable path to development. Later, as firms gain sufficient potentiality and turn competitive internationally, the state provides several incentives for its promotion. However, the state in a parental position has an upper hand vis-à-vis the private entrepreneurs. It makes qualitative assessment of firms' productive capacities and extends fiscal and other kinds of investment and export-related incentives accordingly. The assessment is done on an annual basis.

Elaborating on some of the economic functions of the state for promoting industrialization, Wade suggests that the state must undertake following measures:

1. Controlling finance capital and making private finance capital subordinate to industrial capital
2. Maintaining stability of the economic parameters like exchange rates, interest rates and price levels
3. Modulating the impact of foreign competition in the domestic economy and prioritizing the use of foreign exchange
4. Promoting exports
5. Technology acquisition from the multinational companies and building a national technology system
6. Assisting particular industries.[11] (Wade 1990: 27)

The above-mentioned prescriptions clearly opine that the state, according to the governed market approach, must initiate fiscal and trade policies so as to harness the benefits of global integration from time to time. An indiscriminate opening up of the market to foreign companies is not considered worthwhile but for the purpose of knowledge and technology transfer their involvement in the industry is seen as an imperative in the nurturing process. The borrowed technology must be used to upgrade local skills and capabilities and efforts must be directed

11. *Ibid.*, p. 27.

towards creating an indigenous technological base. In a nutshell, the governed market approach proposes that the state must regulate the production and investment related activities of both local entrepreneurs and multinational companies.

A more radical stance is taken by Alice Amsden while theorizing state control over market in East Asian countries. Her comparative study of industrial transformation cites South Korea as an exemplary case of a developmental state. As Wade, Amsden also illustrates the guardian role of state in South Korea by providing several examples of governmental incentives to the 'chaebols'[12] in South Korea. The state in South Korea extended subsidies to the export-oriented firms referred to as chaebols. However, the state fixed an export target for such selective companies which were assessed on an annual basis. The extension of the subsidies was based on meeting the export targets within a stipulated period of time. Amsden termed this kind of industrial strategy as 'qualitative subsidization'. She observed that the state in other developing countries lacked the requisite capacity or was ignorant towards assisting the private entrepreneurs in their respective economies.

The advocacy of soft authoritarianism based on the structural principle of corporate coherence for economic progress is a negation of democratic institutional forms. Democracy is undoubtedly a pre-condition for development as state authoritarianism cannot be justified in the garb of maintaining market discipline and formulating coherent industrial policies. Ideas favouring soft authoritarianism for economic progress in East Asia are at odds with Amartya Sen's theorization of development as freedom. For Sen, freedom is the goal of development. Therefore, the prior agenda of the government must be to enhance the substantive freedoms of the individuals. Development and progress is contingent upon the level of freedom and public accessibility to developmental benefits. Negation of democracy and freedom at the cost of economic progress is thus unjustifiable.

12. Chaebols basically refers to a group of giant business enterprises in South Korea like Samsung, L.G., and so on which are predominantly export-oriented.

Secondly, the governed market theory takes a monolithic view of the state. In reality, the state appears as a heterogeneous entity, with each of its institutional parts having a functional and political logic of its own. In such situation, achieving corporate coherence is a herculean task. Parts of state may combine differently with different interests within the society. Framing of coherent public policies in such socio-political settings becomes a difficult proposition. Ideological clashes within the state may also pose challenges in this regard. The negotiation between old and new ideas and interests is a cumbersome process and is most likely to work in favour of those who are powerful. In such a context, the advocacy of corporatist coherence becomes a utopian alternative.

State-in-Society Approach

The basic assumption of the state-in-society approach is that state autonomy in policy-making operates within a framework of association, collaboration and cooperation with the societal actors. This approach differs from the governed market approach in terms of its understanding regarding the degree and nature of state autonomy in formulating industrial policies. It denies the authoritarian variant of state autonomy as envisaged by the governed market approach but does agree with the proposition that the state's autonomy in decision-making is the key to social and economic progress irrespective of the political system; the logic works well for both democratic and dictatorial regimes. Association and alignments with societal actors, according to it, must feature cooperation and collaboration. The main proponents of the state-in-society approach are Peter Evans, Joel Midgal, Theda Skocpol, Eric Nordlinger, Atul Kohli, and Vivek Chibber.[13] Scholarly interventions by them in the area of comparative development studies have shown that state's critical

13. Joel Midgal (2001), *State in Society: Studying How States and Societies Transform and Constitute One Another,* Cambridge: Cambridge University Press; Theda Skocpol, Peter Evans and Dietrich Rueschemeyer (1985), ed., *Bringing the State Back In,* Cambridge: Cambridge University Press; Atul Kohli (1992), *State Directed Development: Political Power and Industrialization in Global Periphery,* Cambridge: Cambridge University Press; Vivek

role as an economic actor is a necessary condition for economic progress. They have delved into patterns of state and society interaction to understand the degree of autonomy exercised by the state while formulating public policies. Although only few of them have attempted to study state capacities in advancing coherent public policies, the common point of analysis centred around state's economic intervention is extremely useful to assess the efficacy of industrial policies.

Following the assumption of the state-in-society approach, Joel Midgal points out that state autonomy is exercised within a framework of diverse forms of alignments and collaboration with societal groups. Midgal considers state as a purposeful organization with autonomous goals and objectives, using legitimacy as a tool in maintaining social control and implementing appropriate policies. In this context, Midgal refers to two aspects of state autonomy, namely the 'image' and 'practices' of the state. The nature of state has been termed as the image of state which can be located in boundaries maintained at two levels.

1. Territorial boundaries which refers to the boundary between state and other states
2. Social boundaries refers to the boundary between state and societal actors like business groups, labor, and so on.

Since most of the states are politically sovereign the demarcation between the territorial boundaries of different states are clear. However, there are instances of blurred territorial boundaries when other states start claiming parts of the territory or the states may face attacks from other states, as happened in case of US occupation of Iraq and Afghanistan. The fuzziness of social boundaries is apparent in diverse areas of policy-making. Here, the state and its agencies, especially the ones operating at sub-national or grassroot levels often gets influenced by societal groups and fail to exercise absolute discretion while taking policy decisions or managing its implementation.

Chibber (2003), *State-Building and Late Industrialization in India,* New Jersey: Princeton University Press.

Practices refer to policy outcomes that arise out of a continuous process of interaction between state and societal actors. Practices of the state have serious implications for state autonomy and its capacity to formulate policies that conceive larger interests of society than any particularistic goal embodying interest of a dominant group or coalition. This process of interaction may weaken the image of the state if the latter succumbs to the pressures of such vested interests. On the contrary, the state may preserve its image if it takes decisions without being influenced by them. The legitimacy of the state is sustained as long as the policy decisions are acceptable at large.

Practices, in Midgal's view, are often at odds with the image of the state. The contradiction between the two aspects of state emerges particularly when parts or fragments of the state get aligned with dominant groups or coalition to advance their particularistic goals or vested interests. The rules, regulations or policy decisions that emerge out of such an alignment are distinct from those that are independently or autonomously formulated. In the former case, the territorial and social boundaries get neutralized. This kind of contradiction between the image and practices of the state has serious implications for policy making. As Midgal points out that there could be two outcomes of the interconnection between the image and practices of the state which are as follows:

1. The image of the state could be maintained if the state agencies exist as clearly bounded, powerful and unified organization that can be spoken of in singular terms.
2. The practices may, in a contrary case, lead to fragmentation of state agencies loosely connected with each other and the societal actors. This would further result in the formation of ill-defined boundaries between the parts of the state and the societal groupings and often promote conflicting set of rules with one another and with the official law.[14] (Midgal 2001: 22)

14. Joel S. Midgal (2001), *State in Society: Studying How States and Societies Transform and Constitute One Another*, *op. cit.*, p. 22.

Although, Midgal's concern is more about social conflicts begetting from state-society interactions and the management of the same by controlling authorities, the theoretical framework so advanced can also serve to explain how different forms of state-capital alignment may produce varied policy outcomes. States pursuing outward-orientation, for instance would purposefully seek the assistance of private companies while taking important policy measures. The consultation helps in incorporating relevant inputs for key economic decisions and public policies.

The most influential works to broaden the understanding of state-capital relations while accounting for differences in levels of success in developing economies is the embedded autonomy thesis advanced by Peter Evans. Evans methodological approach is largely inductive in which he is attempting at drawing broad generalizations about industrial development in the developing economies through a particularistic account of IT and electronics sector. In his book entitled *Embedded Autonomy: States and Industrial Transformation*, Evans delves into institutional history of policy-making in electronics and computer industry of three emerging economies: South Korea, Brazil and India. By assessing the institutional capacities of the bureaucracy, he accounts for variations in the growth levels achieved by their respective electronics industry.

Theoretically, Evans introduces various models of state based on their institutional capacities to bring about rapid industrial transformation. He classifies states in the developing world into predatory and developmental states. Predatory states lack the capacity to prevent individual incumbents from pursuing particularistic goals. There exists a nexus between the state and patrimonial elements of the society. And this kind of an unproductive alliance makes it difficult for the bureaucracy and other state agencies to pursue autonomous goal and develop appropriate institutional capacities to promote industrial growth. In this regard, Evans says that,

> "The predatory states lack the ability to prevent individual incumbents from pursuing their own goals. Personal ties are the only source of cohesion and individual maximization takes precedence over pursuit of collective goals." (Evans 1995: 12)

The policies pursued by the government lack vision and public commitment and therefore fail to address concerns that are oriented towards long-term development of the society and economy.

On the contrary, a developmental state is one which pursues autonomous goals and works towards promoting collective good. While exercising such discretion, the state officials also collaborate with key economic actors in the society particularly private firms and trade unions. The state co-opts private entrepreneurs in the developmental process and provides necessary assistance to them to venture into more challenging and innovative kinds of production. Industrialization in a developmental state thus appears to be a cooperative venture between state and private capital.

The embedded autonomy thesis suggests that a truly developmental state is one which combines institutional coherence with social connectedness. The two aspects may seem contradictory at the face value; nevertheless they must go together for a state to be developmental. Taking embedded autonomy as a standard for assessing the developmental capacities of state, Evans infers that the state in South Korea approximates closely to the embedded autonomy thesis while India and Brazil provide intermediate cases exhibiting partial or imperfect approximation of embedded autonomy (Evans 1995: 13). The differential impact of corporate coherence and quality and level of embededness is well reflected in differences at the level of production, investment, and technological advancements in the three economies. While the electronics and hardware sector in South Korea advanced rapidly, the Indian and Brazilian IT sector witnessed slow-pace growth.

For Evans, the institutional capacity of state is reflected in its internal organization and networking with prospective social and economic organizations. He observes that the internal organization of developmental states come very close to the institutional forms in Weberian bureaucracy. A Weberian bureaucracy is one that is based on merit and where long-term career advancement schemes promote commitment and generate a culture of corporate coherence in the bureaucratic organizations. And it is this distinct character of corporate coherence that provides bureaucratic organizations a certain degree autonomy vis-à-vis the societal groups.

Substantiating the arguments of Peter Evans, Atul Kohli also attempts to accounts for state abilities and strategies to pursue industrialization in the periphery. According to Kohli, industrialization in some of the peripheral countries was directed by the state and was not left completely in the hands of the private entrepreneurs. The methodological framework used by Kohli is comparative and descriptive involving historical detailing of policy evolution since the colonial period. Following Evans, Kohli's theoretical model also emphasizes upon the kind or quality than the degree of state intervention to explain variations in industrialization. In other words, his central question is 'what kind' than 'how much' of state intervention in the peripheral countries was necessary. Kohli attempts to evaluate the institutional capacities of the state in formulating coherent industrial policies in India, Brazil, Nigeria and South Korea. He concludes that there is a range of variation in state capacities to pursue industrial transformation, from fairly effective growth promoting state in South Korea to a rather ineffective and corrupt state in Nigeria, while India and Brazil providing mixed cases[15] (Kohli 2004: 2).

In analyzing the institutional capacities of the state, Kohli delves into patterns of state authority, and the way politics is organized and state power is used in the peripheral countries. He states that the pattern of politics, bureaucratic organization has a decisive influence on the economic context within which private decisions are made[16] (Kohli 2004: 2). The distinctiveness of Kohli's theoretical explanation is that it underscores the impact of diverse colonial experiences on state formation and state-society relations in post-colonial nations. Citing the case of South Korea, Kohli observes that the state in South Korea adopted the values of discipline and corporate coherence from

15. Atul Kohli (2004), *State Directed Development: Political Power and Industrialization in Global Periphery*, *op. cit.*, p. 2.
16. *Ibid.*

Japan. During the colonial period, the local entrepreneurs in South Korea came in contact with their colonial counterparts and learned the technical skills required for qualitative industrial production from them. Accordingly, the local entrepreneurs got trained in the art of production and technological innovation during the colonial period. Adopting the skills and innovation of Japanese entrepreneurs, local entrepreneurs of South Korea expanded their industrial base into more innovative areas of production like electronics and computer hardware. On the contrary, lack of such opportunities made it difficult to establish a powerful entrepreneurial base in post-colonial India. Moreover, a group of eight eminent industrialists who charted the 'Bombay Plan', a memorandum for future of economic planning in India envisaged a larger role of government in the developmental arena. The document clearly states that, "We think that no development of the kind will be feasible except on the basis of a central directing authority" (Bombay Plan 1944: 2).

However, this optimism did not last long. As the process of nationalization and public-sector monopolization pursued actively during Mrs. Gandhi's regime stifled the growth of private entrepreneurship, the developmental goals of the state based on the principle of mixed economy required serious rethinking. While on one hand, the innovations of the local entrepreneurship in South Korea got boosted by the assistance of the state, lack of state assistance towards private investment and production in India led to further degradation of the local entrepreneurship. Based on these comparative insights, Kohli opines that different kinds of state structures create different capacities for action. Structures define the role that the state is capable of playing. Outcomes depend on how well the roles fit in the context and how well they are executed (Kohli 2004).

Vivek Chibber also attempts to understand the institutional capacities of the state in the late-developing countries of Asia, Africa and Latin America. He observed that the government in these countries embarked upon a comprehensive programme of developmental planning, industrialization being one of its most important components. Accounting for variations in development across nations, Chibber analyzed the institutional capacities of respective governments in producing developmental outcomes. He observed that the adoption of coherent industrial policies was contingent upon the organization of state agencies. To elaborate, Chibber suggests that for adopting a coherent, internally coordinated policy framework the policy agencies must be guided by norms of bureaucratic rationality. Second, proper coordination between nodal agencies like banks, executive departments and ministries has been considered to be an important precondition for cohesiveness of developmental states. Finally, the third important requirement for corporate coherence is that the state must be embedded in a concrete set of ties with the domestic entrepreneurs (Chibber 2003: 13-28).

The Neostatist theory falls short of analyzing the subjective dimensions of these forms of institutional functioning. It takes a static view of political institutions (in our case studies the role of regulatory and promotional institutions) and appears to be prescriptive in its approach. Underscoring what governments ought to do to overcome economic backwardness, it fails to address what it can really do under socio-political constraints. Institutional changes therefore require a broader understanding of the interplay of ideology and interests of the political and social actors who influence such change. Also, the theorization of the state-society relations is more reflective of the internal politics that affects policies. It does little to explain the internationalization of state policies, particularly for sectors (like electronics and telecommunications) that are deeply embedded in global technological and financial networks. The next section would discuss the global impact on internal policies concerning trade and commerce.

Impact of Globalization on Trade and Industrial Development

In present times, policy-making is largely governed by externalities that result from globalization. Policy shifts and economic change pursued worldwide is better understood as a response to the changing dynamics of globalization. However, study of developing economies especially the emerging ones like

India, China and Brazil require special attention in view of their distinct historical experience and socio-political environment.

Globalization has been preceded by liberalization with the adoption of open market policies by the developing economies at different points of time. In fact, it is believed that globalization is a logical culmination of liberalization. Liberalization of industrial policies has been considered as a prerequisite for globalization of their economies. Some of the exponents of this theoretical stance are Baldev Raj Nayyar, Robert Wade and Pallan and Abott. While the commonly held assumption is that globalization is now a universal phenomenon, they differ in their views regarding the merits and demerits of globalization particularly regarding its significance for industrial development in the developing countries. However, the primary concern is not about accepting or rejecting globalization, but regulating globalization in a way that maximizes the advantage of the participant economies. As Nayyar points out that, "Insulation from the global economy is not a viable option for these (developing countries) states, since that too imposes costs. The question for them is to carve out policies that would allow them to make best use of the situation as it exists"[17] (Nayyar 2005: 259).

Baldev Raj Nayyar characterized the nature of economic globalization in the 20th century, particularly after the World War-II as 'truncated'. He observed that the geographic scope of globalization has expanded tremendously. However, its benefits have not flowed uniformly across different parts of the world. It has got concentrated in the industrially and technologically advanced nations of the world, more evidently in 'triad nations' that include United States, Japan and European Union. These countries of the triad are said to have set the pace of globalization. According to Nayyar, by employing a variety of institutional and political mechanisms they have brought globalization to the service of their interests and passed on the

17. Baldev Raj Nayyar (2005), *The Geopolitics of Globalization: The Consequences for Development*, New Delhi: Oxford University Press, p. 259.

cost of adjustment to the less developed or underdeveloped countries of the world. As an illustration of the variations in success, Nayyar provides data for the rise of exports in different countries from 1995 to 2000.

Table 1: Exports as share of world exports of different countries for the years 1995 and 2000

Country/Region	*Exports % 1995*	*Exports % 2000*
Industrial Countries	67.6	63.2
EU	39.8	35.9
Japan	8.7	7.5
US	11.5	12.1
Developing Countries	32.4	36.8
Africa	1.6	1.9
Asia	18.5	19.9
Europe (East-Europe)	4.6	4.9
Middle East	3.1	4.2
Western Hemisphere	4.5	5.8
World	$5071 billion	$6387 billion

Source: Nayyar 2005[18]

Inference: Nayyar concluded that the advanced nations of the world which comprised less than 20% of world's population had a share of almost two-third of the world's exports. Within the developing countries, Asia occupied the largest share of world exports followed by Eastern Europe, Middle East and Africa. Moreover, within Asia the export-rich countries have been identified as the countries of East Asia like South Korea, Hong Kong, Taiwan and Singapore.

Accounting for the rapid industrial growth in East Asian countries Nayyar states that the East Asian countries had to

18. *Ibid.*, p. 40.

design their industrial policies in such a manner so as to make full use of the benefits flowing from global economic transactions. It was believed that movement along the path of globalization involved reduction in transactions costs or large increment in benefits from international economic transactions.

There is a contradiction between the two simultaneous explanations for the impact of globalization on industrialization. On one hand, the idea of truncated globalization presents a negative portrayal of globalization. On the other hand, Nayyar argues that global integration of the East Asian countries into the international economy has facilitated their industrialization. In other words, Nayyar attempts to present two contradictory pictures of globalization; but ultimately like the free market theory prescribes greater discretion to market forces in the economic arena.

Pallan and Abbott (1999) take a closer view at the impact of globalization in the global periphery. They propose a competitive strategy for industrialization wherein state policies will play a critical role in creating a favourable investment climate for both local and global market players, and hence will enhance the competitive advantage of their key economic sectors in the global economy. Presenting an optimistic picture of global integration of economies worldwide, Pallan and Abbott suggest that globalization and the state systems are mutually reinforcing. The interventionist and the proactive role of state in globalization represent what the authors call 'institutionalization of globalization in the state system'[19] (Pallan and Abbott 1999: 6). The term implies that the state strategies and policies have been modified or re-modified in accordance with the changing needs and the demand-supply dynamics of the global market. For example, the Communist State in China, under the regime of Deng Xiaoping, had to advance a series of economic reforms since the late-1970s to encourage private investment and embrace open market policies. On similar lines, Park Chung Hee of South Korea, brought forth a policy strategy that marked a transition from import-substitution industrialization to export-led growth

19. Ronen Pallan and Jason Abbott (1999), *State Strategies in Global Political Economy*, New York: Pinter Publications, p. 6.

providing better avenues for private entrepreneurship through direct state assistance.

Many states in the developing world initiated industrial transformation by harnessing the opportunities of the global market and that the phenomenon of globalization itself produced varieties of state actions to re-orient its policies and programmes and provide ample opportunities for private investment. Additionally, traditional notions about developing countries as supplier of cheap raw materials is now being questioned as newly-emerging economies in Asia like China, South Korea and India make inroads into the global market with incredible performance in most-favoured and sought-after sectors like electronics hardware and ICT services. These countries entered into innovative areas of production and services that were in high demand in United States and West Europe. But amongst these, few of them like South Korea, Taiwan, Hong Kong, and Singapore could grow faster because of their timely intervention in the global economy. Others like China and India had to suffer from prolonged industrial sickness as a result of their closed-door policies.

It can be stated that global opportunities become relevant only when the policies are rightly ordered to avail them. However, global integration of the economies of the developing world needs a more comprehensive understanding. For this purpose, there is a need to delve into the interplay of political and economic factors at the domestic level that determines the nature and the extent to which liberal policies supporting globalization get institutionalized. Does, globalization imply indiscriminate opening-up or policy-makers are selective in the process? Here, it becomes relevant to highlight selective promotion of industrial sectors with the assistance of state and its bureaucratic agencies. This selection is based on the assessment of comparative advantage of such sectors in the global market.

Second, policies corroborating promotional aspects require a desirable political context under which a continuous process of negotiation takes place between the state agencies as well as state and private stakeholders. Pursuing a specific line of policy becomes difficult when countervailing pressures emerge from both state and social sectors. Therefore, embarking upon a developmental path like liberalization and globalization does not guarantee a consistent movement along that path. There may be intermittent fluctuations emerging out of the countervailing pressures from the local business groups, trade unions and multinational players. However, there are possibilities of complementarities of interest and ideology which may necessitate collaboration between the agencies of state and society. In such situation, parts of state may align with groups within the society to compete for certain demands and most-sought after policy decisions.

Above all, globalization or overdependence on international market for economic growth appears to be a misnomer when it is ridden with financial uncertainties. Global economic turmoil may completely debilitate export-oriented firms that face heavy business losses in such situation. This may further hamper employment prospects in global firms or reduction of salaries and perquisites of the working staff. In many cases, the state may rescue companies facing severe economic distress and are at the brink of closure.

Furthermore, globalization also creates international division of labour where certain countries acquire dominant position while others secure subsidiary roles with minimal economic success. For example, the ICT sector involves multifarious activities and tasks exhibiting different levels of skills and capabilities. As a result, different kinds of products and services may either produce greater value-addition or represent low-value added activities. This point will be elaborated in the later part of the book in the context of India.

Other than this, globalization is seen to facilitate mobility of people and jobs across the globe. Increasing outflow may thus create shortage of human resources and technology in the domestic economy. While some states have checked outflow of skilled labour by extending attractive incentives, others have remained reticent to this trend. However, some countries have found alternative ways to check the outflow. For instance, the Indian Government has extended NRI remittances to facilitate investments by NRIs in strengthening the domestic industry and infrastructure.

Industry and State Regulation

Regulation is a central concern in all theories discussed above. While advocates of globalization and the neo-classical theory denounce regulation of any kind, Neo-statism essentializes its role to sustain capitalist economy. In this regard, it becomes relevant to understand different forms of regulation as it would go into defining manifold varieties of state-interventions to promote industrial development. It would also have implications for how policies are negotiated not only between state and domestic actors but also with multinational companies.

Regulation is defined as an essential mechanism of public control over private sector behaviour[20] (Vogel 1996: 9). It is a means through which the government exercises control over private investment and production. The purpose of state regulation in modern economies is not to restrict but facilitate the market by changing the rules of the game. There is a clear line of distinction between regulatory regimes and restrictive regimes. Regulation does not inhibit private investment and production, while restrictions are prohibitive. Restrictions include industrial licensing, heavy taxation, import licensing, and tariffs. The primary aim of a restrictive regime is to establish public sector monopoly and discourage private business. On the other hand, a regulatory regime tends to strike a balance between public sector and private sector involvement in industrialization. However, regulation in its extreme form becomes restriction. At the other extreme, a completely free market regime demands absolute freedom of market. In fact, all three regimes are a part of continuum of government control over private sector.

A process of deregulation began in United States after the Second World War. It resulted from greater interdependence between nations that renounced protection of their domestic

20. Steven K. Vogel (1996), *Free Markets, More Rules: Regulatory Reform in Advanced Industrial Countries,* Ithaca and London: Cornell University Press, p. 9.

industries. Milner in her comparative study of global industries and politics of international trade in US and France observes that, "The greater integration of American industries into the international economy altered the domestic actors' preferences and thus forestalled recourse to protectionism. Though interdependence subjected the economy to new foreign competition, it also greatly augmented international economic ties for some firms"[21] (Milner 1988: 18). The tie-ups between US firms with foreign companies increased rapidly since 1960s. Vogel points out three main reasons behind the deregulation movement:

1. To foster competition in the market
2. Technological advances
3. Global integration of markets.[22]

Recognizing the ill-effects of free markets in recent economic downturns, the governments in the developed countries have resorted to regulatory measures. Re-regulation does not imply control over domestic private business but necessary restrictions on foreign collaboration and other forms of business engagement with foreign companies. In other words, re-regulation involves protectionism to domestic firms facing stiff competition from foreign players.

Steven Vogel proposes a 'model of re-regulation in developed countries' by categorizing regulation into four types:

1. Pro-competitive re-regulation
2. Juridical re-regulation
3. Strategic re-regulation
4. Expansionary re-regulation.

Each of these regulations tends to define government-business relationship more specifically and the scope of government authority to regulate private enterprises. The diagrammatic

21. Helen V. Milner (1988), *Resisting Protectionism: Global Industries and the Politics of International Trade*, New Jersey: Princeton University Press, p. 18.
22. Steven K. Vogel (1996), *Free Markets, More Rules: Regulatory Reform in Advanced Industrial Countries*, *op. cit.*, pp. 14-16.

representation of the typology of regulatory reforms given by Steven Vogel has been shown below[23] (Vogel 1996: 14-16).

	Emphasis on liberalization	**Emphasis on re-regulation**
Undermines government control over the industry	*Pro-competitive re-regulation* (a) Designing regulation to help competitors (b) Adding regulation to facilitate the effective operation of markets (c) Strengthening antitrust regulations and/or their enforcement	*Juridical re-regulation* (a) Putting informal rules into legal forms (b) Putting tacit rules into written form (c) Formalizing consultation/ improving procedures to ensure accountability
Enhances government control over the industry	*Strategic re-regulation* (a) Giving regulatory advantages to domestic firms (b) Using regulation to take away advantages of foreign firms (c) Promoting/ protecting domestic firms so they can cope up with liberalization	*Expansionary re-regulation* (a) Creating new regulations to enhance bureaucratic authority (b) Replacing old regulations within new ones to retain regulatory control (c) Extending regulations to new areas

23. *Ibid.*, p. 17.

The primary concern of different lines of arguments is to resolve the dilemma of state regulation of private business on one hand and free market and free enterprise on the other. Regulation is now believed to be an essential condition for sustained industrial growth. Complete deregulation may lead to uncontrolled capitalism which may have further repercussions for the economy as a whole. The Great Depressions of 1919 and the recent world recession are well indicative of the ill-effects of uncontrolled market. In a globalized world, the recessionary disturbances in few developed countries have had an overarching effect on rest of the world. The oil shocks of 1970s, the East Asian financial crisis and the recent global economic meltdown produced devastating impact worldwide.

Recognizing the essentiality of government regulation even in a market economy, the governments worldwide, particularly in United States, have recently resorted to several regulatory measures. Reregulation has taken the form of strategic reregulation in United States that has recently resorted to protectionist measures to provide security to its domestic firms and the professional employees. Such protectionist measures include immigration checks, stringent visa measures and restrictions on IT and service outsourcing. On one hand, the domestic labour and certain firms facing stiff competition from Indian firms undertaking outsourced services will get the required protection, the Indian software firms may loose out clients abroad. Regulation thus eliminates the insecurities created by the involvement of foreign firms in the domestic economy.

A wave of re-regulation in United States and European Union has, however, resulted in insecurities for Indian IT industry which is largely dependent on these countries for their business. How would Indian government respond to this scenario? Will it be desirable to continue supporting export-oriented IT firms as they face restrictions abroad? Does it become necessary to create business opportunities within India, especially in the government sector that comes as a big package with the e-governance programme? These questions require serious attention as this would provide fresh insights into how IT sector in India and the government together build new perspectives on IT and service sector policies. Further, the re-orientations will be contingent upon the newly formulated developmental goals that require active involvement of private sector, especially the IT companies in various programmes and projects of the government.

The other response would probably be introducing regulatory norms in line with TRAI. Regulatory institutions have facilitated the growth of sectors in India. They serve as facilitators as well as controllers of private industries. The contributions of the Telecom Regulatory Authority of India towards strengthening the telecommunications industry are notable. Absence of similar regulatory institution in case of IT and software industry has disturbed the balance between regulation and promotion through indiscriminate extension of incentives.

State, Regulation and Software Industry in India

Recently, the comparative literature on state and industrialization has focused on the emerging industrial sectors, particularly Information Technology. India, being one of the leading exporters of software products and services has generated scholarly curiosity to explore the development trajectory of the industry and locate the contributions of state and non-state actors in this journey. Some valuable insights in this regard has emerged in the writings of Richard Heeks, E. Sridharan, K.J. Joseph, Anthony D'Costa, and Vibha Pingle. While Vibha Pingle's and Richard Heek's works on software sector in India are confined till the period of mid-1990s, Sridharan's and Anthony D'Costa have analyzed the recent production trends within the software industry. Most of these works go beyond the assumptions of Neo-Classical theory of state and recognize that the government's promotional programmes have been critical for export-led growth. They express their denial of the thesis that proclaims that absolute freedom of market forces will serve as a driving force for the development of newly-emerging technological sectors. Nevertheless, all of these consider the vitality of export-driven investment for sustained growth and development.

Vibha Pingle in her comparative studies of the development trajectories in three major industrial sectors in India namely software, automobile and steel shows how different forms of bureaucratic intervention produced variable performance in each of these sectors. In line with the argument made by the neo-statists on developmental state, Pingle infers that the pro-active and pro-business orientation of the bureaucrats in the software industry helped in its consistent growth as compared to steel and automobile. Automobile serves as an intermediate case in this comparative frame of analysis. Pingle points out that,

> "Developmental activity also requires autonomous bureaucrats, who are more likely to adopt policies beneficial to the industry as a whole than are bureaucrats captured by one or another societal interest.... If industrial policy is to promote overall industrialization, not only enable a select group of firms or a class of people to prosper, state autonomy would appear to be essential."[24]

To illustrate the developmental role of state, that includes political leadership and the bureaucrats, Pingle mentions the following conditions in the form of a diagram:

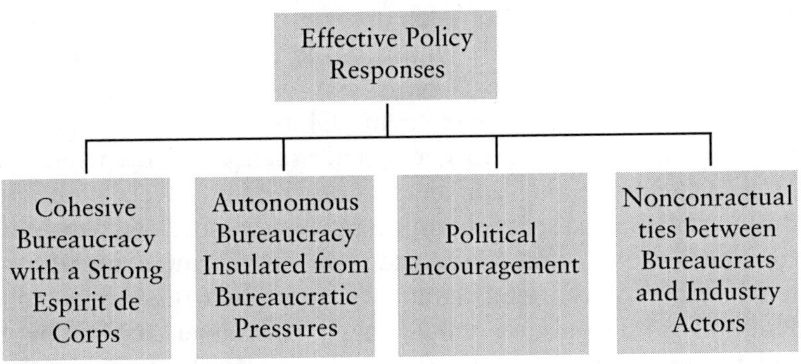

Source: Pingle (2000)[25]

The diagram indicates four important conditions for the formulation of effective industrial policies. All these conditions reflect the autonomous role of political leadership and bureaucrats

24. Vibha Pingle (2000), *Rethinking the Developmental State: India's Industry in Comparative Perspective*, New Delhi: Oxford University Press, p. 7.
25. *Ibid.*

but suggest development as a collaboration venture between political leadership, bureaucrats and the industry actors. Pingle termed these conditions, taken collectively, as 'developmental ensemble.' She uses this formulation to assess the developmental trajectories of the three industrial sectors.

Evans' embedded autonomy thesis also corroborates the developmental ensemble model of Pingle. In both the studies, the focal point of analysis in accounting for industrial transformation is the developmental orientation of policy-makers coupled with the autonomy of bureaucracy in the implementation process. Based on this conceptualization, Pingle inferred that software policies in India closely fit into the development ensemble framework. It is shown that bureaucratic activism informed by a powerful developmental orientation within the DoE and the cooperative ventures with prominent industrialists-cum-technocrats in the emerging software sector triggered its growth. On the other hand, cooperation and trust deficit between bureaucrats and entrepreneurs in steel and automobile sectors is seen to produce dismal growth in these sectors.

The development state theory delineates an exaggerated picture of success in the industry. It ignores the lob-sided growth patterns resulting from pressures of globalization and the strategies to overcome them. Global integration of the industry has given rise to new predicaments like involvement of firms in low-value added tasks, increasing levels of brain drain, imbalance between domestic and export segments of the industry, pressures to withstand the increasing competition from other developing countries, particularly China and Philippines. Second, it would be a misnomer to compare India's software story with Korean or Japanese success in the electronics sector. Unlike these two countries, the Indian system of government incentivization has not involved systematic appraisal of the beneficiaries' performance. The STP scheme for instance leaves little scope for a firm's performance assessment while incentivizing them. In contrast, the practice of qualitative subsidization prevalent in South Korea extended financial subsidies to chaebols on the basis of a systematic assessment of the annual targets achieved.

Moreover, both governed market and state-in-society approaches have not taken into consideration the political constrains that may inhibit the government to follow preferred policies marked by developmental innovations. The political constraints may emerge from within the state like the opposition party or the constituents of the ruling coalition. A consistent investment and export-related governmental support is also a difficult proposition amidst pressures from other ministries like Finance and Commerce and industry. In India, few ministries have off and on expressed their opposition to import liberalization, tax concessions in STPs, and so on, as happened in the late-1980s. While they haven't outrightly rejected the demands of the industry and the DoE (and now the Ministry of IT) they have shown serious concerns over financial implications of extending tax concessions to software exporters.

The globalization argument has inadvertently lost sight of the domestic political constraints that pose difficulties for the government to liberalize policies with the aim of triggering industrial growth. It is observed that while there was a general consensus over liberalization since 1991 economic reforms, the late-1980s witnessed political opposition against import liberalization for software exports. This resulted in significant policy backtracks during this period. Second, the advocates of globalization present a picture of exaggerated optimism about global opportunities and the rationality to harness them at proper time with correct strategies. Over-dependence on the global market may sometimes prove detrimental for the qualitative growth of an industry. In the wake of profit making, the prospective exporters may confine their business to low-end services and lack the conviction to upgrade their capabilities. Inordinate freedom to such market players on the pretext of globalization may worsen the position of the industry as the absence of regulatory pressures may end all possibilities of upward mobility in the global market. The two factors taken together may have debilitating effects on industrial growth itself. State's regulatory presence as a guardian may be crucial for desirable skill upgradation and consistent performance of the firms in both global and local markets.

Reliance on global opportunities may also not be a desirable strategy given the economic and political uncertainties of the global market. Economic uncertainties have been produced in the form of depressions and recessions due to uneven growth of capitalism. Waves of protectionism have re-emerged lately in the Western world due to both economic and political pressures. In such situation, over-attachment with the global may give rise to predicaments for the local. At times, the decisions favouring openness or protectionism in the Western world are predominantly political. And, therefore, the level of volatility of such policy decisions is very high. Short of being objective formulations reinforcing some economic logic, they end up reflecting the subjective preferences of the political incumbents. As Helen Milner points out that, "Choices about the degree of openness of a state's market are quintessentially political ones. They entail decisions about the societal allocations of the costs and benefits of economic change. Moreover, these policy choices have undeniable political significance"[26] (Milner 1988: 3). In a comparative study of policies of international trade in United States and France, Milner observed that the key political issue in the late-1980s in United States was that in response to economic distress should it close its market to foreign products or not.

Empirically, globalization has dictated the domestic industrial policies of the state from time to time. But in a democracy like India it has also been resisted in situations of economic distress and by ideological positions that see it as a cause of increasing vulnerability of the masses. Pressures from non-state and state actors like the political opposition, other institutions of governance have mainly emerged to resist attempts to globalize mass-based sectors which have a wider consumer base and an active labour force. In the perceived elite-based sectors like software, opposition is mellowed as it only comes from within the state, sometimes even within the ruling party. But, globalization occasionally face resistance in such sectors as software due to its apolitical character. Reasons for this could be

26. Helen Milner (1988), *Resisting Protectionism: Global Industries and the Politics of International Trade*, *op. cit.*, p. 3.

better understood in the light of its comparison to other sectors that are mass-based.

Regulation of Industrial Sectors: A Comparative Perspective

While certain regulatory standards for the industry are commonly defined under Industrial Development and Regulation Act of 1951, specific institutions have been created for regulation of certain industrial sectors. The specificity of regulatory norms in each sector is determined by its nature and its implications for the overall development of the economy and society. For instance, a sector like pharmaceuticals that is directly concerned with the health of the people requires greater state control over private industry. Similarly, telecom which affects the connectivity between people by facilitating communication and information-dissemination also becomes a necessary public good requiring governmental regulation. Such regulations may not always been seen in a negative light. They are not antithetical to private investment, a belief that was commonly held in the 1960s and 1970s. The real goal of such regulatory institutions is to ensure best practices in business from the standpoint of collective good and human development. Its objective is public welfare and not anti-business.

Technology-drive industrial sectors like pharmaceuticals, telecommunications and computer software have followed different trajectories of policy shifts and regulations in India. While partly regulations have resulted from the specific needs of the sector and their respective contribution towards socio-economic development, the political circumstances and nature of bureaucracy have been equally deterministic. The inveterate vested interests of bureaucrats regulating such sectors have posed difficulties for implementing structural transformation decisions taken at the macro level. The lock-in industrialization of the 1960s and 1970s created vested interests in certain sectors more than others.

Second, the market has been dominated by the public sector units with nadir presence of private companies. Regulation for justifying prevention of concentration of wealth and socialist goals of the economy has often eclipsed the monopolistic tendencies of the public sector units supported by their bureaucratic agencies, for instance in the telecom sector. On the contrary, regulation seemed absolutely genuine in pharmaceuticals sector in the wake of increasing drug prices. IT was quick to change and respond to needs of a global market but could not create appropriate regulatory measures in the process of integration.

Pharmaceuticals: Pharmaceuticals industry is undoubtedly a mass-based sector as it is directly concerned with the health and life of people. Its importance in developing countries of Asia, Africa and Latin America can be gauged from the fact that they suffer myriad problems of poverty, malnutrition, and fatal diseases like malaria, typhoid, cholera, diarrhea, HIV/AIDS, cancer, tuberculosis, measles, tetanus, meningitis, and several others. Health hazards thus pose serious challenge to governance in these countries including India. The pharmaceuticals industry in India is one of the leading producers of drugs and medicines of international standards. It has not only developed drugs and medicines for the domestic consumers but also exported them to the poor countries of Asia and Africa. Its annual growth rate is between 8-9%.

The government of India has passed several Acts to regulate this sector. The most prominent amongst these are the Drugs and Cosmetics Act 1940 for regulating the manufacture, import, distribution and sale of drugs and medicines in India; the Pharmacy Act 1948 to regulate the profession of pharmacy in India; and the Narcotics Drugs and Psychotropic Substances Act 1985 concerning the regulation of operations related to narcotics drugs and psychotropic substances. The two major regulatory bodies in this sector are Central Drugs Standard Control Organization and Drugs Control General of India within the Department of Health of the Ministry of Health and Family Welfare. Additionally, the pharmaceuticals industry comes directly under the control of the Ministry of Chemicals and Fertilizers which is responsible for policy-making, planning, development, and regulation of the pharmaceuticals industry in the country.

One of the most politicized areas in pharmaceutical industry has been the issue of drug pricing. There has been a long-standing demand on the government to control the prices of drugs. The DPCO (Drug Price Control Order) 1995 is one of the most recent Acts meant for controlling the prices of certain drugs. The Order provides a list of price controlled drugs, procedure for fixation of such prices, and methods of implementation. A new regulatory institution namely the National Pharmaceutical Pricing Authority was established for implementing the provisions of DPCO. NPPA gave serious considerations over expanding the scope of price control, and in view of its recommendations, 20 new drugs were brought under price control. Under the new dispensation, a price increase of 10% would invite scrutiny by the regulator. This would be applicable to even non-scheduled drugs. Statistics show the drug companies owe over ₹ 1410 crore to the NPPA for alleged cases of overcharging. The stringent price-control norms have created a rift between industrialists and the regulator.

Recently, the Pharmaceuticals Policy 2002 and the National Pharmaceuticals Policy 2006 have sought to encourage R&D in focusing on research and drug development with clinical trials especially for the treatment of HIV/AIDS and cancer. Regulatory institutions are being entrusted with the role of ensuring R&D investments by the private establishments. The regulatory regime in pharmaceuticals sector has not been antithetical to private competition. The concerned institutions have encouraged competition in the market but have remained strongly vigilant about the quality and prices of drugs. As pricing of drugs has been a politically-sensitive issue, it has not been left onto the modalities of market mechanisms.

Telecommunication: Telecom regulation has followed a different trajectory whereby the creation of TRAI (Telecom Regulatory Authority of India) led to the breakdown of the monopoly of DoT (Department of Telecommunications) and encouragement for healthy competition between the private players in the telecom market. DoT functioned as a policy-maker, a regulator and a service provider. While the liberalization was underway since mid-1980s, DoT officials showed reluctance in facilitating openness in the telecom sector. The DoT served as a guardian to retain the monopoly of public sector enterprises MTNL and VSNL in providing telecom services. While MTNL catered to the telecom needs of the domestic market, VSNL provided international services in India. Both the PSEs were able to monopolize the telecom market under the aegis of DoT. This resulted in extremely high costs and poor quality telecom services.

DoT's negative approach towards private sector participation in the telecom market created a rift between the DoT and PMO (Prime Minister's Office). PMO favouring private competition in telecom found it difficult to withstand the resistance of DoT. As a solution, the government constituted the Athreya Committee that submitted its report in 1991. Most of the recommendations favouring openness and market competition were vehemently opposed by DoT. But the major bone of contention was the recommendation regarding separation of roles of policy-maker, service provider and regulator.

The National Telecom Policy 1994 was one of the first moves in the direction of privatization. But it was only a half-hearted move with DoT still retaining most of the powers to take policy decisions. It only created certain favourable conditions for the entry of private players in the telecom market. As Rahul Mukherji observes that, "The National Telecom Policy of 1994 permitted private investment in basic telecommunications services. This was a minor concession because basic services in the government sector were cross-subsidized by domestic and international long distances services. This privilege would not be available to the private players"[27] (Mukherji 2009).

The birth of the regulator TRAI (Telecom Regulatory Authority of India) on 27 January 1996 to counterbalance the powers of DoT opened new avenues for private sector participation in the telecom market. Like DoE, the TRAI favoured entry of private players in the domestic market

27. Rahul Mukherji (2 May 2009), "Interests, Wireless Technology, and Institutional Change: From Government Monopoly to Regulated Competition in Indian Telecommunications", *The Journal of Asian Studies*, vol. 68, no. 2.

particularly in the area of cellular or mobile business. Many a times it gave its verdict in favour of private players in case of disputes between private service providers and MTNL. Quite contrary to the desires of DoT, TRAI wished to end the monopoly of MTNL in the domestic market. Unfortunately, the TRAI was given limited powers till the National Telecom Policy of 1999. Under the aegis of ITA (Indian Telegraph Act) 1885 the DoT enjoyed enormous powers. For instance, the TRAI could settle disputes between two service providers but not between DoT and a service provider.

The Telecom Policy of 1999 finally transferred most fundamental decision-making powers to TRAI. Under the new dispensation, the DoT was required to consult TRAI in matters of granting license to the service providers. The Department of Telecom Services within the DoT was corporatized into BSNL (Bharat Sanchar Nigam Limited) in 2000. This was followed by disinvestment in VSNL, the long distance service provider, with Tata Group holding majority shares.

Liberalization and favourable regulation in telecom was met with consistent opposition from the short-sighted bureaucracy that favoured public-sector monopoly and disfavoured private investment. The high-cost telecom services offered by the public enterprises could only be afforded by the richer classes in the urban centres. Privatization and the birth of TRAI broke this monopoly and facilitated public access to telecom services by promoting competitive prices in the market.

Computer Software: DoE (Department of Electronics), established in 1970 served as the regulator of electronics sector that encompassed both hardware and software segments. To begin with, the DoE provided a protectionist shield to the dominant public sector enterprise in electronics and computers namely ECIL (Electronics Corporation of India Ltd.). The monopoly of ECIL and the already existing restrictive laws like MRTP and FERA inhibited the entry of private players in the computer market. The only private player in computers was TCS at this time. Regulation took the form of restrictions which was manifested in high taxes and heavy duties, restrictions on imports, licensing, checks on capacity expansion and new investments.

The challenge to the monopoly of ECIL mainly came from the two major foreign players in the domestic market namely IBM and ICL. Therefore, in order to establish the dominance of ECIL the government passed several regulatory Acts like MRTP and FERA that forced the foreign players out of the Indian market. DoE thus acted liked the DoT in the 1970s by favouring the monopoly of ECIL and showing reluctance towards private investment in the electronics sector. One reason why the DoE showed disinclination towards privatization was that the market for computers and electronics was still limited to government departments and few big private players and business families. The computers were produced mainly for the defence sector of the government.

Nevertheless, the DoE was quick to change its role from regulator to a facilitator during the 1980s with the support of a technocratic leadership. In fact, the top-level bureaucrats took special interest towards working in close alliance with the PMO for encouraging liberalization and privatization with the objective of exploring new business opportunities offered by the global market in software and services. The guise of an export-oriented sector also made computer software less people-oriented or mass-based in contrast with pharmaceuticals and telecom. Whether export-promotion strategy was a political strategy of the government and corporate bodies to present computer software as an elite domain and thereby deliberately minimizing the chances of its politicization is a matter of speculation. Nevertheless, the perception of software being an elite-based sector of the industry with its client-base being confined to the big companies in US was gradually questioned and challenged by the fact it has tremendous potential to facilitate social development and serve as a product of mass utility. This justified the necessity of greater government intervention in the form of e-governance. However, with global integration the matter got diluted and the need for its mass utility did not receive proper cognizance. NASSCOM, the main pressure body for IT and BPO companies has primarily focused on export-oriented strategies of promotion and has negotiated with the government for liberal policies from time to time. Regulation has also been kept at bay as politics in the form of trade unionism has not driven the attention of workers within the industry. Contrarily, absence of worker's union is a political strategy to confirm the elitist image and obscure its mass character well evident in the labour vulnerabilities. In this way, bereft of any political issue so clearly expressed in the false consciousness of the stakeholders, the absence of regulation whether in the form of new institutional mechanisms or labour laws gets politically justified. NASSCOM, that emerged as quasi-regulatory body lacks adequate grievance mechanism and workers lack the initiative for forming their associations. To top it all, the position becomes worse as the IT-BPO sector does not come in the purview of labour law regulations. In short, deficiency of political consciousness sheds the covert mass character and hence the political image of the industry. This creates an open space for labour exploitation and labour vulnerabilities in the industry. These points will be taken up in detail in the last chapter of the book.

Conclusion

The comparative studies on industrial transformation have provided a comprehensive understanding of the patterns of state involvement in developing economies. Scholarly works of Atul Kohli, Vibha Pingle and Peter Evans have involved micro-level analysis of sectoral dynamics showing how a monolithic view of state may not help understand the specificities of policy developments and growth patterns of industrial sectors. Most of such studies delve into patterns of state-capital alliance ascribing the credit to corporate coherence, bureaucratic autonomy and state embeddedness for the success of industrialization.

The role of state in the developing countries has itself been redefined in view of its managerial, corporate and technocratic orientation. Different models of state are seen to have evolved as a result of its developmental role and the likely shifts in its policy strategies. This pattern of theorization is built upon the analysis of variable state responses to new business opportunities in the global market and the emerging technological revolution. It underscores the critical interventions by the state in the economy and industry for harnessing opportunities offered by the global market for technology-intensive products and services. Governments in developing countries like India, China and Philippines have evolved new strategies to promote their computer hardware and software sectors and exercise this comparative advantage to reap maximum benefits from the market offerings.

The East Asian experience of fast-track industrialization and technological advancement, particularly in the fields of electronics and computer hardware has been exemplary. The exploration of the factors behind their economic success is the core theme of all theories discussed in this chapter. However, as observed, their positions and interpretations about institutional dynamics behind industrial transformation are nuanced and clearly distinguishable. While scholars like Bhagwati and Friedman, belonging to the Neoclassical school, cite full autonomy of private entrepreneurs and export-oriented strategy of industrialization as two crucial factors behind the success of East Asian development; Neostatist scholars like Peter Evans, Robert Wade and Alice Amsden pay greater attention to the guardian role of state that involves two basic forms of intervention namely, extending export-oriented incentives to selective firms and ensuring adherence to quality standards through opportune regulatory checks. Irrespective of this fundamental difference, the two theories converge while highlighting the significance of export-oriented strategy for a consistently high-performance of East Asian economies.

The theoretical interventions in the area of state's economic role in post-colonial nations have provided valuable insights into the political economy dynamics of industrial policy-making in the developing countries. The paradox between the ideas of free enterprise and state intervention, that forms the kernel of recent theoretical discourses, still remains a core concern for policy-makers and bureaucrats. While competitive pressures produced by global capitalism require governments to create investment-friendly climate for private entrepreneurs, political pressures of democracy inhibit opening-up beyond prescribed limits. In such dilemmatic situation, that state appears in heterogeneous forms with political masters and bureaucrats exhibiting multifaceted interests and nuanced views about economic policies and programmes. Further, it also becomes important to locate arenas and issues on which state and non-state actors align to support a certain line of policy and others where dissensions within the state inhibit it.

The debilitating effects of intensive global integration require prior attention so that the state may take necessary measures to overcome them from time to time. A truly developmental state is therefore one that maintains its autonomy vis-à-vis the market forces and attempts to regulate the industry in a manner that reaps long-term benefits. Incentives for industrial development must therefore be complimented by regulatory measures so that the excesses of global integration may be checked from time to time.

Finally, the conceptual framework to understand state responses to globalization in IT-BPO sector draws upon the themes and conceptual categories of Neo-statism and theories of globalization and industrialization. In this regard, some analytical points addressed further are mentioned below.

1. Internal political pressures on state may pull parts of state in different directions but largely remains receptive to the agenda of the major pressure group. This may require coherent networking or what is often referred to as corporate coherence between industry and bureaucratic agencies.
2. External economic pressures that on one hand necessitates globalization to reap the benefits of the mammoth market for technological services and at the same time creates dependency that may result in loss of business and foreign exchange under economic distress.
3. Political uncertainties in host countries may hamper economic prospects of the private companies and quite possibly re-orient government policies towards local market and social sectors, at least temporarily.
4. Political salience of a sector determines the extent of regulation to check both globalization-induced predicaments and internal exploitative tendencies.

❐

Chapter 2

IT Sector in Emerging Asian Economies: Comparing China, South Korea and India

The industrial policies in post-colonial developing nations underwent rapid transformation to adjust to the fast-changing technologies globally. The private companies adopted new strategies to modify their existing patterns of production. In this process, they ventured into innovative areas of production and manufacturing. The international market that was characterized by high levels of competition demanded greater skills and innovation from the newly developing nations in Asia and Latin America. As a result, few prospective newly developing economies like China, India, Brazil, Philippines and South Korea entered into such new sectors of economy in order to make their mark in the international market and counterbalance the dominant position of developed countries of West Europe, United States and Japan. Some of such new industrial sectors included computer hardware and software, telecommunications, biotechnology, and pharmaceuticals.

The promotion of such technology-intensive industrial sectors required a favourable political environment and special strategies for promotion. Why was this so? It was realized that the private companies traditionally involved in manufacturing could not afford to take the risk of new initiatives. For newly-emerging firms it was even more precarious to enter such business primarily due to lack of financial resources and technological skills and capabilities required to meet the desired quality standards. Industrial sectors like computer software and hardware, biotechnology, pharmaceuticals and telecommunications were both knowledge-based and capital-intensive different from the conventional ones. Therefore, such industrial sectors required advanced technology as a basic input to gain competitive edge in the international market.

The level of state assistance for the private companies has varied for different countries. Also the changing political contexts have determined the nature and level of state support for private business within a country at different points of time. In view of this, the nature of state-capital relationship has prescribed the path of industrial development creating new avenues of production, investment and foreign collaboration. The conventional patterns of relations between state agencies and private entrepreneurship based on mutual hostility was unsuitable in the context of a globally integrated market. A slow-paced bureaucratic arrangement had to be replaced by dynamic institutions that could support prospective export-oriented firms in their innovative ventures. In this regard industrial policies in most of the newly developing economies followed an export-oriented strategy replacing import-substitution industrialization. In addition, the need for higher foreign exchange was required for speedy economic development.

This chapter attempts to study the industrial policies of three leading economies of Asia namely, China, Korea and India in the changing scenario of the international market which demanded greater integration of the economies and at the same necessitated high levels of technological innovation to compete with the advanced technologies of the West. It examines the governmental initiatives and policies pursued in these countries to establish their electronics and IT sectors for achieving high levels of growth and enriching foreign exchange. The correlation between the nature of state intervention and patterns of industrial growth with reference to the electronics and IT (software and hardware) sector will thus be understood from a comparative perspective.

China

China is one of the fastest growing economies of the world today. The Chinese economy grew at an average rate of almost 10% during the period 1979-95 and at 8% thereafter. The policy of liberalization and economic reforms that were initiated in the late-1970s brought several structural changes in the patterns and modes of production and shifted the focus of economic policy from centralized planning to market reforms. The command economy initiated under Mao's regime in 1950s established centralized management of the economy. In this pattern, the agrarian economy was re-organized by replacing individual farming with collectivization and state ownership; whereas the industrial enterprises were brought under complete state ownership. As large investments were channelled to build heavy industries particularly iron, steel and machine building; light consumer-based industries remained grossly neglected. As a result, China achieved an industrial growth of nearly 10% from 1949 to 1980. But, as Susan Shirk (1993) observes that, the costs of industrial growth were directly felt by the consumers. It did not bring trickle-down effect and the living standards remained abysmal due to poor infrastructure facilities.

State-run heavy industrialization also contributed less towards building technology-intensive electronics and communications industry that was coming up in a big way in some of the neighbouring states like Japan, South Korea, Taiwan, and Singapore. The growth strategy in these states saw clear opportunities in global integration of their economies but decided that the state will assume the lead role and autonomy in industrialization. The South Korean case will be discussed in the latter part of this chapter to indicate the success of this strategy. But this served as a lesson for Chinese Communist Party which was already loosing popular legitimacy due to its authoritative and coercive actions during the Cultural Revolution on one hand and poor public delivery system on the other. The new leadership in the CCP under the leadership of Deng Xiaoping seriously thought of propelling a fundamental shift in economic policies by abandoning close-door policies and initiating market reforms.

The economic reforms that were initiated in the late-1970s also had a political logic behind it. It was a result of competition for succession between the political leaders Hua

Guofeng and Deng Xiaoping. Deng was an ambitious leader and had a strong acumen towards bringing about radical structural changes in the economy. In this regard Susan L. Shirk points out that, "The question of why the Chinese embarked on a set of ambitious market reforms during the decade after 1978 cannot be answered simply by pointing to the poor performance of China's prior economic system or the post-Cultural Revolution crisis of confidence at elite and mass levels. The proximate cause of the 1978 initiatives was the succession contest between Deng Xiaoping and Hua Guofeng. Deng acted as political entrepreneur, using innovations in economic policy to discredit Hua Guofeng and attract support among groups in the CCP (Communist Party of China) Central Committee and Politburo"[1] (Shirk 1993: 37).

The economic reforms initiated in 1978 identified computer hardware and electronics amongst others for inviting both private and foreign investment. Few landmark developments of the market reforms are: "import-led growth policy in 1978; the large scale and open-foreign borrowing in 1979; the decision to establish special economic zones in 1979; the opening of the Shenzhen Economic Zone in 1980; relaxation of tax and tariff rules in 1983 mainly applicable to foreign companies; and the opening up of number of coastal cities to foreign investment in 1980"[2] (Ellman 1986: 423). The most innovative scheme to achieve rapid economic growth and improve external business engagement was opening up Special Economic Zones, mainly in the coastal areas of Guangdong and Fujian. The Central party leaders at Beijing offered special incentives to these regions for foreign investment. In response to the preferential treatment for coastal regions, the inland and mainland provinces also began demanding for such incentives especially to support investments in new technologies.

Since the initiation of reforms in 1978 the Chinese industrial policy has been oriented towards developing and then

1. Susan L. Shirk (1993), *The Political Logic of Economic Reform in China*, Berkeley: University of California Press, p. 37.
2. Michael Ellman, "Economic Reform in China", *International Affairs*, 62(3), Summer 1986, p. 423.

strengthening the technology-intensive sectors of the economy. The government led by the Communist Party of China under the leadership of Deng Xiaoping renounced its hostility towards private entrepreneurship and developed close ties with them. But, the support mainly came in the form for export-related incentives for prospective enterprises. This further meant that the core agenda of the new economic policy was to facilitate exports. The Proposal of the Central Committee of the Chinese Communist Party for the Seventh Plan for national economic and social programme adopted in September 1985 stated that, "The key to implementing the open policy with an increased use of foreign funds and imported technology is to increase foreign exchange earnings through exports"[3] (Ellman 1986: 129). Further, it sought to open up its economy for foreign investment and foreign collaboration both for technology transfer and foreign exchange. The underlying purpose behind the open-door policy was also to upgrade indigenous technology through 'learning by borrowing' process.

However, the reformist programme was piecemeal. The dissenting voices within the party organization particularly those coming from the rank-and-file expected that Deng along with his trusted supporters within the party and bureaucracy moved slowly in their reformist agenda. This meant that indiscriminate opening-up was objectionable and promotional measures were expected to be taken up judiciously both for economic and political reasons. The government also followed a selective approach while extending incentives. The electronics and the emerging computer hardware industry remained the chief recipients of the benefits. In this background of strategic thinking within government circles, the Communist Party of China undertook selective initiatives for the electronics and computer hardware industry. As Zemin points out, "Since the reform and opening up of China in the late-1970s, the IT industry of China has seen rapid growth"[4] (Zemin 2009: 9).

3. Quoted in Michael Ellman, "Economic Reform in China", *International Affairs*, 62(3), Summer 1986, p. 430.
4. Jiang Zemin, "Development of IT industry in China in the New Age", J. Shanghai Jiaotong University (Science), 2009, vol. 14, no. 1, p. 9.

To begin with, the Chinese government encouraged collaboration with foreign firms like Hewlett-Packard, Toshiba and Compaq. The Ministry of Electronics Industry also concluded a joint venture agreement with IBM in the early-1980s although later the US giant decided to go on its own for some time. Finally, it entered into a pact with an emerging local Chinese company called Great Wall in 1994. While this helped IBM get an access to local distribution and marketing channels, the local company could upgrade its technological capabilities by gaining access to IBM's technological and manufacturing know-how (Kraemer 2002: 31). In this manner, many other local PC companies like Tontru, Legend, Star and Shida entered into joint ventures with foreign companies at different stages.

Besides these ad-hoc arrangements to support the newly emerging computer industry, formal arrangements to establish the electronics industry were introduced in the Seventh Development Plan in 1986. The vitality of the industry in strengthening the entire economy was well recognized in the Plan programme. Thereafter, the Ninth Five-year Development Plan focused mainly on the production of Chinese-assembled computers and the computer peripherals such as monitors, printers, disk-drives, add-on-cards and high definition displays. It also paid due attention to the development of IT infrastructure that was found to be lagging in the country (Kraemer 2002: 30).

The Chinese government has strongly supported its software and hardware industry with tax concessions, export incentives, duty free imports and export-processing zones, and so on during the 1980s and 1990s. New programmes and schemes like '908' and '909' projects meant for the development of integrated circuits were started during this decade. Since the hardware sector of the IT industry in China has greater comparative advantage over the software counterpart, it has been a recipient of greater incentives and benefits. Nollen and Siddharthan have observed that, "Chinese import policies for machinery and components have been less restrictive than India's, and custom delays less frequent. These differences mostly apply to hardware manufacturing firms which engage in sizable imports of components"[5] (Nollen and Siddharthan 2008: 25).

Chinese companies have also ventured in several areas of software production and are now providing a stiff competition to Indian firms. In the software segment, Chinese firms have focused on the production of packaged software than services. Packaged software requires high-technology inputs and demand greater skill on the part of the software engineers. China has followed a balanced developmental strategy by paying equal attention to the growth of hardware and software segments. The Ministry of Industry and Information Technology reported that, "China's software growth generated 329.14 billion yuan ($48.19 billion)...Sales of software products surged 24.2% to 115.22 billion yuan, accounting for 35% of the total software industry revenue in 2009"[6] (*China Daily* 2009). The policy focus on software and services could be traced back to the Ninth Development Plan which affirmed its commitment, as it says, "to support the information technology industry specifically the hardware, software and information service sectors in computers and telecommunications" (Kraemer 2002: 30).

The turning point for the Chinese software industry came at the beginning of 2000, a landmark year for IT boom world over. The government made certain determined and concerted efforts towards promoting its software industry. The first step taken in this regard was the advancement of the policy package under the 'No. 18 document' which is also called "Some policy to encourage the development of software and IT industry" dated July 24, 2000. Following this, in 2002, the government launched a second very important document called "No. 47" with the caption "The principle of rejuvenating the software industry" which covers wide areas of assistance for the industry including financing, exporting, human resources, government

5. Stanley Nollen and N.S. Siddharthan (2008), "Software and Hardware Firms in India and China: How they differ", in S.R. Hashim's and N.S. Siddharthan's, ed., *High Tech Industries, Employment and Global Competitiveness*, London: Routledge, p. 25.
6. *China Daily*, 27 June 2009, http://www.chinadaily.com.cn/bizchina/2009-06/27/content_8329730.htm

procurement and others. Additionally since the year 2000, the government invested heavily on R&D in the ICT industry. Ministry of Industry's "Fund for electronics and information industry", "863 high-tech program", "National S&T Breaking-through Program", "Fund for S&T based SME innovation" of MOST (Ministry of Science and Technology), and others were policy interventions for encouraging in-house R&D. It is observed that as a result of such efforts and initiatives of the Ministry of Industry and Information Technology, "By 2000, the weight of investment products representing technological level and higher added value had approached 40%"[7] (Zemin 2009: 10).

Since 2000 the Chinese IT industry has witnessed rapid growth in both software and hardware segments. Kharbanda and Suman observe that,

> "In the hardware sector, China is on its way to becoming the world's biggest base for computers, mobile phones, and information products manufacturing. In case of PCs alone it accounted for 36% of the Asia-Pacific market, with 7.17 million PCs sold in 2000."[8] (Kharbanda and Suman 2002: 1450)

Between 2000-2011, the Chinese information technology industry emerged as one of the largest in Asia-Pacific region. As given, the annual gross income of the industry jumped from RMB 1000 billion yuan in 2000 to RMB 7800 billion yuan in 2010[9] (China Economic Net).

The Chinese government has followed a balanced approach towards the promotion of its IT industry in export and domestic markets. In addition to extending export-oriented incentives to the software and hardware segments, it has paid substantial attention to strengthen the domestic base of the IT industry. Still,

7. Jiang Zemin, "Development of IT industry in China in the New Age", *op. cit.*, p. 10.
8. Kharbanda and Suman, "Chinese initiative in the software industry: quest to leap", *Current Science*, 25 December 2002, vol. 83, no. 12, p. 1450.
9. China Economic Net, http://en.ce.cn/Insight/201104/02/t20110402_22343698.shtml

the Chinese companies mainly concentrate on manufacturing computer hardware, telecommunications systems and accessories for the domestic market. Therefore, while producing for the international market they do not loose sight of the growing business opportunities in the domestic market. As Hashim and Siddharthan point out that,

> "The Chinese software industry is equally productive and efficient but has been purposely oriented towards the domestic market to spread the infusion of IT across a wide spectrum of domestic industries. This may be one of the important factors in the export competitiveness of the Chinese manufacturing sector as a whole.[10] (Hashim and Siddharthan 2008: 9)

Additionally, the Chinese government took necessary steps to keep pace with fast-changing global technologies. The government has taken special efforts to ensure the induction of advanced technology by the IT companies and this was primarily a reflection of the new orientation towards economic modernization as opposed to the ideological conservatism during the Maoist regime (Gabriele 2002: 328). R&D mainly remained confined to defence-related projects and not productive enterprises in the market. The position changed since the early-1980s when the government encouraged research centres to sell their knowledge intensive inputs to productive companies. The government financial assistance for R&D in priority sectors like space, laser technology and supercomputing increased substantially by the end of the decade. In this regard, a network of government institutions in synergy with private companies work towards strengthening R&D under the overall guidance of Ministry of Electronics Industry and SSTC (State Science and Technology Commission), now MOST (Ministry of Science and Technology) that report directly to the State Council, the administrative arm of the National People's Congress. The institutions in the network include The Electronic Technology Information Research Institute, China Computer

10. S.R. Hashim and N.S. Siddharthan (2008), *High-tech Industries, Employment and Global Competitiveness*, London: Routledge, p. 9.

and Microelectronics Information Research Institute, China National Electronics Import Export Corporation, The Chengdu Electronics Research Institute, and the Great Wall Computing Corporation. The primary responsibility for promoting in-house R&D lies with the MOST. It aims at fostering, "commercialization, industrialization and globalization of scientific and technological achievements, administer the management of the national high technology industry and to formulate policies, laws and regulations regarding technology market" (Gabriele 2002: 334).

One of the innovative programmes started by the SSTC in 1988 was the 'Torch Programme' that mainly channelizes the developmental efforts of new technology industries like electronics and computers, promotes product innovation and creation of high-technology development zones (Gabriele 2002: 334). The uniqueness of the Torch programme was that it supported the R&D efforts of several SMEs that later grew into large industrial enterprises. In 1986, the SSTC launched the National High Technology Research and Development Programme, commonly known as 863 spreading over 15 years, focusing mainly on the promotion of seven R&D-intensive areas namely: automation, biotechnology, energy, information technology, laser technology, new materials and space technology. The pace of R&D investment was accelerated by the mid-1990s when the draft proposal on 'Decision to Accelerate the Development of Science Technology' embodying new strategies to promote R&D was approved at the National Science Conference in 1995. A target of 1.5% of GDP on R&D especially in electronics and high-technology areas was set for the year 2000 (Gabriele 2002: 337).

As a result of these efforts, the Chinese IT firms devoted a substantial portion of their investment on R&D. Their innovations have provided them a competitive edge and made them world leaders in the production of digital programmable exchange, mobile communication, digital mobile trunked communication, Tera-scale large computer systems, high performance computers and servers, general purpose CPUs (central processing unit), home-made middleware, financial and enterprises management software and anti-virus software.

The Chinese government has also been highly instrumental in facilitating reverse brain drain of their IT engineers working at Silicon Valley in United States and other countries of West Europe. AnnaLee Saxenian (2004) observes that China developed strong transnational networks between the Silicon Valley and the domestic IT industry. According to Saxenian, the Chinese government took a series of initiatives to encourage participation and contribution of the foreign-educated Chinese IT engineers and those employed in the Silicon Valley towards the development of domestic industries, particularly the infrastructure sectors. In this regard, many technical and business exchange programmes were started by the government. This included organizing a number of conferences, investigation tours, joint research projects, joint research projects and exhibitions. Such exercises were undertaken to promote technology transfer to the domestic industry. One of such popular initiative was the 'Chunhui Programme' that was started by the Ministry of Education. Under this programme, the government financed short-term trips by the Chinese overseas students to participate in R&D-related activities and conferences[11] (Saxenian 2004: 179). Other initiatives of the government in this direction include the creation of 'Returning Students Venture Parks' within the Development Zones of High Technology and Enterprise exclusively for the returnees. Many benefits like relaxation of bureaucratic restrictions, infrastructural facilities, financial incentives, and so on are provided in these zones[12] (Saxenian 2004: 180).

In totality, it can be stated that since the initiation of reforms in late-1970s the Chinese government has embarked on a series of measures to promote its IT industry. Although, concrete initiatives through planning were taken most seriously

11. AnnaLee Saxenian (2004), "The Silicon Valley Connection: Transnational Networks and Regional Development in Taiwan, China and India" in Anthony P. D'Costa and E. Sriddharan (eds.) *India in the Global Software Industry: Innovation, Firm Strategies and Development*, New York: Palgrave Macmillan, p. 179.
12. *Ibid.*, p. 180.

since the mid-1990s, joint venture programmes supported by the government had begun in the late-1970s. The government extended various types of incentives and facilities to both hardware and software companies by establishing Special Economic Zones and technology parks. This kind of partnership between state and corporate bodies is also visible in India; but a fundamental difference that requires careful attention is that while the Chinese state maintained its autonomy and control over the private sector and followed a balanced growth strategy, India's IT policies since early-1990s were fully oriented towards export market and little effort was taken to encourage investment on in-house R&D. The rapid growth of IT exports from China is indicated in Table 1.

Table 1: Export of IT products from China from 1989-2007 in US billion dollars

Year	Total Exports
1989	28
1992	69
1995	165
1998	324
2001	650
2004	2075
2007	4595

Source: J. Shanghai Jiaotong University (Science) 2009[13]

The IT sector in China, particularly the software segment has adequately met the demand of the domestic market. It has found wide-scale application in the military establishments. It is observed that since 1990s in the wake of modernization of national defence the IT industry has been involved in several R&D projects for developing military IT equipments. The industry has expanded its reach in both industrial and civil sectors. In this

13. Jiang Zemin, "Development of IT industry in China in the New Age", *op. cit.*, p. 9.

regard, Saxenian observes that, "The new technology regime has been extremely successful in development of IT manufacturing capabilities, where relationship between domestic firms and foreign investors, particularly from Taiwan and Hong Kong, have contributed to rapid development of the domestic capacity for low-cost manufacture of computers, consumer electronics, and communication equipments"[14] (Saxenian 2003: 11).

Table 2: Country-wise data on the use of computer and IT by the civilians in the FY2000/2001

Countries	Personal Computers (per 1000 people), 2000	Internet Users (thousands), 2000	ICT Expenditures % of GDP, 2000
China	15.9	22,500	5.4
India	4.5	5,000	3.8
Brazil	44.1	5,000	8.4
Israel	253.6	1,270	7.4
United States	585.2	95,354	8.1

Source: AnnaLee Saxenian, 2003

Inference: It is well indicated that China had the second highest number of internet users in 2000. In all three indicators, China leads India. China's success story in IT and telecommunications has redefined the role of state in promoting knowledge-based, technology-intensive industrial sectors of the economy. The IT industry under the guardianship of the state has been excelling in both local and global markets.

South Korea

One of the biggest success stories in automobiles, electronics and computer manufacturing is that of South Korea. South Korean electronics giants particularly LG and Samsung have

14. AnnaLee Saxenian, "Government and Guanxi: The Chinese Software Industry in Transition", DRC Working Papers, March 2003, no. 19, *Global Software in Emerging Markets*, Centre for New and Emerging Markets, London Business School, p. 11.

come to own a significant share of global business in mobile, computer hardware, and other electronic consumer goods like refrigerators, air-conditioners, microwaves and many other home appliances. They are also the major DRAM, SRAM, ASIC design approaches, electronics material and packaging, and new information technology product suppliers in the world. South Korea, as it stands today, is a global leader in state-of-the-art R&D, foreign ventures, and world-class science and technology programmes.

The success of South Korea in industrialization and technological modernization has aroused scholarly attention amongst economists, political scientists, and scientists worldwide. Political economists like Jagdish Bhagwati, Alice Amsden, Peter Evans and Robert Wade acredited the success of industrialization in South Korea to its unique export-led growth strategy assisted by an autonomous bureaucracy. In contrast, the lacklustre performance of India and Brazil is seen to be emerging from their close-door import substitution policy. As mentioned earlier, there are two lines of argument on understanding the reasons behind the rapid industrial and economic growth of South Korea: one that recognizes the uniqueness of the policy of liberalization and market reforms supported by minimal state intervention; and other that underscores the vitality of state-private collaboration under the overall guidance and supervision of a coherent and autonomous state bureaucracy. Bhagwati, belonging to the former school of thought, cites the cases of India and South Korea to justify the superiority of liberal trade regimes and the danger of protectionist policies. Figures indicating growth rates of the two countries have been compared by him. Bhagwati observed that the growth rates of South Korea has shown a consistent upward trend since 1960s when it made a shift towards export-led growth. Indian economy and industry which was far ahead of South Korea in the 1950s and 1960s remained stagnant thereafter due to its protectionist policies. To cite, "South Korea's manufacturing products, negligible in 1962, amounted by 1980s to nearly four times those of India. The manufacturing sector of South Korea was less than 25% as large as India's in 1970s; by 1980s it was already upto 60%"[15] (Bhagwati 1988: 93). Elaborating on the government strategy for promoting South Korea's electronics industry, Mahalingam observes that, "Deficient in internal demand, South Korea resorted to a successful export orientation and selective import-substitution policy, aggressively targeting on selective segments of the world's electronics industry"[16] (Mahalingam 1989: 2376).

On the other hand, scholars like Peter Evans, Alice Amsden and Robert Wade underscore the significance of the symbiotic relationship between state and chaebols. Evans (1995), in his 'embedded autonomy thesis' observes that the development trajectory of IT industry in South Korea clearly shows the prevalence of embedded autonomy. Wade (1990) takes a more radical position while defining the role of state in the arenas of industrialization and international trade. He recognized the contribution of a corporate state with its coherent structures in South Korea to justify its rapid success in the sphere of industrialization. Likewise, Alice Amsden observes that the state in South Korea played the role of a guardian in nurturing its industries. The state encouraged the firms to export by advancing subsidies and other kinds of incentives. The subsidies extended were of two kinds:

1. Tax breaks that included the reduction of import and corporate income taxes especially depreciation allowances incurred in establishing export markets for electronics.
2. Direct fiscal subsidies for investment in domestic electronic firms for increasing exports and for the purchase of required foreign technology.[17] (Villa and Han 1990: 273-92)

15. Jagdish Bhagwati (1988), *Protectionism*, MIT Press, p. 93.
16. Sudha Mahalingam, "Computer Industry in India: Strategies for Late-Comer Entry", *Economic and Political Weekly*, 21 October 1989, vol. 24, no. 42, p. 2376.
17. Luis Suarez Villa and Pyo-Hwan Han, "The Rise of Korea's Electronic Industry: Technological Change, Growth and Territorial Distribution", *Economic Geography*, 1990, vol. 66, no. 3, pp. 273-92.

government and chaebols—a symbiotic partnership

'he government was involved in a corporate relationship a cooperative venture with the chaebols. This was ularly visible at the time of formulating industrial policies. Ernest has pointed four major factors behind the success Korean Electronics and Informatics Industry. These are ws:

The symbiotic relationship between the 'developmental state' and huge-family owned conglomerates known as haebols.

ubsidized credits and tax privileges combined with rict performance requirements.

port protection to the infant industry during the tial stages of development coupled with offsetting entives for export sale.

trictions on the inflow and outflow of capital. (Ernest 8: 251)[22]

industrial strategy was initiated by the government Chung Hee's regime a period that witnessed fast-nization of the Korean economy and industry. period which is marked by rapid growth and n the economic history of the country is popularly s the period of 'South Korean miracle.' The ring this period adopted an export-led growth ustrialization. It harnessed the best practices and ertise of its private entrepreneurship in order rialization. By allocating capital and moderate overnment promoted some leading companies , Samsung, LG and Kia in the international aewoo is a leading producer of automobiles, are global giants in electronics and computer

n of finances through credit, loans and ictly based on the annual performance of

"Catching-up, crisis and industrial upgrading: cts of technological learning in Korea's electronics p. 251.

However, these incentives have been performance-based which meant that the government fixed prior export targets for selective companies and the annual extension of incentives was based on meeting the set targets. This kind of performance-based industrial policy has been termed as 'qualitative subsidization.' Neo-statism mainly highlights the two-fold strategy of the government in building national economy and infrastructure; these are as follows:

1. It encouraged private investment in selective industrial sectors like electronics and automobiles by extending both monetary as well as non-monetary incentives but maintaining control.
2. It adopted export-led growth strategy of industrialization and made heavy investments in infrastructural development.

The push factors, so mentioned, helped South Korea emerge as one of the leading producers of semiconductor chips, computers and peripherals. Today, the country holds the distinction of being one of the biggest exporters of personal computers, microcomputers, color graphic terminals, and disk drives. Semiconductor chips account for nearly 10% of the total exports in South Korea. Some of the VSLI-level semiconductors (a more advanced version of semiconductors) produced are integrated circuits, transistors, diodes, memory devices and logic elements[18] (*Korea Business* 1994: 81). Recognizing the successes of the semiconductor industry in South Korea, Dieter Ernest points out that,

> "The pace and scale of the capacity and market share expansion of Korea's semiconductor industry is unprecedented in the history of the electronics industry. Never before has a country been able to move so rapidly from the position of an insignificant outsider to that of the market leader in a highly capital-intensive industry saddled with incredibly high risks and entry barriers."[19] (Ernest 1998: 254)

18. Atul Kohli, *Korea Business* (1994), World Trade Press, p. 81.
19. Dieter Ernest, "Catching-up, crisis and industrial upgrading: evolutionary aspects of technological learning in Korea's electronics

Table 3: Korea's electronics exports in different segments placed rank-wise (million dollars) for the year 2006

Rank	Electronic Product	Export (million dollars)
1	Integrated circuit	34,386
2	Wireless communication equipment	30,889
3	Flat display	14,522
4	Video/audio equipment	6322
5	Computer ephemerals	5717
6	Rotary equipment for home use	4406
7	Passive and apparatus parts	3872
8	Computer ephemerals (memory device)	2297
9	Dry battery and storage cell	1638
10	Semiconductor device	1516
11	Electron tube	1357
12	Wired communication equipment	997
13	Computer body	376

Source: Korea International Trade Association (2007)

Like China, the Korean electronics and computer hardware industry has primarily focused on enhancing the quality of its products which is done through the use of state-of-the-art technology. Technology innovations were facilitated by R&D, an area that involved substantial investment since 1970s when

industry", *Asia Pacific Journal of Management*, 1998, vol. 15, p. 254.

the sector was at its take-off stage. As Lui
that,

"Indeed, the electronics indus
spending was three to four tim
the manufacturing sector over
reflecting a rise in domestic
sophistication in product de
Han 1990: 281)

The electronics industry of So
external borrowing but adapting
technology. A combination of wel
and low-cost disciplined labour fo
in electronics, semiconductor an
it is observed that South Kore
ventured into software busines
substantially on R&D in that

Table 4: Ratios of
amount in ea

Capital	Less than 1 billion won
IT Service	10.10 (177.09)
IT Equipment	20.99 (379)
Software	17.76 (431.29
Total	15.81 (361.7

Note: The number in
per capital amount, i
Inference: The data
of software sector.
software is reason

20. Luis Suarez
Electronic
Distributi
21. P.R. Kin
Telecom
vol. 15.

The

and
partic
Dieter
of the
as follo

1.

2. S
3. In
in
inc
4. Re
199

Such an
during Park
track moder
This golden
development
referred to a
government d
strategy for inc
managerial exp
to pursue indus
incentives, the g
such as Daewo
market. While D
LG and Samsung
hardware.

The allocatio
subsidies were str

22. Dieter Ernest,
evolutionary asp
industry", *op. cit.*

industries on the export front. The government nationalized the banks in order to centralize financial control. Furthermore, the government employed tight control on interest rates and directed credit loans to support specific sectors and industries allocating more than half of the bank credits in supporting the programmes. Performance evaluation was based on confirmation to policy guidelines framed by the government. Managers carefully executed government decisions and prudently avoided visible failures such as large loan defaults. They were made to monitor the loans closely, held responsible for the failure of any discretionary lending and were encouraged to make the directed loans profitable. These checks by the government disciplined the firms involved in the transaction business. The government, being the creditor could not only cut off official credit but also impose punitive measures against the borrowers in case of dissatisfaction with their performance. Also the guardian role of the state was reflected in their support to the firms in bailing them out during financial distress.

On the other side, the chaebols devised effective channels of communication to provide required market information to the government from time to time and assisted in effective translation of policy goals into industrial activities. Furthermore, monthly meetings on export promotion and briefings on market trends were organized which were chaired by the president and attended by senior government officials, bankers, business representatives and labor union leaders. The basic purpose behind this joint exercise was to develop common understandings on various export, economic, market and development-related issues. In these meetings, the officials of the Ministry of Trade and Industry prepared reports that not only fixed export targets but also incorporated the difficulties faced by the chaebols in meeting their export targets. The process of assessment of exports involved an item by item scrutiny of the performance. After the discussions and deliberations over these matters the president in consultation with other members from various segments prescribed ways of resolving the bottlenecks. This process of collective involvement in policy-making indicates that the government, labor, private entrepreneurs and bankers shared a common responsibility towards achieving the prescribed goals. The triad—industry, bank, and government—has been termed as 'government-led-internal organization' by Thomas Hellmann and Yoon Je Choo[23] (Hellmann and Choo 1994).

In addition to these collaborative ventures between the government and private entrepreneurs, the government took certain specific initiatives for strengthening the electronics sector. First, it enacted various laws with regard to national banking regulations, low-interest loans, tax incentives and duty-free import of selected capital goods for the growth of the high-technology industries. Second, the Ministry of Science and Technology; Ministry of Trade, Industry and Energy; Ministry of Information and Communication have extended financial support to various institutions, universities and research bodies for R&D from time to time. Further, the government has created 'Science Parks' which provide various infrastructure facilities including internet services and buildings with state-of-the-art technology. The most famous amongst them is Taedok, situated nearly 150 km south of Seoul. Additionally, highways and new transportation systems were established to improve public delivery. Lastly, the government has devised special schemes and programmes for promoting SMEs. The Korean Electronics Technology Institute assists the SMEs and emerging high-tech industries in product development, augmenting their tool bases and providing other kinds of specialized services.

The chaebols have also grown consistently with continuous state support for all their innovative ventures. They have taken full advantage of the subsidized loans and tax breaks provided by the government. Table 5 shows the rising trends of South Korea's electronics exports since the late-1980s.

In the final analysis, it could be stated that the collaboration between state, private entrepreneurs and other stakeholders in the industry has resulted in rapid industrial development in South Korea. The government bureaucracy has remained autonomous from sectarian or particularistic interests but at the same time served as a guardian to the flourishing business

23. Thomas Hellmann and Yoon Je Choo (1994), "The Government's Role in Japan and Korean Credit Markets: A New Institutional Perspective", *Seoul Journal of Economics*.

conglomerates; carrying out functions of regulation and promotion simultaneously.

Table 5: South Korea's Electronics Exports from late-1980 to mid-1990s

Companies	1987	1991	1993	1995
Samsung	$1.8 billion	$5.00 billion	$7.00 billion	$10.00 billion
LG	$1.8 billion	$2.1 billion	$2.9 billion	$5.00 billion
Hyundai	$390 million	$730 million	$1.1 billion	$4.1 billion
Daewoo	$800 million	$1.2 billion	$1.5 billion	$1.9 billion

Source: WTEC Report on the Korean Electronics Industry[24]

Indian IT Sector in Comparative Perspective

The transformation towards a promotional and market-driven model of industrialization in India was a way-long journey. A strong sense of commitment towards socialist pattern of industrialization during the Nehruvian era led to planned industrial development and the concomitant creation of a public sector monopoly. The drive towards state-led industrialization gained further momentum with nationalization of industries and private banks, industrial licensing, and high levels of corporate taxation during Mrs. Gandhi's first tenure as the prime minister. These policy changes resulted from the political compulsion of gaining the support of CPI to continue in the government. Therefore, the political alliance between CPI and Congress exacerbated the possibilities of privatization and liberalization. Transition to industrial liberalization only began in the mid-1980s with the initiatives of Shri Rajiv Gandhi which continued thereafter. The change in political scenario marked by greater proximity between government and corporate sector has facilitated the process of liberalization and privatization since then. Globalization was however not in the immediate political agenda.

In this background, the software industry in India followed a different growth trajectory as compared to electronics

24. www.wtec.org

and hardware sectors in South Korea and China. During the initial stages of development of the computer sector in India, the government followed strict regulation and focused on strengthening the hardware industry for the domestic industry. This stage began in the late-1960s and culminated into a tussle between IBM and the government in the mid-1970s. On the contrary, the Korean government had already begun supporting its electronics industry during this period by removing restrictions on private investment and production. In case of China, the inter-party conflicts over succession had sown the seeds of liberalization during the mid-1980s. Second, import substitution industrialization provided the foundation for India's industrial policy till the late-1970s. In South Korea, the Park Chung Hee government preferred export-led growth as a model of industrial development under which a number of export-related incentives were extended to the chaebols. Export-led industrialization became a critical subject of economic reforms that were initiated in the late-1970s by Deng Xiaoping. China locked out its industrial sectors to the international market and encouraged foreign investment and foreign collaborations. However, political advocates of socialist pattern of industrialization informed by the agenda of establishing public sector monopoly inhibited the transition to liberalization for a consistently long period of time.

The software sector became the foremost recipient of business incentives resulting from the industrial liberalization of mid-1980s. However, the incentives were not supplemented by adequate performance assessment and effective regulation unlike China and South Korea. This led to the emergence of a new set of predicaments within the sector like brain drain, performance of low skilled tasks, imbalance between export and domestic market, lesser investment on R&D, and so on. Comparing Indian and Chinese hardware and software firms with respect to their R&D contributions Hashim and Siddharthan point out that,

> "Chinese spend more on R&D and they introduce more products and processes. Until recently, Indian software firms participated mainly in the less-technologically

advanced segments of the customized software business such as programming, testing and maintenance for which R&D and product or process innovation was scarcely necessary."[25]

Second, while the Indian software firms were primarily export-oriented the Chinese counterparts produced more for the domestic market. As a result, despite having a large market domestically the Indian software sector until very recently could not harness the opportunities therein as much as the Chinese firms did.

The only area that served as a disadvantage for China in the global service industry was the lack of English-speaking professionals in the country. On the contrary, abundant supply of skilled software professionals with English-speaking backgrounds provided immense business opportunities to the BPOs and KPOs in India. Lately, the Chinese government has sponsored several courses in order to overcome this shortcoming. Such an initiative is directed towards enhancing the competitive potential of the Chinese software firms in the global market.

Table 6: High-technology industry value-added, selected years 1990-2002 in US$ million

Country	1990	1992	1994	1996	1998	2000	2001	2002
India	1401	1891	2416	2722	3516	3734	3886	4076
China	9224	13157	20139	25596	34532	59042	67596	86770
South Korea	10959	12448	16397	22577	20375	38407	36958	41652

Source: National Science Foundation[26]

25. S.R. Hashim and N.S. Siddharthan (2008), *High-tech Industries, Employment and Global Competitiveness*, London: Routledge, p. 33.
26. http://www.nsf.gov/statistics/nsf07319/content.cfm?pub_id=1874&id=7, "Asia's Rising Science and Technology Strength: Comparative Indicators for Asia, the European Union, and the United States", National Science Foundation, National Centre for Science and Engineering Statistics.

The comparative data on the growth of high-value added technology-intensive industries clearly indicates that even after a decade of liberalization (in 1991). India's high-tech industry has lagged behind China and South Korea. In fact, China's growth story in this regard has been unprecedented and has made it emerge as a global economic powerhouse.

Conclusion

An analysis of the patterns of state's intervention in industrialization clearly indicates that the trajectories followed by the three emerging Asian economic giants were different from each other. With the culmination of independence in India and South Korea and the consolidation Communism in China, these countries embarked upon a comprehensive planning for development. While industrialization became the core agenda of economic planning in India and South Korea, reforming the agrarian structure became the major area of attention in China. However, with the changing scenario of international market marked by rapid growth of technology these countries began recasting their economic and industrial policies. In the process, government's involvement in the economy also underwent marked shifts. The difference in the orientation of political leadership at different points of time produced different policy responses to globalization. Taking full advantage of the opportunities in the international market, the South Korean state drove its economy with the strategy of export-led industrialization and translated its policy goals into desirable growth outcomes. Contrarily, because of the restrictive industrial policies in China and India industry remained stagnant for a relatively longer period. In their study of Indian software industry, Patibandla, Kapur and Petersen observe that,

> "While the South Korean semiconductor industry became internationally highly competitive, the Indian industry (referring to computer industry) remained non-competitive.... Indian governments' organizational efforts fell short of making the industry internationally competitive. The South Korean government nurtured

> the industry by investing adequate amount of capital in a targeted and systematic way (unlike India's blanket import substitution) and building up a good network between government and private producers. In India's case the close-door policy and licensing controls stifled the industry and thereby contributed to making it non-competitive."[27] (Patibandla, Kapur and Petersen 2000: 1265)

The lack of foreign collaboration and FDI inhibited technology transfer that immensely hampered efficiency and innovation in Chinese and Indian industries. It was not until late-1970s that the Chinese state realized the need to abandon closed-door policies and encourage foreign investment and collaboration especially in high-technology sectors. Thereafter, the Chinese government took direct responsibility in assisting the IT and software companies through its R&D initiatives and later provided attractive incentives to facilitate reverse brain drain of the software and IT engineers in Silicon Valley. The Indian software firms also received consistent government support since the advent of industrial liberalization in the mid-1980s; but only for exports. Also, little effort was made to retrieve the young talents that were working for US and European companies.

The nature and quality of state intervention in industrialization is a defining feature of state's role in developing economies. Quality here entails both the right choice of industrial strategy and the state's involvement with market forces. Involvement in economy can take two forms: 'promotion with effective regulation' and 'regulation informed by restriction and prohibitions.' China and South Korea witnessed rapid industrialization by opting for the former type of state involvement. The Indian state adopted public-sector driven import-substitution industrialization in 1950s within the purview of planned development and took almost three decades to realize its debilitating effect on industrial growth. Liberalization that was initiated during 1980s confronted political opposition

27. Patibandla, Kapur and Petersen, "Import Substitution with Free Trade: Case of India's Software Industry", *Economic and Political Weekly*, April 8-14, 2000, vol. 35, no. 15, p. 1265.

especially from the old-guards within Congress party but remained reasonably acceptable since the advancement of New Economic Policy in 1991. While achieving high growth levels particularly since the year 2000, the Indian software companies face several challenges under pressures of globalization. One of it is certainly the stiff competition that comes from the newly emerging Asian economies like Philippines, Indonesia and China.

❐

Chapter 3

Software Industry in Early Stages: From State Control to Liberalization

The computer software industry emerged in India during the mid-1970s. However, it was not recognized as a sector that needed special attention for getting incentives until the mid-1980s. Therefore, for almost a decade it remained an important constituent of electronics sector. Throughout the 1970s, policies for electronics and computers were applicable to software as well. Further, the central focus of computer industry was on hardware production. During the first phase of its development of the computer industry the primary objective of the government was to develop the hardware sector mainly to meet the needs of the defence sector. The focus shifted to software mainly in the mid-1980s when under Rajiv Gandhi's regime the government advanced a number of policies specially meant for the promotion of the software sector.

The initial phase of growth in the computer industry is marked by the dominance of the public sector unit, ECIL (Electronics Corporation of India Limited). ECIL was established in 1969. The emphasis of ECIL was on the production of hardware, though some preliminary attempts were made to produce software packages as well. The other peripheral industries that were established for production of computers were Bharat Electronics Limited, CMC, and Hindustan Teleprinters Limited. These public sector units came up in the background of the recommendations of the Committee on Minicomputers that proposed adequate public investment in R&D, design, assembly testing, software, maintenance and sales.

The domestic entrepreneurship was virtually absent in the computer software industry of 1970s. As stated, ECIL was mainly involved in the production of computer hardware and it was only during late-1970s that ECIL entered the software segment. The domestic market was mainly dominated by two multinational companies, namely IBM and ICL. However, since the government was inclined to maintain the dominance of ECIL, the companies were forced to retreat. While, ICL compromised with the conditions laid by the government, IBM retreated.

The process of liberalization, starting from the early 1980s and gaining momentum in the mid-1980s, converged with the recognition of software sector as an 'industry' having a strong future potential in domestic and global business. The government adopted an export-oriented policy for the software recognizing the long-term advantages of strengthening the sunrise industries, namely computer software, telecommunications and biotechnology. The shift was largely a result of declining industrial growth and burgeoning of sick industries. The failure to meet the goals of industrialization was contingent upon the inefficiency and incapacity of public sector enterprises that had assumed a monopoly position in the market. Therefore, it became imperative for the government to curb monopolies by providing a level-playing field to private entrepreneurship, particularly in the emerging technology-intensive, knowledge-based industry like computer software. It was with this developmental conviction that during the mid-1980s the computer software industry received exclusive attention by the Rajiv Gandhi government. This phase also witnessed a marked change in the nature and role of DoE (Department of Electronics). The most distinguishing feature of the software industry in India is that this is one industry where the private sector, since the mid-1980s, has received consistent support in its business ventures by its regulatory institution, the DoE.

The late-1980s witnessed some amount of political opposition over liberalization of software policies, especially the measure to reduce import duties. The inconsistency in policy shifts is clearly visible in the emerging policy backtracks at this time. The differences and disagreements were not only over mere policy changes but larger ideological issues related with retreat from socialism. The discomfort with liberal policies was not only expressed by the Left but the socialist old guards within the Congress. The ideological tussle was therefore not really between the government and opposition but two generation of politicians.

The chapter mainly focuses on the initial stages of the development of the software industry and attempts to locate the political and ideological context within which the industry received its initial start-up. The political context is mainly defined in terms of the nature of political leadership and bureaucracy, and political intercourse between state and capital that includes both domestic and foreign capital. Accordingly, the study has been divided across various sub-phases on the basis of the emerging political scenario and resultant regulations and policy shifts during respective periods.

The first phase is between late-1960s and late-1970s when the central focus of the government policy was to maintain the dominance of the public sector enterprise, ECIL. This phase also witnessed the retreat of IBM, the major computer player in the local market till 1978. Nevertheless, the government adopted few preliminary measures to facilitate private investment and export-oriented industrialization in the computer sector. The early-1980s marked the emergence of liberalization, although in a half-hearted manner. However, it may be stated that during both these periods the computer policy was directed towards hardware production. Little was done to develop the software segment of the computer industry. In other words, the software was still not recognized as an 'industry' having some special infrastructural needs and policy incentives. The real shift towards liberalization, export-oriented industrialization, and privatization took place in the mid-1980s when concrete policy packages were advanced for the software sector.

The Early Phase—Bargaining between State and Foreign Players

The inception of foreign players in India, namely IBM and ICL (a UK-based company) marked the beginning of computer software industry in India. IBM entered the India market in 1964 along with two other players, namely ICL and Digital Equipment Corporation. While IBM had a 100% foreign ownership in the Indian market, ICL had a 40% Indian ownership in its manufacturing unit. But virtually the foreign counterpart was fully dominant even in case of ICL as the sales unit took all the major decisions regarding manufacturing, marketing and sales. The total share of IBM and ICL in the market taken together amounted to almost 85% in which IBM alone had a 75% share until about early-1970s. The dominance of IBM and ICL in the computer market in India in the 1960 inhibited the entry of local entrepreneurs in the computer business. As observed, no private entrepreneur could see the future potential of this industry in a developing economy like India and also they felt that it was extremely difficult to compete with international players IBM and ICL.[1]

With the emergence of ECIL with other public sector enterprises like CMC (Computer Maintenance Corporation Pvt. Ltd.) and Hindustan Teleprinters Limited, the foreign players were forced to quit the market. The forcible eviction of foreign players cleared the ground for public sector dominance. Like textiles, automobile, and gems and jewellery, the computer industry also emerged as an import-substituting industry. The DoE wholeheartedly supported the socialist thrust of the government in the electronics and computer sector.

The Retreat of IBM

Facing stiff competition from the foreign players, IBM and ICL, the ECIL was provided a protective shield by the DoE. The DoE recommended that the two foreign companies must move

1. Patibandla, Kapur and Petersen, "Import Substitution with Free Trade: Case of India's Software Industry", *Economic and Political Weekly*, April 8-14, 2000, vol. 35, no. 15, p. 1265.

away from their trading and manufacturing activities. Further, as IBM's presence in India was through a 100% subsidiary of the parent company, it fell within the purview of FERA (Foreign Exchange Regulation Act), 1974. Under this Act, the equity participation of foreign companies in any firm was fixed at 40%. A high stake of 74% was permitted only under the condition of unavailability of the requisite technology in the domestic market. IBM proposed to set up a 100% export unit to manufacture peripherals and another unit to export software worth a million dollar annually. But they required the permission to import computer systems up to 80% of the value of exports. Additionally, it demanded 100% equity in core manufacturing, marketing and maintenance operations.[2] Since these provisions did not fulfill the requirements of the FERA Act, they were not accepted by the government. Consequently, IBM was compelled to wind up its operations by 1978.

ICL, on the other hand agreed to abide by the conditions laid out by the government and diluted its ownership of the resulting enterprise to 40%. As a result the Indian unit assumed the majority ownership. On similar lines, The Burroughs, another foreign company operating in the computer market, formed a joint venture with the Tata's on a 50% ownership basis.[3]

The departure of IBM from the Indian market must be understood within the framework of the interests and ideology of the new political elites who wished to maintain the dominance of ECIL with the patronage of DoE. Self-reliance and socialism became the ideological motivations for developing an indigenous base of the computer industry, no matter how week and unproductive the base was. In the garb of protecting ECIL from internal and external competition, the ministries of trade and finance also came up with series of restrictions on private

2. C.R. Subhramanium (1992), *India and Computer: A Study of Planned Development*, New Delhi: Oxford University Press, p. 193.
3. Joseph Grieco (1984), *Between Dependency and Autonomy: India's Experience with International Computer Industry*, Berkeley and Los Angeles: University of California Press, p. 30.

competition. For instance, the finance and trade aspects of the industry needed the approval of these ministries.[4]

Preliminary Steps towards Private Sector Promotion

The promotional drive of the government began in early-1970s. On September 1970, the DoE issued newspaper advertisements for developing software especially for exports. In 1973, the government established the SEEPZ (Santa Cruz Electronics Export Processing Zone). Further, in the financial year 1973-74 the DoE under the leadership of M.G.K. Menon proposed a Computer Policy. The policy specified that the software industry in India must develop an indigenous base after which it would be transformed into an export-oriented industry. The policy statement also opined that computer industry could be developed as a powerful indigenous industry. It added that all companies entering the industry ought to be incorporated as a firm under the guidelines laid out by the Ministry of Industry.

The Department of Electronics decided to provide hardware facilities to the software producers on a non-profit basis. Many provisions were made at the outset to promote software production. To facilitate this, the DoE permitted the import of additional hardware and software. The provisions made were as follows:

1. The imports to be entirely utilized for exports of software products.
2. Software to the extent of 100% of the total cost of the system, including maintenance costs, is exported.
3. If the firm was unable to export the necessary software, the government retained the option of take-over.

The Computer Policy, 1974 provided impetus to software production and exhorted private investment but with critical regulatory checks. New computers could be imported provided there was no foreign collaboration involved and net foreign exchange earned within a five-year period equalled the amount

4. Vibha Pingle (2000), *Rethinking the Developmental State: India's Industry in Comparative Perspective*, New Delhi: Oxford University Press, p. 136.

spent on imports. The export requirement was further increased to 200% of the cost of the systems. Such restrictions proved to be unfavorable for qualitative production because it would shun the possibilities of technology transfer that happens through foreign partnership.

The preliminary steps towards encouraging private investment in the software sector can be characterized as restrictive and 'half-hearted' in nature. The main loophole with the provisions was that no significant steps were taken to facilitate borrowing and then upgrading advanced technology. Further, there was hardly any measure to streamline the bureaucratic procedures which served as an impediment to private investment and production.

Role of DoE (the Regulator) and the Ministries

In electronics and computers, the DoE wished to preserve the monopoly of ECIL vis-à-vis the foreign players IBM and ICL. The dominant coalition of DoE and ECIL inhibited the entry of foreign and domestic entrepreneurs in the computer market. In his study, Evans found that DoE's leading members and officials came from the Bhabha Committee which was in turn closely associated with the ECIL.[5] In Evans' view, the DoE assumed a custodian role in the computer industry by discouraging private investment and closing the possibilities of their capacity expansion. The true potential of the private sector in the software sector was ignored as the entire focus shifted to maintaining the dominance of ECIL in both hardware and software production. The lack of competition in the market resulted in the production of outmoded computer systems (hardware) and despite the initial motivation that came through the 1974 Computer policy, virtually no efforts were taken by DoE to engage in software production.

Additionally, the DoE also decided to strengthen the position of CMC, the PSE set up in 1975 for the maintenance of computer hardware and software. At that time S.P. Gupta was the Secretary

5. Peter Evans (1995). *Embedded Autonomy: State and Industrial Transformation,* New Jersey: Princeton University Press, p. 113.

of DoE. His preference for maintaining the dominance of CMC in the computer maintenance market provided yet another instance of socialist pattern of industrialization. Advocating national control over computer production in the computer policy of 1971, the DoE sought to provide a protective shield to both CMC and ECIL.[6]

The primary area of production within the computer sector was hardware. Most of the software was imported and there was very little demand for software in the domestic market. Second, the Ministry of Commerce was the nodal agency for formulating trade policies. Export promotion was not in the immediate agenda of the ministry. Moreover, to restrict imports the ministry proposed high duties and tariffs. This approach contrasts with the governmental network of Ministry of Communications, the Ministry of Science and Technology, the Ministry of Trade and Industry, the Blue House, and the National Computerization Agency in South Korea that took significant export promotion measures and developed a performance assessment mechanism for the advancement of incentives.

The private players in the industry were also miniscule in number. Large companies were not keen to involve themselves in the business of consumer electronics, particularly computers as they lacked access to modern technology. Investment in areas involving high technology inputs was particularly difficult due to excessive restrictions by the state on imports and production capacities. As a result they preferred to confine themselves to the conventional sectors like textiles, cement, gems and jewellery, and so on. However, the Tata Group soon entered the computer business by forming Tata Consultancy Systems Ltd. which was later renamed as TCS (Tata Consultancy Services). TCS, since the early-1990s, has become a leading software and service provider.

Policy Shifts since Early 1980s: The Political Context

The decade of 1980s was marked by an overall shift in the strategy of industrialization adopted by the state. The emphasis

6. Dinesh Sharma (2009), *The Long Revolution: The Birth and Growth of India's IT Industry*, Noida: HarperCollins, p. 136.

on public-sector led industrialization and import-substitution industrialization in the 1970s shifted towards export-oriented growth, technology imports, and privatization in the 1980s. The software sector was the foremost beneficiary of this new mode of thinking in the government circles. While there was a general policy shift towards liberalization in the 1980s, specific sectors like computer and textiles received additional impetus for their comparative advantage.

By the early-1980s the government felt the imperative of a special promotional drive for computer software and its potential in bringing about rapid growth of the economy in future. For a modern economy, it was essential to promote the computer industry as computer technology could enhance productivity and efficiency in any economic activity. The decade of 1980s has also been characterized by a breakthrough in microelectronic technology leading to the emergence of new products in the market. Further, the convergence of electronics, computing and telecommunications also referred to as 'New Industrial Revolution' or 'Information Technology Revolution' has brought significant changes in the organizational structure of the industrial activities. The science and technology revolution ushered at the global level drew the attention of the policy-makers in India who came to realize that any further attempt to restrict private investment, particularly in technology-intensive sectors, would hamper industrial growth in the country.

The promotion of the software industry became an important subject of political deliberations on industrial policy since the late-1970s. Since the general focus of the industrial policy shifted towards export-promotion, it became momentous to facilitate sectors that displayed a certain degree of comparative advantage in the international market. Software was one of them. The comparative advantage of this sector could be exercised by utilizing the skills and capabilities of a talented pool of engineering and management graduates from IITs and IIMs. The decade of 1980s was a take-off stage for the sector. The endogenous changes resulting from significant policy advancements at this stage culminated into a large-scale transformation at the tipping point mediated by an external shock in 1991 (Mukherji 2014).

The early-1980s began with Mrs. Gandhi's second tenure and is marked by a greater alignment between the political leadership and the business community. However, the government under the leadership of Mrs. Gandhi did not attempt at any radical restructuring of policies as it may have led to political repercussion from specific corners of the society and political parties. As Frankel points out that,

> "In the early-1980s the government was unwilling to openly embrace a new industrial policy that departed from the established ideology of socialism and still contributed to the claim that Congress was pro-poor."[7]

Elaborating further on this account, Frankel observes that the government extended whole-hearted support to the private sector to promote greater competition in the domestic market and relinquish its jaundiced view of giving priority to the public sector.[8]

The new political context demanded systematic accommodation of competing interests especially in view of Congress party's great debacle of 1977 resulting from its authoritarian rule and failure to aggregate interests in an emerging heterogeneous political community. Business communities were specially let down by the party's negative approach toward privatization in the 1970s. Plus, the socialist policies could not live up to the expectation of bringing about radical social and economic transformation. Public sector enterprises, barring few, proved largely incapable in meeting the developmental goals and consumer needs. ECIL was one amongst them. So, it was no longer possible to stifle competition within the domestic market and restrict private investment to maintain the monopoly of the public sector enterprises.

Atul Kohli points out that the new political strategy of the government was centered on three crucial areas:

7. Francine Frankel (2006), *India's Political Economy: 1947-2006*, New Delhi: Oxford University Press.
8. *Ibid.*, p. 585.

1. To maintain the rhetoric of socialism, self-reliance and people-friendly policy-making.
2. The emerging political difficulties compelled Mrs. Gandhi to pursue the communal appeal to the dominant Hindu community.
3. New economic measures were adopted to secure the political base amongst the business communities.[9]

Extending the argument further Kohli says that after 1980s Mrs. Gandhi seemed to be more concerned about building her base amongst business communities by shifting away from socialism. He added that in her second tenure, Mrs. Gandhi adopted a more pragmatic approach to accelerate economic growth and build her support amongst business and commercial groups.[10] Kohli and Frankel's observation clearly reflect a shift in the political attitude of the government from a prohibitive to a more accommodative approach. The expansion of business communities with the inclusion of a large number of SMEs (small and medium enterprises) also necessitated the introduction of business-friendly policies.

The early-1980s is thus marked by greater alignment between the government and business groups. The period witnessed the emergence of technocratic entrepreneurship whose active involvement was deemed to be necessary for realizing the goals of industrial liberalization. The computer sector was prioritized within the liberalization package in view of its significance for the overall growth of the economy. The government's strategy in this regard was to follow step-wise process of development. Firstly, the structural constraints to private investment were to be minimized incrementally and then incentives for exports would follow. Software was still a part of the computer industry and therefore no special promotional drive was initiated for it. However, a number of initiatives were taken to liberalize measures for the electronics and computer that directly affected the software sector as well.

9. Atul Kohli (1992), *Democracy and Discontent: India's Growing Crisis of Governability*, Cambridge: Cambridge University Press, p. 313.
10. *Ibid.*, p. 311.

To begin with, the government advanced the 'Minicomputer policy' in 1978. This policy granted the permission for setting up system's engineering companies to design and assemble computers. Nevertheless, the policy was accompanied by certain restrictions. A limit of ₹ 20 million was set for annual production. Further, the policy restricted the limit of the types of computers produced to five and that each could not cost more than ₹ 3 lakh. Also, an access to foreign exchange for importing components and peripherals was limited to ₹ 2.6 million.[11] The policy provisions of the Minicomputer policy provided limited scope for capacity expansion to private companies in the field of computers and electronics. However, it could not address various institutional restrictions that the corporate sector intending to enter computer business was facing. Further, the microcomputer policy failed to provide any special concessions to the emerging software sector. However, taking advantage of the policy four private firms embarked upon the microcomputer business by incorporating advanced microprocessor technology.

The advancement of Microcomputer policy was followed by the constitution of a high level Review Committee to look into the relevance of existing computer policies and structural matters. The committee recommended a number of measures in the area of industrial approvals, tariff policies, fiscal arrangements and exports. In short, the committees suggested a host of measures that would eliminate unnecessary controls and procedures that hampered the growth of the industry.[12] Accepting the recommendations of the High level Review Committee, in the Import policy of 1978-79 a large number of electronics and computer systems were placed under the 'OGL (Open General License)' category.

In 1981, the government constituted the Sondhi and Menon committees to review the position and performance of electronics and computer industries in India and suggest measures to enhance

11. Joseph Grieco (1984), *Between Dependency and Autonomy: India's Experience with International Computer Industry, op. cit.*
12. A Report of the Review Committee on Electronics Part-I (March, 1980), *Electronics Information and Planning*, Department of Electronics, Government of India, vol. 7, no. 6, pp. 303-88.

their growth and performance. These committees recognized a series of bureaucratic controls and regulatory procedures that obstructed the growth of this sector. In paragraph 2 of the report it is observed that the government policy on electronics and computers has focused on regulatory aspects and neglected the promotional and developmental aspects. It recognized that the cumbersome procedures and multilateral scrutiny has stifled the initiatives of SMEs and self-employed technocrats. Before preparing its report, these committees held meetings with a number of industrial bodies and professional experts to seek information and views concerning the structural conditions that hampered the growth of the industry. It was observed that these groups were disgruntled with the government's policy approach and the harsh institutional measures that it had adopted to restrict private investment. These groups wanted the government to eliminate the structural bottlenecks that were inflicting the industries in various ways. In response to the grievances of the private firms, the committees suggested to minimize the controls to the extent that it does not subserve the socio-economic objectives envisioned by the political leaders in the past. For instance, in paragraph 3 of the report it is suggested that to avoid excessive time consumption in the clearance of the applications, a time-bound package of maximum 45 days must be fixed.[13]

Another area that figured into the agenda of the committee was R&D (research and development). The committee recognized that the industry needed high technology input and for this R&D was very essential. But, R&D seemed to be missing in the business agenda. The government in the past had also paid lip service in encouraging in-house R&D. In view of this, the committee recommended that the organized sector must be motivated to develop in-house R&D not merely for the sake of fiscal relief but essentially for the growth and upgradation of indigenous technology and for adaptation to imported technology. In order to achieve this, it was suggested that a substantial portion of industrial investment must be towards

13. "Sondhi and Menon committee Reports on Electronics: Government Decisions," para. 3, May 1981, *Electronics Information and Planning*, Department of Electronics, Government of India, p. 595.

R&D which was meaningful, relevant and commercially linked with production. Thereby, the committee mandated the private companies in computer and electronics to invest 20% of their turn-over on R&D.[14]

A closer interaction between the DoE and the industrial groups were recommended by organizing annual meetings to ensure that national specifications get involved over a large spectrum with overall requirements of the industry.[15] The committee also proposed the prioritization of the production of microcomputers and microprocessor-based systems costing not more than ₹ 5 million, with maximum flexibility on the import of computer systems and all computer systems and such sub-systems, peripherals, accessories, software, and so on, as are under production in the country be subject to import duty at 1% and a countervailing duty at par with the excise duty levied on indigenous manufacturers. Substantiating further on this account paragraph 47 of the report recommends that, "The countervailing duty should be reduced to 8%. Full duty must be levied on identifiable discrete units of the above imported systems that are manufactured in India and enjoy protective duty...excise duty on all indigenous computer systems, sub-systems, peripherals and accessories should be reduced from a level of 25% to a general of 8%."[16]

The Budget of 1980-81 incorporated a number of these recommendations as concessions with clauses to private companies. Custom duty was reduced to 25% from the existing levels of duties on specified items of capital goods such as machines and instruments required by the electronics industry not produced within the country. This was a very important concession to an industry which was still at a nascent stage of its development. Further, the excise duty on indigenously manufactured computers was reduced from 25% to 20% ad valorem.[17] Under the new fiscal provisions, the electronics

14. *Ibid.*, para 36, p. 601.
15. *Ibid.*, para 37, p. 601.
16. *Ibid.*, para 47.
17. "Budget Speech 1980-81", Ministry of Finance, Government of India, pp. 27-28.

component industry was included in the Ninth Schedule of the Income Tax Act within which the dividends derived by an Indian electronics component company was completely exempted from income tax. In addition to this, the import duty concessions were extended to fifty-nine new items of capital equipments and twenty-three items of raw materials and components required by the electronics industry including computer hardware and software.

These concessions advanced by the government were in consonance with the DoE's transformed approach in favour of liberalization and privatization. Though no specific provisions were made for the promotion of the software sector, the incentives for electronics and computer were meant for software as well. As the software segment was still at a nascent stage of its development no specific policy was introduced for its development. However, the general policy incentives seemed to be adequate enough for the new technocratic entrepreneurship to start their business in software.

To begin with, Aziz Premji, the chairman of WIPRO entered the computer business. Later, WIPRO became the lead producer and exporter of software. Some other companies that entered the software business included Applied Computer Science Organization, Dowell Consultants, Infosys, Integra Micro Systems, Mascon Technical Services, Mastek, Software Research Group and Kirloskar Computer Services. Pingle also observes that the emergence of new technocratic private entrepreneurship was not simply a result of shifting policy trends at the governmental level. It was also due to a continuous process of formal and informal interactions between the DoE technocrats and these new entrepreneurs. The technocrats in both DoE and private companies shared common educational and social backgrounds.[18] Most of them were the products of IITs and IIMs and had common aspirations for building a strong indigenous base of software industry with greater participation of private firms and companies.

18. Vibha Pingle (2000), *Rethinking the Developmental State: India's Industry in Comparative Perspective*, *op. cit.*, p. 137.

In short, it can be said that the emergence of new entrepreneurship in the field of electronics in general and software in particular was a result of two important developments at the political level:

1. Shifting political interests of the political leadership with an intention of drawing the support of corporate sector.
2. Greater interaction between the emerging software companies and the technocrats within the DoE.

Increasing Momentum in Policy Shifts Since mid-1980s: The Political Context of Industrial Liberalization

The mid-1980s is the most critical period for the growth of software industry because it is here that the process of liberalization gained momentum and the main focus of industrial policy shifted towards developing technology-based sectors like computer hardware and software, telecommunications and electronics in general. The shift in the direction of business-friendly policies and development of these industries resulted from the emergence of the 'New Industrial Revolution' often referred to as 'IT Revolution' worldwide. This paradigm shift in the field of industrialization and technology required a rethinking of the ideological dimensions of industrial policies. There seemed to be an urgent need towards increasing the pace of liberalization to involve greater participation of the private sector in the process of industrialization. However, it was also felt that such paradigm shift was possible only through broad-based political consensus. The second important requirement was to adopt an export-oriented industrial policy in place of import-substitution industrialization. The new strategy necessitated special attention towards those sectors that exhibited a certain degree of comparative advantage in the international market, or at least has strong future potential and also had a critical role to play in the domestic economy. Software sector figured most prominently in this framework as its potential for the future growth of the economy came to be well recognized. It had horizontal linkages with many other sectors of the economy.

Nature of Political Leadership

See the contrast! In the decade of 1970s the political leadership was thoroughly inclined towards an ideological framework that emphasized self-reliance, public-sector dominance and a negative attitude towards private investment. However, under the leadership of Rajiv Gandhi the government policies witnessed a marked shift towards business-friendly policies and private-sector driven industrialization.

Rajiv Gandhi's technical background offered him a modern and technocratic outlook. He was pilot by profession and was completely detached from politics even when his mother was at the zenith of her political power. His brother Sanjay Gandhi had also plunged into politics by the mid-1970s when Rajiv Gandhi preferred to be involved thoroughly in his professional world. Rajiv's personality, educational and professional background played an important role in shaping his ideas that supported liberal, technology-driven, export-oriented policies.

The unfortunate death of his brother in an aircraft accident forced him to enter politics. Rajiv began assisting his mother in her political activities. In June 1981, Rajiv was elected as a member of Lok Sabha from Amethi, his brother's constituency in Uttar Pradesh. Rajiv worked meticulously in reorganizing his party and preparing for the next elections scheduled for January 1985. The first initiative that Rajiv took in this regard was recasting of the entire leadership of 'Youth Congress' by inducting young and motivated individuals within the organization. This was his first attempt to create an organization that would have a larger role to play in establishing a modern and a technocratic society in future.

The next important step that was taken by Rajiv was to modernize and transform the Congress party by using its numerous cells and frontal organizations, while building the district and state congress committees. His new style of political functioning was quite different from that of the earlier Congress leaders. He emphasized discipline and meticulousness, new ideas that were unknown to Congress culture. However, implanting these new ideas was practically difficult in the face of resistance by the old-generation socialists of Congress party who were not open to such innovative ideas and preferred to maintain the status quo. Though this opposition was not very visible during the early years of Rajiv's rule, in the later half of his tenure it became hackneyed. In short, there seemed to be a scintillating gap between the feudalistic and tradition outlook of the old leadership within the Congress and the modern, technocratic and managerial language of politics and public administration under Rajiv Gandhi.

Rajiv worked scrupulously for the scheduled elections. He went to the masses with his new, innovative and modern ideas to reorient the society along the lines of modernization, technological advancement and industrialization. He promised the masses that under his leadership Indian economy and industry would make a great leap forward in the 21st century and would come at par with nations in East Asia like South Korea, Japan, and Singapore. In this regard, Bhabani Sengupta observes that "He projected to the Indian voter a new political sociology of rapid modernization relying primarily on the use of high technology of electronics and computers."[19]

It is well observed that the process of developing technology-intensive industries including computer hardware and software had already begun in the early-1980s under the leadership of Mrs. Gandhi. However, it is important to make a distinction between the reasons behind the shifting focus towards liberalization of industrial policies particularly for technology-intensive industries like those of electronics and computer hardware and software. In the early-1980s the policy shifts were a result of shifting political base of the Congress party. Drawing the support of the organized business class was critical to the new political strategy of broadening social coalition by Mrs. Gandhi in her third tenure. During Rajiv's regime, ideas in favor of liberalization and technological advancement were more important than capturing political power.

Rajiv Gandhi saw the future of India in its 'sunrise industries' and therefore paid special attention to its development. The

19. Bhabani Sengupta (1989), *Rajiv Gandhi: A Political Study*, New Delhi: Konark Publication Private Ltd., p. 34.

earlier stance of public-sector driven industrialization had only produced stagnation of the economy. The burgeoning of sick public sector enterprises by the early-1980s clearly evinced this claim. Technological backwardness was cited as one of the key factors behind industrial sickness and stagnation. The quality of technology used in the industry was outdated and fell miserably short of international standards. This was further due to lack of competitiveness in the industrial arena. In a speech delivered while inaugurating the National Conference on 'Productivity through People in the age of changing technology' in New Delhi on 29 October, 1986 he said that,

> "What India needs today is not just gradual growth of technology and upgradation of technology. We are now ready to take a jump. If we go through the full process of each step, we will never be able to catch up; we will go through all the negative aspects that the developed countries have already gone through."[20]

Third, Rajiv's approach towards industrial policy was to promote competitiveness in the Indian industry. The new policy programme was a balancing act that entailed simultaneous involvement of public and private enterprises in industrialization. The emerging privatization drive did not negate the contribution and future potential of public sector. In fact, Rajiv wanted to make the public sector dynamic and forward-looking through its technological upgradation. He wanted to provide a new life to the public sector units that lacked professionalism and were subject to extreme bureaucratism and nepotism.

Further, Rajiv Gandhi wished to bring technology closer to the people to transform their living conditions. The idea behind promoting telecommunications, electronics, and computer software was to ensure that these technology-intensive public goods will provide a new lease of life to people in the periphery like farmers, labourers, tribal communities, craftsmen and women. In other words, it was believed that the benefits of modern and advanced technology must not remain a prerogative

20. *Rajiv Gandhi's Selected Speeches and Writings: 1986*, vol. 2, May 1989, p. 116.

of the elite, which was the case in the past. It must target the common masses especially for those who fell below poverty line and had no access to proper education, health and employment facilities. Speaking on these lines in his inaugural speech at the National Convention on Small Industry, New Delhi on 17 September 1986, Rajiv said that, "We want the sophisticated computer to study the monsoon so that we can tell the farmer when to plant and what the rainfall is likely to be accurately."[21]

These ideas formed the backbone of the powerful liberalization drive for the software industry. Although export-promotion remained the core strategy, the government expressed rhetorical commitments towards the social utility of technology. This may also appear as a political strategy to maintain the rhetoric of socialism. So, liberalization in action and socialism in rhetoric was the gangplank of connecting with masses while maintaining close proximity with the technocratic entrepreneurs in the new developmental project.

Changing Nature of the Bureaucracy—Regulator as well as Facilitator

Ideas of the political leadership were not sufficient to produce the envisioned economic change. In democracies, ideas are subject to debates and are likely to fail if they don't gain acceptance amidst multifarious political interests. Political consensus on such ideas is hard to achieve when they mark a radical turning point in the economy. In India, the institutionalization of a socialist pattern of economy was hard to break not only for the ideological embeddedness that it produced but also the vested interests that remained attended adequately in a closed economy. Bureaucracy of the import-substitution economy was its foremost beneficiary. The apprehension was also felt for the bureaucrats of DoE. But the puzzle is that the attitudinal change of DoE was easily accomplished and the apprehension of an unsupportive bureaucracy was broken. The DoE re-positioned itself as a coalitional partner in the liberalization drive of the

21. Inaugural Speech to the "National Convention on Small Industry", New Delhi, 17 September, 1986 in *Rajiv Gandhi's Selected Speeches and Writings*, vol. 2, May 1989, pp. 102-06.

government. Moreover, the DoE since the mid-1980s has been actively pursuing policy matters with the other ministries like finance and commerce.

One of the prime supporters of the liberalization in the mid-1980s was the then Additional Secretary of the DoE Dr. N. Seshgiri. He is considered to be the architect of the software policies during this period. Dr. Seshgiri was thoroughly in favor of speeding up the process of liberalization as he believed that private sector investment in the software sector was critical for its growth in the longer run. The cumbersome bureaucratic procedures and stringent norms of industrial licensing were still existent and therefore delicensing was seen as a prior policy measure.

Dr. Seshgiri ideas converged with those of Rajiv Gandhi and fitted well within the liberalization project that the latter wished to undertake in case of software sector. Elaborating on this account Parthasarathy says that,

> "As Seshgiri's view fitted well with Rajiv Gandhi's own interests in encouraging the widespread of application of computers, Seshgiri came to be one of Rajiv's 'computer boys', as the Prime Minister's team of advisors were popularly referred to. With political backing at the highest level, Seshgiri was able to push through his policies."[22]

Elaborating on a similar note, Heeks points out that, "Seshgiri's convictions formed one of the strongest pro-liberalization factors within software policy-making, and none of the other bureaucrats spoke up whole-heartedly in favour of liberalization as Seshgiri did during the 1980s."[23]

Initially, in the 1970s the DoE seemed to be apprehensive towards open competition in the computer sector as it was

22. Balaji Parthasarathy, "Globalizing Information Technology: The Domestic Political Context for India's Software Production and Exports", *An Interdisciplinary Journal of Software History*, 3 May 2014, p. 13.
23. Richard Heeks (1996), *India's Software Industry*: *State Policy, Liberalization and Industrial Development*, New Delhi: Sage Publications, p. 320.

inclined towards maintaining the dominance of ECIL in the domestic market. This idea was also in consonance with the broader framework of industrial policy that sought to give priority to public sector in industrialization. However, the position of DoE changed dramatically in the 1980s when other regulatory institutions felt uneasy with the fast pace of liberalization. Elaborating on this account, Peter Evans states the reasons behind the transformation in attitude. They are as follows:

1. Informatics and Computers was a sector that could not possibly be used as a plank for power aggrandizement by either politicians or bureaucrats.
2. The sector neither represented a major political constituency nor was it a source of political patronage. Therefore, no clientele relationship could be visible.
3. The DoE comprised technically-oriented managers who took adequate interest in the growth of the sector and were generally without any political affiliations.[24]

Therefore, it can be inferred that it was rather easy to adopt liberal policies for the software sector as the level of political opposition that was generated against other sectors of the economy because of strong lobbies outside the government and the rigidity of the ministries, departments and the older generation of Congress leaders was much less. In fact, there was a general political consensus over facilitating technology-intensive industries, particularly software.

Policy Innovations and Regulatory Standards in the mid-1980s

The foremost step towards liberalization was the 1984 Computer Policy. The main objective of this policy was to remove the institutional barriers that inhibited private investment in the computer sector. Furthermore, the policy spelled out the need to induce advanced technology, strengthen the manufacturing capabilities, simplify procedures, and promote application

24. Peter Evans (1995), *Embedded Autonomy: State and Industrial Transformation*, *op. cit.*

of software development. The underlying objective was to encourage best business practices for capacity expansion in technology production.

Under the new policy framework, no restrictions were to be imposed on the entry of firms including the large industrial houses that included the MRTP companies. However, the FERA restrictions on foreign collaboration remained intact. There was complete relaxation on the import of computer technology, components and capital goods. The policy thus encouraged greater involvement of the large companies in the computer sector which were otherwise discouraged from investing in innovative areas of production under the existing policy framework. Though some degree of delicensing was already in place in the early-1980s, the big industrial houses including the foreign companies were still excluded from the policy benefits. Therefore, a provision facilitating the re-entry of big companies in computers and electronics was a noteworthy measure towards policy innovation.

The stringent bureaucratic procedures that were involved in obtaining a license were simplified with the introduction of a single window clearance system. Under the new dispensation, the manufacturers interested in acquiring a license for production, foreign collaboration, import of capital, technology, components, and so on had to approach only the DoE for the clearance. This was followed by the requirement of evaluation of the Inter-Ministerial Standing Committee that was to meet once every 15 days. The meeting was to be chaired by the Additional Secretary of the DoE and attended by a representative each from the Directorate General of Technical Development, Ministry of Finance, Ministry of Commerce, and the Planning Commission.

A few relaxations were also made on the import front. In the earlier policies, all purchases related with importing computer equipments or software export had to be rooted through the DoE. The DoE was assigned the task of finalizing the purchases and negotiating with sellers on behalf of the actual users. Under the new dispensation, the interested entrepreneurs were permitted to select from a list of computer systems prepared by the DoE and the concerned entrepreneur was allowed to negotiate directly with the seller without the involvement of the DoE in the negotiation process.

The software sector received special attention in this new policy framework. For the first time it was recognized as an industry eligible for allowance, investment and other policy benefits. This was a decisive move considering the preoccupation of policies with computer hardware and apathy towards software in the past. The duty on imported software was lowered. However, the duty on application software was still kept high. On the technology and R&D front, a 'National Microelectronics Council' was to be established to plan and coordinate the R&D centres all throughout the country.

The 1984 Computer policy opened a new window of opportunity for prospective private companies intending to enter the software business. It recognized the failure of ECIL in meeting the growth targets and the technology standards. Therefore, the Computer policy made headway in checking the monopoly of ECIL by promoting competition in the computer market. To do this, it addressed the structural constraints that inhibited private investment and encouraged monopoly practices. It was first-of-its kind policies that gave priority to computer software recognizing its comparative advantage in global business and its social utility in the longer run.

However, the impact of rising imports on balance of payment and foreign exchange reserves were fully recognized. In one the questions-answer sessions in Lok Sabha following the advancement of the Computer policy of 1984, the DoE observed that the software industry in India was heavily dependent on imported parts including semiconductor devices, professional grade active and passive components, multilayer printed circuit boards or peripheral devices which are the major cost-contributing constituents of a typical computer system.[25] But these apprehensions did not deter the government from lowering the import duties for software exports in 1986.

25. *Lok Sabha Debates*, August 1984, Government of India, p. 713.

The next in line was the 'Computer Software Export, Development and Training Policy', announced in 18 December 1986. The focus of this policy was to devise measures and strategies that would increase software production and facilitate India's software export besides increasing its share in the domestic market. The 1986 policy eased the accessibility of a firm to the most advanced software technology and software tools available in the global market. The South Korean business strategy of upgrading the borrowed technology was followed in this regard. The most important provision of this policy was the placement of software imports in the OGL category, which meant that software could be imported in any form, in any quantity and by anybody by paying 60% ad valorem duty. Being placed in the OGL meant that an item could be imported by merely paying the import duty without obtaining the import license.

It was felt that hardware and software were two sides of the same coin. Availability of advanced hardware was a critical necessity for the development of software. In view of this, the policy incorporated a very important provision that made accessibility to the required hardware easy. Under this policy framework, those wanting to import hardware for software could now apply through IMSC. Another route for obtaining such a license was the EXIM Bank. Moreover, those who took the latter route were to be given a 50% rebate.

There is a critical difference between the 1984 and 1986 policies. First, the 1986 policy provided a special incentive package for software as against the earlier policy that paid general attention to the computer sector. Second, the latter measure introduced performance standards for the exporters which were missing in the earlier one. The entrepreneurs had to meet certain targets in order to get these benefits. Importers who were intending to follow the IMSC route and required foreign exchange from the government were required to generate net export equivalent to 250% of the amount. Those taking the EXIM (Export and Import Bank) route had an export obligation of 350% of the total amount. The period for meeting the export target was fixed at 4 years. Any shortfall in meeting the set targets within the stipulated period of time was liable for heavy penalty. The policy also encouraged foreign investment in the field of software and decided to make venture capital available to new firms in this area.

The nature of 1986 software policy clearly marked a shift in the attitude of the government towards emerging software companies. These companies were placed in the priority list of government incentives. However, as observed, there were certain conditions that were attached to such incentives. These conditions ensured that the private companies met their export targets within the given time if they were to continue receiving the benefits. The performance-oriented approach of the government manifested in the 1986 policy redefined the role of state as an economic actor. In the new format, the state assumed the role of a 'guardian' from a 'regulator.' Here, it is possible to draw parallels with South Korea's strategy of 'qualitative subsidization' for its electronics and computer hardware industry.

Emerging Differences at the Political Level over Liberalization in the late-1980s—Back to Regulation

The end of 1980s witnessed a policy backtrack over opposition to speedy liberalization as labelled by some opposition parties and bureaucrats. While the DoE was completely in consonance with the government over liberalization of software policies, the bureaucrats in other ministries and departments felt deeply concerned about the pace of liberalization. Diverse opinions over liberalization emerged in political circles. The interplay of ideas and interests is what shaped the policy preferences of the politicians and bureaucrats. But cutting across party lines, a new line of division was created between the old and new generation of politicians and bureaucrats. The status quoist in the old generation of Congress party felt restless with the sudden spree of liberalization as they saw it as a radical departure from the constitutional obligation of a socialist economy. The initial fanfare of Congress's grand success in elections and the freshness of ideas concerning professionalization of administration and new technological innovations produced high public optimism and subdued opposing voices. But, slowly the dissenting voices within Congress especially amongst the older generation and their bureaucrat affiliates made consensus over liberalization difficult to achieve.

The feudalistic orientation of the old leadership within the Congress often conflicted with the managerial and technocratic orientation of Rajiv Gandhi and his supporters in the DoE. As Frankel observes that, "The Left within the Congress as well as the old-style Congressmen attached to the socialist pattern of economy and society resisted any deviation from the Nehru's policy of self-reliance and Mrs. Gandhi's pro-poor policies."[26] Further, in the later half of the mid-1980s, growing dissensions between Rajiv Gandhi and Finance Minister V.P. Singh also impacted the pace of industrial liberalization that had a spill-over effect on software.

The liberal orientation of the DoE officials and the prime minister towards software industry was not supported whole-heartedly by the Ministry of Finance. The main concern of the ministry was over matters related to foreign exchange and balance of payments. Therefore, it had reservations over import liberalization. It expressed its disapproval of the DoE's decision to lower the import duties on software from 60% to 25% in 1986. It proposed to renew regulatory checks and controls on import liberalization. Later, in 1989, it was because of the political pressure from the ministry that the import duties on software were raised.[27] The opposition to import liberalization in the software industry was found baseless by the DoE officials. In this regard, both Seshgiri and Vittal were of the view that liberalization of import duties would result in higher growth of the industry, which would generate greater government revenue from other taxes. Therefore, they believed that at the initial stages of its development, the software industry must be

26. Francine Frankel (2006), *India's Political Economy: 1947-2006*, *op. cit.*, p. 586.
27. Richard Heeks (1996), *India's Software Industry: State Policy, Liberalization and Industrial Development*, *op. cit.*, pp. 322-23.

exempted from high import duties. Lack of advanced technology input was also cited as an important reason behind import liberalization. Despite these logical claims made by DoE's top officials, the finance ministry was still not ready to compromise on the area of taxation and high import duties. Disgruntled with the attitude of finance ministry, one of the lobbyists in the industry commented that, "whatever the DoE wants, the Ministry of Finance can veto it."[28]

Further, the opposition parties also raised serious concerns over the policy of import liberalization in electronics industry. For instance, a prolonged debate took place in Lok Sabha over the liberalization of imports of sophisticated electronics equipments and technology. In one of the questions, Prof. Madhu Dandawate raised the concern of free import of electronics equipments and technology, including computer equipments, on a large scale. She expressed the apprehension of its adverse impact on foreign exchange reserves. Further, in justifying her observation she raised one of the previous statement made by the government with regard to electronics policy which said that the government feels that there was a need to accelerate the use of electronics equipments such as communication equipments, computerized control equipment, data communication and data processing equipments, and therefore, import of technology would be permitted freely to develop an appropriate electronics base in the country. Prof. Dandawate recognized that the indigenous production was likely to suffer adversely under the impact of import liberalization of electronics and computer equipments.[29]

The combined pressure of political opposition and Congress old guards with their bureaucrat affiliates forced the government retreat from its policy positions. The Software policy of 1987 was an important step in this direction. New norms and regulations were introduced with regard to the import of software under OGL. It was now restricted to actual users, including government

28. Richard Heeks (1996), *India's Software Industry: State Policy, Liberalization and Industrial Development*, *op. cit.*, p. 323.
29. *Lok Sabha Debate*, 1985, Government of India, p. 146.

departments and computer manufactures, the DoE, and the firms registered with DoE as distributors of foreign software. Also, a 15% foreign exchange conservation tax was imposed. Later, in 1988 the duty on imported software was raised from 60% to 65%. Further, in 1989 the import duties were raised to a greater extent.

Rajiv Gandhi by the late-1980s had come to feel the political unease in realizing the goals of liberalization. Radical policy shifts marking a departure from socialism that gave prominence to public sector and state regulation had created rift between the old and the new generation of leader within Congress party. Encouragement for foreign investment and the entry of multinationals in software business was yet another area of ideological conflict. Therefore for the future prospects of the party, many of the liberal measures were untenable. The policy rollback of 1987 is an outcome of this thinking.

Production and Export Profile

The export-oriented, incentive-based policies of the government had a positive impact upon software exports through the 1980s. Table 1 provides data on computer production, software and hardware exports between 1984 and 1988.

Table 1: Software and Hardware Exports (1984-1988)

Production and Exports	1984	1985	1986	1987	1988
Computer Production	66	111	200	268	347
Hardware Exports	0.6	0.5	3.00	3.00	
Software Exports	17	20	30	41	

It can be inferred that the production of computer has increased substantially from 1984 to 1988. While the export of computer hardware has witnessed a fluctuating trend and has been abysmally low, there has been a consistent rise in software exports in this period.

The actual involvement of the private companies in software exports will indicate that there is a positive correlation between the advancement of business-friendly policies by the government and the number of software companies involved in export-related production. Table 2 gives the figures of the total number of software export companies registered with DoE from 1981 to 1988.

Table 2: Software Export Companies Registered with DoE (1981-1988)

Year	DoE-registered software export companies
1981	21
1982	15
1983	20
1984	35
1985	35
1986	60
1987	85
1988	90

Source: Heeks (1996)[30]

Table 2 clearly indicates a rising trend in the number of software companies involved in exports. However, the trend has not been consistent. There was marked decline in the number of registered companies from 21 to 15 from 1981 to 1982. While the number of companies registered increased sharply from 1983 to 1984, the number remained the same in 1984 and 1985. However, from 1985 to 1986 again the number increased dramatically from 35 to 60 after which the figures have shown a rising trend. Nevertheless, the rate of increase has

30. Richard Heeks (1996), *India's Software Industry: State Policy, Liberalization and Industrial Development*, *op. cit.*, p. 87.

been increasingly low between 1987 and 1988 which clearly indicates that the reversal of government policies on import liberalization affected the interest of the private companies in software exports. The given data clearly indicates that there exists a positive correlation between liberalization of software policies and entry of software companies into export business.

By the late-1980s a number of domestic companies and a few big multinational companies got involved in software production. Along with the big software giants like Wipro, Infosys, Patni Computers, TCS and so on, a number of medium and small-sized software producers also came up. Though, the FERA regulations were still intact, not many multinational companies entered the software business in India. However, taking advantage of the liberal measures a few multinationals made an entry subsequently. One such liberal policy was that a 100% export multinational company could operate without an Indian partner.

Critical Analysis and Conclusion

Computer policies have undergone metamorphosis since the late-1960s. The state-controlled model of import substitution industrialization in the 1970s resulted in ECIL's monopoly in the computer market under the stewardship of DoE. Subsequently, the change in strategy towards export-led growth with liberalization and privatization in the 1980s gave a new direction and orientation to the computer industry, especially by acting as a driving force for the software industry. The policy shifts that followed were not only driven by the logic of economic growth but a new political dynamism embodied in the ideas and interests of state actors. But clash of ideas often impeded the pace of liberalization. Sometimes democratic compulsions of political accommodation may pose difficulties in pursuing a desirable growth strategy because the policy shifts brought therein may challenge the ideology or pose a threat to the interests of the political gerentocrats. It is not easy to challenge a system that is long established and has been protective of the interest and position of its office holders. Continuities are not easy to break especially where ideology is deep-rooted and interests turn into rigid ambitions.

The political context of the late-1960s and 1970s necessitated inward-looking policies with stringent bureaucratic controls on the private sector and monopoly of public sector enterprises in almost all segments of the Indian industry. Computer policies of this time were also shaped by this political necessity. ECIL became the dominant public sector enterprise in producing electronics goods and computers. Preference for public-sector driven industrialization also closed the possibilities of foreign investment in the computer sector. The foreign players, IBM and ICL, were compelled to wind up their operations or compromise with the conditions imposed by the government under FERA (Foreign Exchange Regulation Act) regulations. The idea of maintaining the dominance of ECIL in the computer market provided little scope for the local private entrepreneurs to invest in new innovative ventures in the field of computers, electronics and even telecommunications.

Second, import-substitution was the principle strategy of industrial development. Policies governed by the principles of self-reliance and import substitution encouraged the development of indigenous technology and the public sector enterprises were to play a key role in this regard. In computer industry, mostly hardware faced the brunt of import-substitution because software till the late-1970s had still not figured in the policy agenda of the government. Unwittingly, the low priority to software under import substitution went to its advantage as by the time its salience was recognized liberalization had already taken roots. So, liberalization that envisaged open competition and an intensive participation of private players in industrialization converged with the autonomy of software from computer and electronics. In this regard it is observed that, "Indian software industry represented an island of competitiveness as import-substitution was not directed at it.... It took birth as a by-product of the general policy framework and the import-substitution was directed at the hardware industry."[31]

31. Patibandla, Kapur and Petersen, "Import Substitution with Free Trade: Case of India's Software Industry", *Economic and Political Weekly*, April 8-14, 2000, vol. 35, no. 15, p. 1264.

Also, the software sector had not figured as an autonomous segment within the computer sector that needed special attention by the government in its policy decisions. Till almost mid-1980s, it was treated as a segment of the electronics and computer industry. Subsequently software found its special recognition within the electronics industry even when hardware was prioritized. The recommendations of Sondhi and Menon committees in 1981, budgets of 1981-82 and 1982-83 included provisions that liberalized the rules and regulations for the software sector. A number of initiatives were taken to address the institutional barriers that inhibited private investment. The recommendations of Sondhi and Menon committee to relax the bureaucratic rules and regulations for software sector were well incorporated in some of the policies of the government and the budgets of 1981-82 and 1982-83. One of the important recommendations of these committees was to suggest greater synergy between DoE and private companies in devising strategies to enhance production and technological innovations. These liberal measures and motivational elements encouraged the entry of prospective private players in software business. However, during this period little attention was paid to the aspect of technological upgradation. The quest for liberalization did not take the government very far as any radical policy shift in this direction would have threatened the brand image of party's socialism.

Liberalization of software policies gained momentum in mid-1980s under the leadership of Rajiv Gandhi. Rajiv's managerial and technocratic approach to public administration and governance and his preference for export-oriented industrialization provided an impetus to liberalization. His association with a set of liberal economic advisors along with his 'computer boys' created a policy architecture with a powerful developmental agenda and a futuristic outlook towards establishing an investor-friendly environment. One could say that this was the real starting point for India's great future in the IT world. Technology became the focal point in the new industrial policy architecture. As a result, technology-intensive industries like computer software, electronics, telecommunication, automobile and biotechnology became priority industries for policy incentives. Rajiv's approach towards technology was inclusive. He intended to bring the benefits of technology closer to masses and for the overall development of the economy. Software technology was believed to have a strong future potential in strengthening the industrial, agrarian, and even infrastructural sectors of the economy.

The other important shift in industrial policy under Rajiv Gandhi was the adoption of export-oriented industrialization. To begin with, software was recognized as one of the critical export-oriented sectors. To promote exports the government incentivized prospective claimants. It liberalized imports of hardware and electronics components required to produce software for exports. This was also done to promote the use of best equipments for the production of software which was abundantly available in the international market.

The wider political consensus for liberalization and privatization in technology-driven sectors accrued from the coalition of PMO, technocrats and economic advisors and the DoE bureaucrats. In this trio, the DoE appeared to be at the forefront in supporting the new change as against DoT and other regulatory bodies that had shielded their respective PSEs from competition. The new technocratic coalition brought the 1984 and 1986 computer policies that opened new gateways for doing business by the emerging technocratic entrepreneurship. Without undermining the FERA regulations, these policies also provided business opportunities for multinational companies in the software sector. Adoption of export-promotion measures was yet another notable feature of these policies. Highlighting the necessity of export-led growth, R. Schware points out that the exports and marketing measures are crucial for software promotion. Some of the export measures are direct in nature like reduction of taxes in export revenues, exempting duty on imported hardware, and so on, while there are others that are indirect in nature such as setting joint venture training institutes, sponsoring business delegations to explore overseas markets and supporting software market groups.[32] These ideas got actualized in 1986 and 1984 computer policies.

The liberalization drive for software sector could not remain consistent in the 1980s. The late-1980s witnessed a policy backtrack that resulted from the emerging political dissensions over policy issues, ideological clashes and the approaching BoP crisis. Import liberalization, in particular, appeared as the main bone of contention. While the finance ministry expressed its disapproval for import liberalization for its foreign exchange and public debt implications, the opposition parties and the old leadership within the Congress were skeptical about its impact on the business of the indigenous producers of electronics equipments. The logic of opposition had both political and economic overtones. The politics of disagreement and scepticism entailed ideological clashes and interest subversions. The economic logic was centred around the impact of liberalization on the economy as a whole. But, the economic logic was adequately highlighted to shed the ideological conservatism and interest politics of the inward-looking politicians and bureaucrats.

Both the decades of 1970s and 1980s were critical for the development of the software sector in India. The policies of the government particularly in the mid-1980s laid a groundwork for the emergence of a potent software industry in the 1990s. However, the opposition to import liberalization in the late-1980s and the resultant policy backtrack clearly indicated that the state was more sensitive to policies like import liberalization and tax incentives and the principle of checks and balances was widely employed to see that the internationalization of the industry was not stretched beyond a certain limit.

❐

32. Robert Schware, "Software Industry Development in the Third World: Policy Guidelines, Institutional Options and Constraints", *World Development*, 1987, vol. 15, no. 11, p. 1263.

Chapter 4

Software Industry Since 1991: Contours of Globalization and Institutional Change

The face of the economy changed since 1991 when the government embarked upon the path of liberalization and globalization in response to the macroeconomic crisis that had engulfed the country in the late-1980s. The crisis began as the balance of payment situation deteriorated with mismanagement of the economy during the mid-1980s. There was a shift from 'import-substitution industrialization' to 'import-intensive industrialization' that led to an imbalance between imports and exports. This further led to borrowings from abroad and the resultant external debt. In order to rescue the economy from this crisis, the government took the refuge of IMF (International Monetary Fund) which dictated the state to undertake a comprehensive package of 'SAP (Structural Adjustment Programme)' opining deregulation and delicensing and encouraging private investment. Following SAP, the government passed the 'New Economic Policy' adopting a series of measures that incentivized both local and global capital. Export-promotion appeared as the fundamental growth strategy of the government. The new economic policy provided new windows of opportunity for both local and foreign investors.

The underlying idea behind this deep-seated change at the policy level was to achieve high levels of economic growth and that the fulfilment of this objective would itself guarantee equitable distribution of wealth, social welfare and improved standards of living. The newly-carved growth strategy necessitated the promotion of those industrial sectors that exhibited comparative advantage in the international market. Secondly, with rapid advances in global technology it became imperative to establish and strengthen technology-driven sectors; it became equally important to do so in the face of stiff competition from emerging Asian economies in the global market.

The software industry was one such industrial sector that was seen to play a critical role in the building the Indian economy. The technology evolution in India was marked by the emergence of IT-ITES (Information Technology-Information Technology Enabled Service) industry in the mid-1990s and by the year 2000 India became a leading producer software products and services. As Upadhya points out that,

> "The emergence of India's IT industry coincided with an acceleration in the internationalization of the production, distribution and management of goods and services in the 1990s.... While global restructuring provided the space for the emergence of the IT-ITES industries in India, their rapid growth can also be attributed to specific political and economic processes that have unfolded in the country since the 1980s."[1] (Upadhya and Vasavi 2008: 13)

This chapter begins by discussing the emergence and role of new institutions that were created to support the new class of technocratic entrepreneurship in a bigger way. These institutions were an outcome of political ideas that favoured corporatization and global integration of the Indian economy. In politics, the interest of the powerful matters and shapes policy preferences. By the early-1990s the dominant coalition of a pro-LPG regime involving state and non-state actors pursed an enduring process of globalization stretching it to its logical extreme. The IT and software industry played the lead role in

1. Carol Upadhya and A.R. Vasavi (2008), "Outposts of the Global Information Economy: Work and Workers in India's Outsourcing Industry", in Carol Upadhya and A.R. Vasavi, ed., *In an Outpost of the Global Economy: Work and Workers in India's Information Technology Industry*, New Delhi: Routledge.

this process and continued with its export junket that it had started in the mid-1980s. The organizational pressure for the export-drive through state support came from NASSCOM the umbrella body for software and services firms in India, and its association with the government, particularly the DoE (and later the Ministry of Communications and Information Technology). NASSCOM's involvement with the government has triggered the process of globalization embodying greater incentivization for service companies and the growing BPO industry. Although the process of liberalization and globalization has been relatively consistent in the 1990s and 2000s as compared with the 1980s, differences over its pace and outreach has remained a matter of political deliberation and inter-ministerial, inter-departmental differences have surfaced from time to time over some of the demands of the private industry. The disagreements have mainly been centred around the extent of state support to the export-oriented firms. Second, institutional change in support of the industry was not any easy process. Conflict of interests between predatory institutions and the liberal ones produced difficulties in negotiating policies and schemes for supporting the private industry. In the light of clashes between DoT and PMO the difficulties in pursuing institutional change are clearly identifiable.

Policy change has resulted from a corporatist alliance between state and non-state institutions manned by its respective actors. The joint endeavour of industrial development bringing key advantages to the prospective service exporters has made them devise policy strategies for the adaptability of the industry to the changing nature of global technology, increasing demand for quality services and growing global competitiveness with economies of scale. The chapter would attempt to show how the policy strategies helped in addressing the key concerns of the industry. In addition, it accounts for the limits of state regulation to check the emerging challenges of globalization in the form of brain drain, cyber security, low-end business servicing, etc. Globalization has brought a mixed baggage of benefits and constraints. Its intensification therefore demands a more autonomous and active role of state to address the key constraints through definitive policy and regulatory measures. For instance, a legal mechanism ensuring R&D investment by firms or cyber security laws could be good illustrations.

The support system for the newly-emerging IT industry and the ways and means to intensify the process of global integration could readily be understood in the light of the emergence of new institutions at state and societal levels. This includes NASSCOM, Software Technology Parks, Ministry of Information and Communication Technology, the IT Act and the new Cyber security regime. The first section of the chapter accounts for the institutional change that broadened the support system for the software industry.

SECTION 1: INSTITUTIONAL INNOVATIONS IN THE POST-1991 PERIOD

NASSCOM—The Industrial Association

NASSCOM is the apex and umbrella organization of IT software and services industry in India. It acts as an advisor, consultant and coordinating body for such private companies. Further, its aim is to facilitate business and trade in software and services and to encourage advancement in software technology by taking a number of R&D (research and development) initiatives. NASSCOM was established in 1988 with the initiative of some of the big players in the field of software like Wipro, Infosys, TCS (Tata Consultancy Services), Satyam, and so on. To begin with, it had 38 members. Currently, 1749 member companies/ firms are registered with the organization and account for nearly 95% of the total revenues generated by the industry (NASSCOM website).

The membership profile of NASSCOM has changed over a period of time with the inclusion of SMEs within its organization. Its members include all those software and services companies that are incorporated or registered in India, which have a positive contribution to make to the computer software industry and a good record in business operations, and have a strong financial commitment and a significant local value-added component in products and services offered. The expansion in the membership profile of NASSCOM shows the growing salience and influence of smaller firms in manifold policy matters.

Strategic Review (NASSCOM) clearly states some of the main objectives of the industrial organization. These are as follows:

1. Maintaining a continuous process of interaction with the Government of India and various state governments in formulating national IT policies with a special emphasis on the promotion of software and services segments.
2. Collaborating with global stakeholders for promoting the software and services industry in the global market and thereby strengthening the 'brand equity' of India as a global sourcing destination.
3. Engaging with all member companies and stakeholders to devise strategies to achieve common aspirations for the industry.
4. Taking effective measures to check software piracy by proposing the adoption of a proper legal framework for the same.
5. Taking active steps in the development and management of human resources required for the software-driven IT industry.[2] (NASSCOM 2001: 14)

NASSCOM has been involved in a continuous interaction with the government. It has its representatives in various committees of the Government of India as well as the Ministry of Communications and Information Technology, Ministry of Commerce, Ministry of Finance, Department of Telecommunications, Ministry of Human Resource Development, Ministry of Labor, and the Ministry of External Affairs who voice the interests of the industry in policy matters. NASSCOM also acts as a consulting body for various state governments. This is especially visible in case of states like Karnataka, Andhra Pradesh and Tamil Nadu where special policy initiatives were taken to establish their IT industry. By late-

2. *Strategic Review 2001*, *op. cit.*, p. 14.

1990s, virtually every state had an IT policy, at least on paper, and the city of Bengaluru came to be recognized and referred to as the 'next silicon valley.' But the states mentioned above superseded even the national government by creating a support system through sound infrastructure, telecommunication networks, tax exemptions and easy administrative clearance that helped the industry flourish alarmingly in their respective regions. The NASSCOM fulfilled its aims by pegging its hope on the support of these state governments and therefore initiated some of its programmes with their cooperation. One of the recent schemes is the 'Start-up Warehouse' with the aim of providing world-class infrastructure to 'tech-start ups' at reasonable costs. The scheme was first launched in the Diamond City at Bengaluru in collaboration with the Karnataka government. The facilities provided include 10,000 sq.ft. of working space, 100% power back-up, a leased internet line and four meeting rooms (NASSCOM website).

Subsequently, NASSCOM worked closely with the central government in many of its IT-related schemes. It has acted as a catalyst for the consistent growth of the IT-ITES industry and has been a proponent of free trade, arguing for zero tariff protection, deregulation of the telecom market, and greater privatization of technical education. It was instrumental behind the creation of STPs and has collaborated with the government in a wide range of activities that are essential for the growth of software industry.

NASSCOM has developed a wide network with the central and state governments and influenced their IT policies by proposing necessary business strategies to cope up with emerging global challenges. It has come a long way in helping the government create a regulatory environment compatible with the needs of the IT sector. The IT regulatory framework consists of seven elements: cyber laws, telecom regulations, investment policies, capital market regulations, bureaucratic procedures, labour laws and taxation. While government is seen to have made headway in many regards, few bottlenecks still continue. One of these is the concern of high taxes in e-business. Similarly, NASSCOM feels that a restrictive labour regime still exists in a number of states that prohibits the companies to use the services of its employees in late hours. Due to time lag, the foreign clients have to be served at night or during late evening hours. So, round-the-clock service is essential to run an IT firm. A committed and dextrous labour force is thus a prior necessity for running IT-BPO business[3] (NASSCOM 2001: 36).

NASSCOM has thereby proposed certain changes in the regulatory regime and has emphasized areas that require prompt action of the government. They are as follows:

1. Securing agreements with user countries and regional hubs on India specific visas and work permits.
2. Tax and fiscal incentives for the offshore parks in the countries where software services are being provided.
3. Active promotion of training and education amongst the skilled workforce by the government through the advancement of fiscal and non-fiscal incentives like tax holidays and relaxation of rules for hiring global experts in the area of software technology.[4] (NASSCOM 2001: 40)

Taxation has been an area of prior policy concern for NASSCOM. During 1991, when the process of industrial liberalization reached its matrix, NASSCOM lobbied with the government and for the first time secured income tax exemptions on the profits of software exports. Later, due to the pressure by NASSCOM, the government lowered the import duties from a high 114% to almost nil[5] (NASSCOM 2002: 126). The major areas of concern in the arena of taxation are transfer pricing, expiry of tax holidays for STPI and minimum alternate tax imposed on SEZ units. Such tax burdens imposed in the Annual Budget 2012-13 were seen to solidify the tax regime and tighten financial control on the IT industry (NASSCOM website).

While on many counts the development network between NASSCOM and the government helped in triggering the pace of globalization, there are a number of grey areas where the

3. *Strategic Review 2001*, *op. cit.*, p. 36.
4. *Ibid.*, p. 40.
5. *Strategic Review 2002*, New Delhi: NASSCOM, p. 126.

government has disagreed to abide by the demands of NASSCOM. Inter-ministerial disagreements over policy matters have sometimes impeded the process of incentiviation and thrown up new challenges before the industry. This is particularly noticeable in areas of taxation, availability of data communication links, the bandwidth issue, reduction of government holdings in incumbent companies, removal of foreign ownership restrictions in telecom companies, and reduction of tariff barriers on telecom equipment exports[6] (NASSCOM 2002: 87). Recognizing the lack of consensus over policy matters amongst various ministries and government bodies, NASSCOM clearly states that, "To make changes happen, the Ministry of IT will need to play an active catalytic role—lobbying on behalf of the industry with multiple government bodies"[7] (NASSCOM 2001: 36).

It is henceforth observed that there have been areas of convergence and divergence over policy matters between NASSCOM and the government. In regulatory matters, NASSCOM has always desired a liberal approach of the government so as to support the best business practices of the industry. The development networks partly resemble a relationship of embedded autonomy between state and private capital. Ministry of IT's close alliance with NASSCOM exhibits the embeddedness, while state's decisions in altering rules of the game from time to time displays its autonomy. But, the autonomy often takes a toll in the state's inability to meet the infirmities and bottlenecks through necessary policy action. Autonomy is also a function state's developmental capabilities which often get revealed in its policy decisions. State's capabilities in rightsizing strategies to promote growth of the software industry are registered through its necessary interventions.

State Institutions

The nature of state intervention in industrialization changed dramatically since 1991. The new economic advisors to the Prime Minister favoured liberalization and globalization of the

6. *Ibid.*, p. 87.
7. *Strategic Review 2001*, *op. cit.*, p. 36.

Indian industry. The software industry received prior attention in view of its future potential and ability to realize the goal of high economic growth. Second, the creation of NASSCOM was in itself an important landmark in the development of software sector as it provided a collective voice to the policy demands of the industry. Right from its inception, NASSCOM established a long-lasting relation with government bodies and has remained a close partner to the government in its policies and programmes for IT development.

The collective and shared vision of 'India as an IT superpower' oriented the government policies towards providing some key infrastructural facilities to the emerging software firms. This led to the creation of STP (Software Technology Park) and other tax-concession zones whereby the software firms were provided working space, tax exemption, telecommunication links and incessant power supply. The continuity of the support system however seemed capricious due to uncertainties over political consensus for incentivization, a crisis-ridden global market and changing political preferences in favour of local development than export-led growth. In some cases there was difference in opinion between the ministries over the extension of these benefits, while in others cases there was a clash between bureaucratic agencies like DoE (Department of Electronics) and DoT (Department of Telecommunications) over the issue of data communication facilities.

The STPI Scheme

The two major pronouncements to support software industry in the back-drop of the New Economic Policy 1991 were:

1. Income tax exemption on export profits which had been earlier granted only to goods was extended to computer software.
2. The DoE announced the STP scheme, whereby software exporters were given a flexible policy environment with certain key infrastructural facilities particularly core

computers and high speed data links that seemed to be lacking earlier. (Ministry of Finance 1992-93: 136)

The STP Scheme was launched in 1988 by the government. The main objective of this scheme is to promote software exports with desirable institutional support to prospective software firms. It gives tax-free status to 100% export-oriented units for a period of 5 years within first eight years of operation. The STPs provide the facility of office space and computer equipments, access to high-speed satellite links and continuous supply of electricity. Established software firms that are 100% export-oriented units can also register with STPs to enjoy the benefits provided by the scheme. The firms registered under it are freed from regular bureaucratic procedures, rules and regulations and get single window clearance. For smaller projects, that is less than ₹ 30 million only STP clearance is required, 100% foreign equity is permitted and there are no restrictions on location.

The STPs were providing similar facilities as those in EOUs (export-oriented units) and EPZs (export-processing zones). Nevertheless, the need for special zones for software arose in view of preventing hording with other industries. Justifying the separateness, Parthasarathy points out that, "Though the scheme is in principle no different from 100% EOUs or the EPZs established by the commerce ministry, the DoE had its own reasons for establishing separate facilities." These are as follows:

1. Considering the export potential of the software industry, it needed special attention compared with the other industrial sectors.
2. As wide range of industries avail the facilities of EOUs and EPZs, the people who administer them do not have the requisite expertise to understand the specific requirements of the software industry.
3. Many regulations governing the EOU and EPZ schemes were not meaningful when applied to the software industry as the issue of disposal of obsolete hardware showed.

4. It was felt that the export obligations in EPZs and EOUs, which had an unrealistic value added criteria, were not suitable for the software industry.[8] (Parthasarathy 2004)

The first three STPs were established at Pune, Bangalore and Bhubaneshwar respectively in 1990. Further, in January 1991 more STPs were set up at Gandhinagar, Noida, Thiruvananthapuram and Hyderabad. Initially, the DoE decided to set up these parks through autonomous societies. It meant that each of these zones would work at their respective levels. However, due to Planning Commission's reluctance the idea was given up and the provision of setting up large number of autonomous societies under the supervision of DoE was made, and these autonomous societies were merged under one institution STPI (Software Technology Park of India), New Delhi in June 1991. Each park had its own management board consisting of representatives from the industry. However, as stated earlier, all zones operated under the single body STPI. The director of STPs was given adequate autonomy to approve new projects from the industry.

On February 1991, a National Advisory Board for Software Technology Park was constituted under the chairmanship of N. Vittal. The Board included representatives from some of the big software companies like TCS, Infosys and Digital Equipment India Ltd. The main agenda of the meeting was to rethink the possibilities of support that could be extended to export aspirants in the software sector and the necessity of setting performance standards for them. The first crucial issue that emerged during the course of discussion was the availability of data communication links. The Board emphasized that an international gateway with 64 kbps data links was needed by the exporters and the same had to provided. The other major recommendation was that the export obligation for the software exporters should be raised to 4.5 times the salary bill of the unit.

8. Balaji Parthasarathy (3 May 2004), "Globalizing Information Technology: The Domestic Policy Context for India's Software Production and Exports", *Iterations: An Interdisciplinary Journal of Software History 3*.

Incentives for the exporters registered with STPs have been revised from time to time. The input requirements of the industry have changed with transformation in their business practices and efforts to upgrade their information services to foreign clients. So, the incentive package introduced in 1991 was found insufficient to meet the emerging requirements of the industry. STPs have responded well to these changes by extending and ordering its incentives in such a manner so as to provide for better adaptability of the industry to the demands of the global market. Some important steps in this regard are as follows:

1. Shifting focus to offshore projects which contributes 85% of national offshore exports
2. 50% contribution to national exports
3. Expansion of STPs to other areas like Pune, Thiruvananthapuram, Gandhinagar, Bhubaneshwar in addition to the conventional areas like those in Bengaluru, Hyderabad, Chennai, and so on
4. Nurturing and developing of 100% reliable, high-speed data communication links to the software exporters to overcome impediments like physical distances and time constraints
5. Single window concept to overcome procedural complications that still inflict the software industry
6. Expanding infrastructural facilities to SMEs (small and medium enterprises).[9] (DoE 1997-98: 54)

Recently, the issue of extending the term of STPI scheme by another 5 years has come under political spotlight. The 10-year tax holiday provided in the STPI scheme was to expire by the end of year 2010. The software firms under the umbrella of NASSCOM pressurized the government to extend the term by another 5 years. A delegation of the IT industrial body NASSCOM met A. Raja, the then Minister of State for Communications and Information Technology to put forward this proposal before the government. In the background of the discussion, the President

9. *Annual Report 1997-98*, Department of Electronics, Government of India, p. 54.

of NASSCOM Mr. Som Mittal commented that, "It was Raja who had brought about the extension of STPI for one more year and we are hopeful that the government will look into the industry's demand"[10] (*Financial Express* June 2009). As per one of the reports from the software industry, A. Raja had stated that instead of extending the term for 5 years it would push for a 3-year extension of the tax holiday[11] (*Financial Express* June 2009).

The ministries of commerce and finance had also given their recommendations regarding the extension of tax-holidays under the STPI Act and those set up in EOUs (export oriented units). The Ministry of Finance was keen to extend the term by another year. As pointed out that, "The ministry is likely to extend the income tax benefits enjoyed by units under STPI Act and those set in EOUs by another year upto 30 March 2011"[12] (*Business Standard* June 2009: 6). Further, the commerce ministry had its independent position on the issue of term extension of the tax holiday. In response to the wish-list presented before the commerce ministry, the ministry recommended a 3-year extension of the scheme. Both commerce and IT ministries demanded that the tax concessions must be extended for a 3-year period since the export community had been hit hard by the slowdown in western markets. The government however expressed reluctance in extending the tax holidays beyond 2011. Minister of State Jyotiraditya Scindia referred to the sunset clause that this would be the final year for tax holidays as announced by the finance ministry. But he promised that he would use all his good offices to persuade the ministry. Despite all efforts the tax holidays came to an end in the year 2011 and the direct tax code came into force on 1 April 2014.

The un-sustainability of the liberal tax regime could be understood in the light of greater reluctance by the finance ministry to continue the incentives. Although the commerce and IT ministries half-heartedly accepted the demand for extension, all efforts to persuade the finance ministry were

10. *Financial Express*, 24 June 2009.
11. *Ibid.*
12. *Business Standard*, 24 June 2009, p. 6.

abortive and the industry had to finally forgo its demand as the term came to an end. The political pressures of the industry did not therefore deter the government from terminating the tax holiday. The view of the finance ministry prevailed even when the NASSCOM supported by the ministries of IT and commerce remained steadfast in its persuasion. As pointed out by one of the government officials, "The issue concerning extension of the term for tax-holidays under the STPI scheme and those under the EOUs will be more of a political decision than an economic one. If the tax benefits are withdrawn, units operating under the EOUs and STPI schemes will loose export-related advantages. This could result in closure of units and job losses, something the government does not want"[13] (*Business Standard* June 2009: 6). This political logic however did not work for software as the workers did not yet constitute a powerful political constituency requiring appeasement by government bodies. But, these steps to block incentives also show the diminishing possibilities of export support in future and credible move of the government in re-orienting the industry towards domestic sector. E-governance and other IT related welfare programmes for gaining political currency required partnership with private sector. Minimizing support for exports was also a way of drawing the attention of software companies towards the objective of home-grown development.

Auxiliary Institutions

In addition to the provisions of tax rebates and infrastructural support in the STPs, the government proposed various other concessions for the software sector. These concessions were extended in view of a fast-expanding IT and ITES industry in the country. It was well recognized that the industry had a long way to go and had great contribution towards building the national economy. A number of free-trade zones were established to promote off-shore servicing by IT and ITES companies. These free-trade zones are as follows:

1. DTA (Domestic Tariff Area): All normal laws apply to such units set up in India. In addition to this, the special

13. *Ibid.*, p. 6.

EPCG (Export Promotion Capital Goods) Scheme of Ministry of Commerce could also be availed by units in the DTA.[14]

2. SEZ (Special Economic Zone): The government announced the setting up of SEZs in 2000. The SEZs are meant to provide a duty-free environment for the exporters involved in manufacturing, trading and services activities. In SEZs, the companies are permitted to import capital goods and are exempt from custom duties. In addition to this, they are also exempted from Central Sales Tax and excise duties from DTA, subject to certain specific conditions.
3. EPZ (Export Processing Zone): EPZs are designed to provide an internationally competitive duty-free environment for export production. Each of these provide basic infrastructural facilities such as developed land, standard design factory buildings, roads, power, water supply, drainage and customs clearance facilities to companies housed in them. EPZs can push domestic sales upto 50% of FOB (free on board) value of exports, subject to fulfilment of export obligations and on payment of applicable duties. Zero import duty and a special 10-year income tax rebate are few of the other incentives provided to the companies under EPZ.
4. Special concessions to 100% EOUs: These concessions include single window clearance, allowance of 100% foreign equity, duty-free exports, allowance of the import of second hand capital goods, exemption/reimbursement of excise duty and CST for domestic purchases, sales in domestic market permitted upto 50% of exports subject

14. "The EPCG scheme allows the import of new and second hand capital goods upto 10 years of age, including computer software with concessional custom duty, but demands a commitment of export obligation. The company or the exporter is required to undertake export obligation, which is equivalent to eight times the duty saved on capital goods. This has to be fulfilled over a period of eight years from the date of issuance of license." *Strategic Review 2004*, New Delhi: NASSCOM.

to achieving net foreign exchange earnings and payment of applicable duties.

These schemes were primarily aimed at addressing the issue of taxation and bureaucratic procedures in getting the clearance for investment proposals. The firms had various options for establishing their export business. They could choose any one of the schemes that would be most suited to their requirement. These schemes were also meant to provide a sound infrastructure for running business. Availing the benefits the industry showed impressive growth since the mid-1990s well indicated in Table 1.

Table 1: Software Production (in ₹ Crores)

	1996-97	1997-98	1998-99	1999-2000	2000-01
Software for Exports	3700	6500	10,940	17,150	28,350
Domestic Software	2600	3470	4950	7200	9400
Total	6300	9970	15,890	24,350	37,750

Source: *Electronics Information and Planning* 2001: 170[15]

Inference: The data given in Table 1 clearly indicates that there has been consistent growth of software exports from 1996-97 to 2000-01. The domestic segment also grew but at a pace slower than exports. Export-based incentives of the government produced this pattern of growth.

The government also perceived the new line of policy with great optimism and enthusiasm. According to the *Annual Report 1992-93*, Department of Electronics, the STP scheme launched by the government resulted in a positive growth of the sector. In addition to the 7 STPs established by the DoE, a large number of private STPs were approved and were made operational. The government also decided to commission the

15. *Electronics Information and Planning*, Department of Electronics and Information Technology, Ministry of Information and Communication Technology, Government of India, p. 170.

Satellite Earth Station at Bengaluru by July 1993 to enhance telecommunication links at STPI[16] (DoE 1992-93: 3). Data shows that the approval for clearance and registration with STP went up sharply since the establishment of STPs. There is also a positive correlation between the investment approvals and export growth in the software sector. As per the report of Economic Survey 1996-97, "Among the 521 units accorded approval so far under the STP scheme, 157 received approval in 1995-96 only." Further, it clearly indicated that the exports from the STP units accounted for a CAGR (compound annual growth rate) of 160% with the export figures of STP units standing at ₹ 727 crores during 1995-96[17] (Ministry of Finance 1995-96: 130).

Telecom Regulation Institutions—Birth of TRAI

Data communication facility is a prior infrastructural requirement of the industry. Shortage of internet connectivity had forced the firms into onsite business. In onsite services, the professionals were required to work at the client's site which had two major repercussions. First, the company had to bear the travel cost of the employee who would visit the site. Since most of the clients were based in US or Europe, the cost of travel was extremely high. Second, it also restricted the nature of contracts they could undertake. As Dinesh C. Sharma points out that, "Since they (the Indian software companies) could not afford to send large teams to America to work for a single client, Indian firms were restricted to relatively small jobs or they acted as sub-contractors in large projects"[18] (Sharma 2009: 335).

The main cause for the inability of the government to provide high-speed internet data was the monopoly of DoT as the service provider in the telecom market. The DoT could charge exorbitant rates from the software exporters because of this monopoly.

16. *Annual Report 1992-93*, Department of Electronics, Government of India, p. 3.
17. *Economic Survey 1995-96*, Ministry of Finance, Government of India, p. 130.
18. Dinesh C. Sharma (2009), *The Long Revolution: The Birth and Growth of India's IT Industry*, New Delhi: HarperCollins, p. 335.

Lack of competition made the software firms totally dependent on the DoT for data services. The government recognized the urgency of curbing monopoly and facilitating competition in telecom services not only for its benefits to private operators and its general customers but also for the growing data needs of the software exporters. However, breaking the monopoly of DoT was not an easy task. The protectionist interests were embedded in DoT and it was not ready to forgo its monopoly position even when liberalization became institutionalized since 1991. As Rahul Mukherji points out that, "It was not easy to undermine the DoT's monopoly power over telecommunications service provision in India"[19] (Mukherji 2009: 493). Considering, that high-speed data link was a vital input for the software companies, it became extremely important to find an alternative to DoT.

Initially, the DoE approached the DoT for providing the facility of high speed data communication links. The DoT finally agreed to provide data links at STPs through satellite stations under the condition that in order to avail this facility the software units were required to pay in advance the annual charges while applying for high-speed leased line, citing this as the standard procedure. This was found to be an extremely stringent condition as the cost incurred was very high and the software units were not necessarily aware of their bandwidth requirements. Second, the DoT had not mentioned the time-frame within which it would provide the data communication links to the software units. Finally, a sum of ₹ 12 crores was diverted for rebuilding SCL to set up earth stations at Bengaluru, Hyderabad, Thiruvananthapuram, Gandhinagar and Bhubaneshwar. The DoE decided to procure the necessary equipments by itself, while the task of building earth stations was given to VSNL (Videsh Sanchar Nigam Limited).

The DoE also found other means to improve the availability of data communication links to the software units in the STPs.

19. Rahul Mukherji (2 May 2009), "Interests, Wireless Technology, and Institutional Change: From Government Monopoly to Regulated Competition in Indian Telecommunications", *The Journal of Asian Studies*, vol. 68, no. 2, p. 493.

In this background, a bilateral agreement was signed between India and France whereby French companies were to provide communication equipments required by the software units. Responding to the deal, the DoE imported communication equipments from a French firm, CGR, and set it up for satellite data links at STPs parallel to the earth stations controlled and operated by VSNL. The advantage of this was that the software firms were getting the necessary data communication links from the DoE at much cheaper rates than those offered by VSNL. There was a large difference between the charges of DoT/VSNL (₹ 65 lakhs) and DoE (₹ 14.5 lakhs). Consequently, the DoE pruned its rate further and a competitive environment for providing high-speed data communication links to the software exporting firms was created. The result of this was that the number of high-speed data links availed by the software exporters increased from just three in 1992 to 200 in 1994 in which 60 data links were provided at the DoE earth stations.

In the NDA (National Democratic Alliance) government, the impetus to improve telecom services came from the desire to promote the IT industry that was believed to play a significant role in the future growth of the Indian economy. As Rahul Mukherji points out that,

> "The Prime Minister's Office became deeply interested in modernizing telecommunications and promoting India's Information Technology exports when Atal Bihari Vajpayee assumed office for the second time (March 1998-May 2004). The PMO (Prime Minister's Office) evolved a model of inter-ministerial coordination through the formation of National Task Force on Information Technology. The Task Force, which was formed in March 1998 soon after Vajpayee's assuming office, had paved the way for ending DoT's monopoly over India's long distance carrier (VSNL) and over Internet service provision."[20] (Mukherji 2009: 504-05)

20. *Ibid.*, pp. 504-05.

The end of DoT's monopoly was thus a landmark development in the evolution of IT industry in India. It provided multiple options to the software exporters to avail data and internet services. The entry of private operators in the telecom market generated competition for providing telecom services that was not possible under the DoT regime. It created greater avenues to connect with rest of the world through a range of communication networks available to the software exporters.

Elaborating upon some of the advantages of easy accessibility of data communication links by the software exporters, one of the reports of Department of Electronics points out that,

> "With the increased awareness of potentiality of data communication and Internet/Intranet, in addition to 'Local Area Networking', greater adaptation of the 'Wide Area Network' based solutions has resulted in overall expansion of these services at a rapid rate. This has led to the opening of the internet services, which has increased the usage of computers as information accessing tools by individuals and corporate sector. As an augmentation to the terrestrial telecommunication infrastructure, satellite based networking solution has reduced the introduction time of these services at remote locations."[21] (DoE 1997-98: 12)

Henceforth, the end of DoT's monopoly was a significant move. More importantly, it suggests that protectionism was not easy to break as vested interests in favour of import substitution and public-sector driven industrialization remained firmly entrenched.

Policies and Institutions under NDA Regime

The software industry received a strong impetus under the BJP-led NDA regime. Its economic ideology favouring intensive globalization provided greater impetus to globally-oriented sectors of which IT was identified as the most significant one.

21. *Annual Report 1997-98*, Department of Electronics, Government of India, p. 12.

Two main components of its economic policy were disinvestment and incentives for export-oriented sectors. Policy measures so adopted were not simply aimed at supporting export business but also identify ways and means to deal with fast-changing technologies and business models followed worldwide. These policies attempted at providing level-playing field not only to the local entrepreneurs but also the multinational companies that had by now emerged as major players in the Indian economy.

The economic ideology of the BJP was completely at dissonance with that of its parent social organization, namely RSS that strongly adhered to the idea of 'Swadeshi' envisaging 'development of indigenous base of the Indian industry.' The RSS resisted the policies of BJP that sought to intensify the process of globalization. Further, some of the important leaders within the party and the coalitional partners within NDA also raised apprehensions against the pace and pattern of economic liberalization and globalization. Globalization directly contradicted with the ideology of Swadeshi or self-reliance whose basic thrust was to promote indigenous industry for enhancing local skills and capabilities.

However, there was less opposition to the globalization of the software sector as compared to other industrial sectors. This is because the main political lobby for the industry, namely NASSCOM, strongly favoured liberalization and global integration of the industry by working in close quarters with the government departments and ministries. Secondly, due to absence of trade unions and other politically-influential groups that could oppose the globalization drive the possibilities of opposition to government's liberal policies towards software was bleak. There was some apprehension regarding the entry of foreign firms. The main concern here for the domestic players was the competition for hiring talented and skilled labour in India. Since the foreign and the Indian companies hardly made any competing products, there was lesser possibility for opposition to the entry of foreign companies on that score. In absence of the uncertainties that had gripped other industrial sectors, the government found it easy in furthering the process of globalization of the software industry.

On 1 June 1998 while delivering the Budget Speech, Mr. Yashwant Sinha, Minister of Finance elaborated on the importance of IT sector for the economic growth of the country and the institutional changes that were needed to accommodate the new advancements that have taken place in the field of IT and computer software. In his speech, Mr. Sinha said that,

> "IT is the fastest growing sector of the Indian economy as indeed of the world economy. It has tremendous potential for the generation of employment, income and export earnings.... Our specialists are second to none in the world.... The government has set itself a target of making India a 'Global Information Technology Power' and one of the largest generators and exporters of software in the world within 10 years.... Our software companies operate in a highly competitive global market and the skilled professionals working in these companies have attracted opportunities abroad. They have sought permission to offer stock option schemes to their Indian employees linked to ADR/GDR issues abroad, under which the employees will be eligible for ADR/GDR stock options. In recognition of the excellent work being done in this sector, and its very special circumstances, the government had decided to formulate a special scheme to allow such options for the software sector."[22] (Budget Speech 1998-99: 35-37)

Mr. Yashwant Sinha presented an elaborate account of the future prospects of the IT industry. He emphasized on some of the incentives that were needed for strengthening the industry and extending its outreach in the global market. His speech clearly recognizes the extent of external competition that the industry was likely to face particularly on the front of labour market.

---

22. Budget Speech, *Budget for 1998-99 (Part A)*, Ministry of Finance, Government of India, 1 June 1998, pp. 35-37.

The National Information Technology Task Force and the IT Action Plan[23]

The foremost step of the NDA government was the setting up of a 'National Information Technology Task Force' on 22 May 1998[24] headed by the Deputy Chairman, Planning Commission to formulate a National Informatics policy to realize the objectives highlighted in the Budget speech. The Task Force submitted the Information Technology Action Plan comprising 108 recommendations on 4 July 1998. It set an export target of $50 billion by 2008 for the software sector and a target of $10 billion for computer hardware and telecom. It was also targeted that the CAGR for the software sector which was around 55% between 1992 and 1997 should increase to almost 80% by 2008.

There was a proposal to facilitate greater private investment in software and IT and make the policy environment more conducive for the same. Although the Task Force appreciated the liberal measures that were in force since 1991, it found them insufficient in addressing structural hindrances like existence of complicated procedures for getting approvals from the authorities and certain stringent taxes and duties. As a result, a number of tax-related incentives were proposed under the 108-point Action Plan that included zero customs and excise duties on IT software, income tax exemption to software and services exports, gift tax exemption on computers, 1-3 per cent of Budget of every Ministry/Department for IT Applications.

One of the main areas of concerns was human resources in the IT industry. It was recognized that the key advantage that the Indian software industry has over other countries is the availability of a talented pool of engineers. With its English-speaking, technically skilled professionals Indian IT industry had a comparative advantage over its counterparts in other

---

23. The Policy Documents and the Reports are available online on the Official website of National Task Force on Information Technology and Software Development, Government of India, http://it-taskforce.nic.in/index.html
24. http://it-taskforce.nic.in/index.html, Official Website of National Task Force on Information Technology and Software Development, Government of India.

countries. Henceforth, the National Task Force gave a number of recommendations to strengthen the human resource base of the industry. The most important amongst these was the proposal to launch 'An Operation Knowledge' for universalizing IT education and IT-based education in a phased manner. It was also proposed that US Dollar linked stock options must be allowed for employees in Indian software companies. Other schemes were proposed to promote and facilitate IT education at the school and college levels. For this, it was recommended that attractive packages must be granted to students for buying computers[25] (Ministry of Finance 1998-99: 109).

The National Task Force mainly addressed four important issues concerning the software industry, namely simplification of bureaucratic procedures, lowering the taxes and duties, provision of proper infrastructure particularly high speed data links, and qualitative training and education to the software professionals. Although some of these concerns were addressed by the government through initial policy changes and the introduction of the STPI scheme, the industry required further impetus to cope up with challenges thrown up by the expansion of mobile and internet technology at the global level. Second, the entry of Asian countries like Philippines and China in the software business posed stiffer competition to Indian exporters. Such new concerns for enhancing competiveness necessitated upgradation of infrastructure particularly telecommunication facilities so that the companies could switch over to offshore services.

Following the recommendations of the Task Force, the principle strategy of the Ninth Plan was 'Export, Employment, Productivity-led Growth' of Electronics and Information Technology[26] (DoE 1997-98: 1). In view of this, the DoE advanced a number of programmes to improve training and education in IT and software production. It included developmental programmes for manpower, quality upgradation,

---

25. *Economic Survey 1998-99*, Ministry of Finance, Government of India, p. 109.
26. *Annual Report 1997-98*, Department of Electronics, Government of India, p. 1.

stimulation of software engineering and research, and so on. This programme was later renamed as 'National Software Capability Enhancement Programme.' It was also decided that a National Institute of Advanced Software Education and Research for imparting qualitative education and specialized training for software engineers and professionals will be established. Recognizing the growing significance of JAVA in computer applications, the DoE also took the initiative of establishing the JAVA Competency Centre at CMC R&D Centre, Hyderabad in collaboration with Sun Microsystems Ltd. and NASSCOM for enhancing the quality at high end software capability in software and IT education and R&D sectors. Further, a 'Special Manpower Programme for VLSI Design' was launched recognizing the significance of this design for testing and application development. The main objective of launching this training programme was to increase India's global share in VLSI Design and related services from a level of 0.5% to 5% by the end of Ninth Plan[27] (DoE 1997-98: 31).

Prior to the submission of the IT-Action Plan-III, a prolonged parliamentary debate followed on the future course of development and policy initiatives for the IT sector. The underlying purpose was to find ways to strengthen the industry and its export prospects. Concerned about the achieving the export targets in the software industry, Prof. Umma Reddy Venkateshwari asked about the details of the multi-prolonged strategy for the development of the IT sector. Further, she drew the attention of the government towards the achievement of the set target of $60 billion for exports in the IT sector. Responding to the questions of Ms. Venkateshwari, the Minister of IT and Parliamentary Affairs, Shri Pramod Mahajan replied that first and foremost the government has established the Ministry of IT to undertake a number of initiatives for facilitating the growth IT-ITES sector manifold and that a comprehensive Action Plan for the IT sector was being drafted to achieve the target of $50 billion by the year 2008. He further added that the Ministry of IT has identified a number of action areas for achieving the export targets in the software sector. These were: software productivity

27. *Ibid.*, p. 31.

improvement, quality of software development, human resources development, communication infrastructure, national information infrastructure, e-commerce regulatory framework, promotion of venture capital funds, convertibility of capital account, promotion of brand equity, simplification of custom procedures, electronic governance, generation of strong data bases, increase in PC (personal computers) penetration, vibrant domestic IT services market, strategy for business development, and creation of Indian IT multinational companies[28] (*Lok Sabha Debates* 1999: 71-73).

The political debates on the new IT policy clearly suggest growing concerns over ways and means to meet the ambitious export targets. The issue of human resource development in the service sector appeared to a prior concern for the government in the policy agenda. But more importantly it would be condign to suggest that the IT policy was still export-oriented as the underlying purpose behind the task force recommendations and the concomitant policy changes in the Ninth Five-year Plan was to follow a multi-pronged strategy for export-led growth in the sector. This large-scale initiative of export promotion necessitated the establishment of a separate ministry for IT that would be action-oriented and work closely with NASSCOM to attend to the needs of the IT sector and yet regulate effectively to promote a consistent growth. For this purpose, the Ministry of Information and Communication Technology came into being.

Ministry of Information and Communication Technology

The Ministry of Information and Communication Technology was set up in October 1999. It served as the nodal agency for undertaking various measures to promote an overarching development of the IT industry in collaboration with the Central government, state governments, academia, the private industry, and successful Indian IT professionals abroad. The ministry clearly stated its underlying objective of making India an IT superpower and achieve a target of $50 billion by

28. *Lok Sabha Debates*, 15 December 1999, vol. 3, no. 13, New Delhi: Lok Sabha Secretariat, pp. 71-73, Q. 259.

2008. It underscored the need to bring about a series of policy changes[29] (Ministry of Finance 1999-2000: 125) that included promotion of IT-enabled services, IT education, electronics and computer hardware manufacturing and exports, silicon facility, e-commerce, internet-based enterprises and internet-based distant education programmes in collaboration with leading academic institutions like the IITs, IIMs and other leading engineering and management colleges in India.

The Ministry of Communication and Information Technology comprises the Department of Electronics and Information Technology. The department is administered by the Minister of State for Communication and Information Technology who is its political head. Broadly, the administration is divided into two branches, namely the Secretary and Cyber Appellate Tribunal (CAT). The secretariat of the ministry is further divided into five branches: Groups and their Heads in the Ministry, attached offices, autonomous councils, Section 25 companies, and advisory councils/committees. CAT mainly deals with legal cases related to cyber security and other matters (ministry website).

The newly born IT Ministry took on to its task of recommending IT-specific programmes and concomitant funding in the Annual Budget of 2000-2001. As observed in *The Strategic Review* published by NASSCOM, "IT Minister Pramod Mahajan and Finance Minister Yashwant Sinha proved that two heads were better than one by introducing a budget that was extremely IT friendly"[30] (NASSCOM 2001: 41). In view of the ministry's recommendation the budget pruned the existing taxes and duties for IT sector. The Income Tax holiday for EOUs, EPZs was extended till 2010 and the ESOP tax was rationalized and reduced. In addition to this, the Venture Capital funds came to be exempted from income tax. A decision was also taken regarding abolishing of sale tax on IT products. Further, the government allowed 100% FDI in the IT industry,

29. *Economic Survey 1999-2000*, Ministry of Finance, Government of India, p. 125.
30. *Strategic Review 2001*, New Delhi: NASSCOM, p. 41.

a long-standing demand of the industry. Also, the Ministry of IT recommended that each ministry must allocate a minimum of 2%-3% of its budget on IT promotion.

Clearly, government support for the industry scaled new heights with the formation of the MIT. Since its formation, it has worked closely with NASSCOM attending to the needs of the industry in the face of emerging challenges of globalization. Like NASSCOM, the ministry has also been a voice to the demands of the industry but has remained committed to socializing IT by facilitating its outreach to masses. Thus, IT education has been a subject of prior action and implementation for the ministry. Its e-learning exercise is committed to create a knowledge society and development of e-skills. In this regard, the Department has provided grant-in-aid for R&D projects in areas of content development, technology development projects, human resource development projects, and faculty training to improve literacy through distant learning using information technology (ministry website). Some of the major projects launched during Tenth and Eleventh Plan periods were: Design and development of an online course content on cyber security to be offered in e-learning mode; Enhancing Competency of IT Teachers and Industry Professionals; Development of content delivery tools to enhance the existing experimental education technology services and Training of trainers in e-learning.

Also, it is realized that gearing up software and services exports has become extremely crucial in the wake of stiff competition from a number of Asian countries like China, Philippines, Indonesia, Malaysia, and so on. As observed that, "The government inaction will spell doom. The current advantages of Indian companies will disappear and they will become marginalized in the global arena. Other countries such as Philippines, China, Indonesia whose governments are actively encouraging software and services exports will overtake India as the preferred skill surplus countries.... Overall failure to act will have an adverse impact on the economy"[31] (NASSCOM 2001: 40).

31. *Ibid.*, p. 40.

The creation of the Ministry of IT has certainly increased the bargaining power of the industry with the government. DoE had a similar approach but it took time for it to evolve from a controller to a facilitator. The ministry was born as a facilitator with a largely action-oriented approach towards development. Second, the vision of the ministry was broader and multi-faceted. Its span of attention was much larger ranging from exports to e-governance. Ministry of ICT was a bold initiative towards institutionalizing the goals of IT and technological innovation. Finally, the ministry served as a channel of communication between the industry and the cabinet and a negotiating point for the private players.

Ministry's close-knit involvement with the industry has given a boost to its growth. This is well illustrated by the data on revenues generated through software exports between 2002 and 2008 given in Table 2.

Table 2: Software exports (₹ Crores) from 2002 to 2008

Year	Software Exports (₹ Crore)
2002-03	46,100
2003-04	58,240
2004-05	80,180
2005-06	104,100
2006-07	141,000
2007-08	163,000

Source: Annual Report 2007-08, DeitY; 11[32]

Inference: The data clearly indicates that there has been a consistent increase in the export revenue from the software sector.

32. *Annual Report 2007-08*, Department of Information Technology, Ministry of Communications and Information Technology, Government of India, p. 11.

The Cyber Security Regime

Cyber security and protection of IPR has emerged as prior areas of concern with the rapid spread of information technology. It has drawn the attention of policy-makers and corporate players worldwide. The *Annual Report 2002-03* of the Ministry of IT observes that, "The rapid growth of Internet as a universal communication medium to transact business, over recent years has major ramifications for computer and network security. The spread of Internet-based electronic commerce added substantially to the incentives for the intruders to attack computer and network security in recent years"[33] (DeitY 2002-03: 19).

To check software piracy and ensure cyber security, the government introduced the Information Technology Bill in 1991. Cyber laws for facilitating electronics commerce, recognizing electronic contracts, preventing computer crimes; and electronic filing/documents were incorporated. In May 2000, both the Houses of Parliament passed the Information Technology Bill. The Bill received the assent of the President in August 2000 and came into force since 17 October 2000.

Under the IT Act 2000, the Office of Controller of Certifying Authorities was set up in the year 2000 for issuing digital signature certificates and ensuring cyber security. In addition to this, three more certifying authorities, namely National Informatics Centre, Institute for Development and Research in Banking Technology, and TCS were given the license to issue digital signatures.

In its endeavour of preventing software piracy and cyber crime, the government has sought the support and cooperation of NASSCOM and other big companies like TCS, Wipro and Infosys at individual levels from time to time. For instance, TCS is authorized by the government to certify digital signatures. NASSCOM's involvement in the cyber security regime is also noteworthy. One of the primary objectives of NASSCOM is to

33. *Annual Report 2002-03*, Department of Information Technology, Ministry of Communications and Information Technology, Government of India, p. 19.

take effective measures to campaign against software piracy[34] (NASSCOM 2001: 14). To begin with, NASSCOM created an independent organization named DSCI (Data Security Council of India) which further constituted the CSPF (Cyber Security Policy Forum). The organization makes necessary recommendations to the government on cyber security measures from time to time. One of such reports titled "Securing our Cyber Frontiers" was released by the then Union Finance Minsiter P. Chidambaram in April 2012. The report highlighted the joint role of the government and industry for ensuring cyber security. Its proposal for establishing a National Structure for Cyber Security envisaged information sharing between government and industry through public-private partnership and appointing the Head of Cyber Security as a high-level government functionary. Further, it suggested the development of a competency framework to develop a skilled workforce for cyber security. Providing training to law enforcement agencies like police in investigating cyber crime cases was yet another valuable input.

In accordance with the legal provisions of the IT Act 2000, the Department of Information Technology has set up an ISTDC (Information Security Technology Development Council) with experts drawn from User, Industry and Developer/R&D agencies. The main objective of this newly established institution is, "To facilitate, coordinate and promote technological advancements and to respond to Information Security incidents and threats and mitigating attacks at the national level"[35] (DeitY 2002-03; 19). The ISTDC with the support of the government and the private industry has consistently worked towards devising new techniques and mechanisms to address security issues related to internet and software, electronic commerce, cyber forensics, and so on. In this regard, it has been extensively involved in R&D projects. One such recent projects is called 'Design & Implementation of Secure, Authenticated Systems for E-Commerce' which was completed at TIFR, Mumbai.

34. *Strategic Review 2001*, New Delhi: NASSCOM, p. 14.
35. *Annual Report 2002-03*, Department of Information Technology, Ministry of Communications and Information Technology, Government of India, p. 19.

Recently, the government has established the office of STQC (Standard, Testing and Quality Certification) Directorate which is attached directly to the Department of Information Technology. The STQC has a wide network of Electronics Test and Development Centres and Electronics Regional Test Laboratories that provides the services of testing and calibration. One of the main tasks of STQC is to provide certification for QMS, EMS, Safety and EMC and training in the areas of quality assurance, reliability, manufacturing technology, industrial automation, Test Engineering and Metrology. In alignment with the Department's policies and programmes to ensure cyber security it has provided a range of security-related services like Information Security Management Certification, IT Security Product Testing, Penetration Testing and vulnerability analysis of IT networks and Systems, Software Testing Evaluation Certification, Certification of IT Service Management, and Quality Assurance and Conformity Assessment Support for electronics-governance products and services[36] (DeitY 2007-08: 45).

The government has also collaborated with other countries and international agencies to promote cyber security. Recently, an Indo US Cyber Security Forum took place under which the Working Group on Information Security Assurance undertook the responsibility of promoting development and review of security standards and guidelines for the IT industry. It will ensure that the Indian organizations would strictly comply with US Information Security Requirements for international trade in the network economy.

Thus, we find that there has been an overarching collaboration and cooperation between the government, NASSCOM, domestic software firms at the individual level, and other countries to create a secured IT environment in the country. This collaboration has resulted in devising new institutional mechanisms that would ensure compliance to the security rules and guidelines by the software firms. More importantly, a global concern for cyber

36. *Annual Report 2007-08*, Department of Information Technology, Ministry of Communications and Information Technology, Government of India, p. 45.

security has gelled with the interests of local firms to support a national-level cyber security regime. As stated, the NASSCOM with some major IT players in India have worked close doors with the ministry to establish the legal framework for IT security. Interestingly, the private players have been drawn in this newly-established regime and are close partners of the government.

SECTION 2: EMERGENCE OF ITES OR THE BPO SECTOR

The emergence of IT-BPO industry is yet another significant outcome of the globalization process. Like many other countries, IT-BPO was a new business model in India to expand the global outreach of its IT industry. ITES also referred to as BPO (business process outsourcing) has emerged as one of the fastest growing segments within the IT industry. The BPO segment involves the outsourcing of processes that can be enabled with IT. ITES covers human-intensive services that are delivered over telecom/internet networks to a range of business segments and vertical organizations. Elaborating on the emergence of the ITES industry in the developing countries in general and India in particular Carol Upadhya says that,

> "A range of white and pink collar work has been outsourced or offshored to sites where cheaper labour enables large amounts of clerical work to be carried out round the clock. Work carried out in these dispersed sites is managed and coordinated through the use of new ICTs (information and communication technology). These economic shifts have created a 'global information economy' based on complex production and services networks that create and support information technology systems and provide remote backend services, linking together workers, managers and customers located across multiple site and borders."[37] (Upadhya and Vasavi 2008: 12-13)

37. Carol Upadhya and A.R. Vasavi (2008), "Outposts of Global Information Economy: Work and Workers in India's Outsourcing Industry" in Carol Upadhya and A.R. Vasavi, ed., *In an Outpost*

It has been indicated that wide ranging global communication networks has led to the emergence of a large pool of technical professionals in the developing world who have become important players in the global information economy. They are the English-speaking software professionals in the IT-BPO sector who constitute the largest section of skilled labour within the service industry. The knowledge industry emerging through BPOs and KPOs with these skilled professionals has given a comparative advantage to Third World countries. As Carol Upadhya points out,

> "Aided by the spread of sophisticated computer technology and telecommunications technology, systems of production are becoming even more geographically dispersed and an increasing array of economic activities are being outsourced and offshored to new destinations, leading to the establishment of new 'knowledge' industries in the countries that were labelled 'Third World."[38] (Upadhya and Vasavi 2008: 1)

What gives comparative advantage to India's IT-BPO industry is its skilled professionals who have excellent command over English language. With their technical and linguistic capabilities they are hired to provide round-the-clock information and business services to clients abroad. Secondly, the conducive policy environment provided by the government has attracted many companies in United States and Europe to the India's ITES industry[39] (NASSCOM 2002: 37). The NASSCOM-McKinsey Report 2005 highlights five major advantages of India in the IT-BPO sector. These are: abundant talent, sound urban infrastructure, operational excellence, conducive business environment and continuous growth in the domestic IT sector (NASSCOM-McKinsey Report 2005: 15).

The software and ITES exports have grown at a rapid rate. From 2000-2005, the software and the ITES industry in India

---

of the Global Economy: Work and Workers in India's Information Technology Industry, New Delhi: Routledge, pp. 12-13.

38. Carol Upadhya and A.R. Vasavi (2008), *op. cit.*, p. 1.
39. *Strategic Review 2002*, New Delhi: NASSCOM, p. 37.

grew at a CAGR of 28% and its contribution to GDP grew at a rate of 4.8% by 2005. By 2005, the exports went upto $17 billion.

Table 3: Industry-wise distribution of ITES/BPO service exports from 2008-13 (in percent)

Activity	2008-09	2009-10	2010-11	2011-12	2012-13
BPO services	84.7	75.6	82.0	84.7	82.5
Customer interaction services	10.7	18.0	12.2	14.4	10.9
Finance and accounting, auditing bookkeeping and tax consultation services	8.3	11.9	13.4	23.5	9.7
HR administration	2.4	1.3	0.5	0.2	0.9
Procurements and logistics	1.2	0.3	0.5	0.0	0.4
Medical Transcription	11.8	0.4	0.6	0.2	0.7
Document Management	—	0.3	0.6	0.4	0.5
Content development and management and publishing	6.5	1.0	0.8	0.7	1.4

Source: *RBI Monthly Bulletin* March 2014: 55

The data shows the pre-eminence of BPO services within the ITES/BPO industry. But within the ITES segment customer interaction and finance and accounting services account for the highest share of business.

According to the *Annual Report of Ministry of Communications and Information Technology 2005-06*, "The Indian ITES and business services (ITES-BPO) have demonstrated superiority, sustained cost advantage and fundamentally-powered value proposition in ITES. Indian companies are expanding their service offerings, enabling customers to deepen their offshore engagements; the shift from low-business process to higher value, knowledge-based processes is having a positive impact on the overall industry growth"[40] (DeitY 2005-06: 1).

Further, it has been estimated that the ITES industry in India created 3 million job opportunities by the year 2005[41] (DeitY 2005-06: 2). The ITES industry in India also expanded its export base from US, Europe, and Canada to countries in the Asia-Pacific region as a result of growing demand of BPO in these countries. In the year 2011, India assumed a share of 58% of the global outsourcing market generating net revenue of $59 billion. United States that registers almost 70% of the overall global outsourcing gets 80% of its business from India.

It has been indicated that the ITES/BPO sector has witnessed vendors moving up the value chain to offer high-end research and analytic services to the clients. Elaborating on this account the Annual Report 2006-07 of the Ministry of IT states that,

> "High offshore component of delivery and superior execution in multi-location delivery continue to be the key features and differentiators of this segment of the IT industry. Broad-based industry structure, IT led by large Indian firms, BPO by a combination of Indian and MNC third-party providers and captives, reflects the depth of the supply base."[42] (DeitY 2006-07: 9)

The BPO/ITES sector has been one of the most successful segments within the IT industry and has a strong future potential. Although, BPO is an export-oriented sector, its share

40. *Annual Report 2005-06*, Department of Information Technology, Ministry of Communications and Information Technology, Government of India, p. 1.
41. *Ibid.*, p. 2.
42. *Annual Report 2006-07*, Department of Information Technology, Ministry of Communications and Information Technology, p. 9.

in the domestic market has also been rising in recent years. As per a NASSCOM study, the domestic IT-BPO market increased from ₹ 932 billion in 2009 to ₹ 1741 billion in 2013. In 2014, the domestic market share has increased to ₹ 1910 billion (*The Hindu*, Chennai ed., 11 May 2014).

SECTION 3: GLOBALIZATION AND CHALLENGES

Globalization has produced both opportunities and constraints for the industry. The institutional change accounted for in earlier sections was initiated to enrich the performance of the industry in the global market. It created a level playing field for SME's along with bigger companies. Today, as discussed above, the SMEs supported by the government especially through STPI assume a sizeable share of the global business. The institutional initiatives assisted in exercising the global opportunities but have often fallen short of addressing the pressures and constraints. While extending support in all possible ways, the government has retreated from certain key areas which require state intervention and accordingly some form of regulation. The real challenge of moving up the value chain with greater investment on in-house R&D has remained unattended. Technological upgradation becomes imperative in view of emerging competitors in the global market like China, Philippines and Malaysia. Above all, the emerging IT demands in domestic market necessitates greater involvement of private companies in local business arenas complimented by state incentives for facilitating reverse brain drain as witnessed in case of China. It is found that a large pool of skilled engineers from the premier institutes like IIT and IIM migrate to US and Europe due to alluring salary packages in those markets. In recent times, a slowdown in the global market has undoubtedly re-oriented firms towards local business especially government projects under public-private partnership, but export business still remains the core agenda of the private players and government.

Nature of Services in the Software Industry—Moving up the Value Chain

The IT/Software industry can be categorized into three types, namely, IT services, ITES, and software products. The service sector may be further divided into onsite services and offshore services. Onsite services involve visiting the site of the client and delivering the required service. It requires an expenditure of great deal of time and money as most of the foreign clients are based in far-off destinations like United States and West Europe. Offshore services involve the delivery of services from the producer country itself. It has many advantages vis-à-vis onsite services as it saves both time and money. However, onsite services require a far more efficient infrastructure particularly continuous availability of data communication links. As the clients are situated in far-off destinations, lack of proper data communication links makes it extremely difficult to provide the services to the clients. Onsite services occupied a major share of Indian software services exports till the year 2000.

Table 4: Share of the export revenues generated through different categories of services (in percent)

Year	Onsite Services	Offshore Services	Software Products and Packages
1990	90.00	5.00	5.00
1993-94	62.01	30.05	7.94
1994-95	60.90	29.59	9.51
1995-96	60.32	31.63	8.05
1996-97	58.69	30.21	11.10
1997-98	59.00	32.20	8.80
1998-99	58.18	33.91	7.91
1999-2000	57.26	34.69	8.05
2000-01	56.09	38.62	5.29

***Source*:** Parthasarathy, 2004[43] and *Strategic Review*, 2001

43. Balaji Parthasarathy (3 May 2004), "Globalizing Information Technology: the Domestic Policy Context for India's Software Production and Exports", *Iterations: An Interdisciplinary Journal of Software History 3*.

Inference: The data given in Table 4 well indicates that the onsite services accounted for a major share of the total software export revenues till 2000. However, the share of offshore services has increased from 5.00% in 1990 to almost 38.62% in 2000-01. On the contrary, the percentage share of onsite services has plummeted from 90.00% in 1990 to 56.09% in 2000-01. As a result, there is a gradual trend towards offshore services which is also referred to as outsourcing. The production of software products and packages remained abysmally low. This category has shown fluctuating trends and the production figures reached a low level of 5.29% in 2000-01.

Although, there is a trend towards an increase in offshore services, the onsite services still occupied a major share of the total software exports till 2000-01. However, today offshoring occupies a major share of service business. In the year 2011, India assumed a 58% share of the global outsourcing market generating net revenue of $59 billion. According to an RBI survey, the share of onsite services in software exports plummeted from 32.2% in 2008-09 to just 15.8% in 2012-13 (RBI Survey on Computer Software and Information Technology Enabled Services Exports: 2012-13; 2014). The offshore services improve the quality of services delivered to the clients abroad. The transformation in nature of services is mainly due to an improvement in data communication links. The data communication links came to be provided by the STPs as well as VSNL at a reasonable cost. One major reason behind the persistence of onsite services was that the clients perceived a high degree of risk in outsourcing work because of their suspicion against Indian firms' skills, ability and quality of work in the export markets. Consequently, they preferred to retain the work at the production site. Only risk-free tasks such as coding, testing and debugging are outsourced. Chakraborty and Gupta (2002) cited policy uncertainty and political volatility as major causes of apprehension against outsourcing. They point out that the foreign clients are apprehensive about the direction of government policies predicting that the frequency of policy changes with shifting political ideologies is very high in India[44] (Chakraborty and Gupta 2002: 12). It is felt that the persistence of high levels of bureaucratic controls despite the liberalization drive can hamper the timely delivery of services.

The studies conducted by Anthony P. D'Costa, E. Sridharan, Chandana Chakraborty and Dilip Gupta indicate that the Indian software firms have not successfully attempted to move up the 'value chain'. By analyzing the innovative behaviour of Indian firms and the nature of services offered to the foreign clients they have shown that IT business still remain concentrated in the low-end services and there is an element of reluctance to move beyond what is given. The low-end services include testing, coding and debugging which capture the largest portion of India's software services. The customized services offered by the Indian software firms which require high skills and have not been able to capture much of the global market include systems integration, packaged software integration, infrastructure management, consulting, turnkey projects, product development and design, embedded software and R&D services.

Elaborating further on this account Chakraborty and Gupta (2002) observe that the process of software development involve two consecutive stages. The initial stage of the software development involves the tasks of analysis and design which demand high degree of technological skill, innovation, expertise and creativity. It requires a high degree of sophistication in terms of experience and innovative capacities. The latter stages of coding and testing entail relatively low level of technological innovation and skill requirements and are generally considered to be non-creative components of the production process. The onsite programming services which fall in the category of coding and testing of software occupied a major share of total services exports. As a result, Indian software professionals have basically worked as programmers rather than system engineers

44. Chandana Chakraborty and Dilip Gupta (2002), "Indian Software Industry: Growth Patterns, Constraints and Government Initiatives", Australian South Asia Research Centre (ASARC) Working Paper, p. 12.

or designers by their foreign clients[45] (Chakraborty and Gupta 2002: 12). On similar lines, Nagesh Kumar (2005) also observes that the export activity of Indian enterprises largely involves onsite services. He recognizes onsite services to be involving low level of skill intensity compared to software product designing and development, and has been derisively termed as 'bodyshopping'[46] (Kumar 2005: 92-130).

D'Costa and Sridharan (2004) have conducted a detailed survey of the nature of services performed by the Indian software firms for the foreign clients.

Table 5: India's global share in various categories of services exports for the year 2001

Software Services	India's Exports (US $ billion)	India's Global Share (%, 2001)
Professional Services	5.3	3.7
IT Consulting	0.1	0.3
Systems Integration	0.1	0.1
Custom Application	4.5	23.1
Network consulting and integration	0.7	3.3
Product Services	0.4	0.3
IT Training and Education	—	—
H/W Support and Installation	—	—
Packaged Software Support Services	0.4	0.7

(contd...)

45. *Ibid.*, p. 12.
46. Nagesh Kumar (2005), "Indian Software Industry: National and International Perspectives", in Ashwani Saith and M. Vijaybaskar ed., *ICTs and Indian Economic Development: Economy, Work and Regulation,* New Delhi: Sage Publications, pp. 92-130.

Outsourcing Services	0.1	0.00
Processing Services	—	—
Information Services Outsourcing	—	—
Application Outsourcing	—	—
Network Infrastructure Management	0.1	0.3

Source: Anthony P. D'Costa, 2004: 10[47]

Inference: The data given in Table 5 well indicates that the category of high-value added services like Systems Integration and Packaged Software Support Services of Indian Companies account for a miniscule part of the global share of these services exports.

The recent decade however witnessed a surge in value-added services of the IT-BPO companies in India. There has been a gradual evolution from application development and maintenance to qualitative testing services, infrastructure services, consulting and even system integration by the IT service providers. BPO services have been upgraded to KPO (knowledge process outsourcing) representing a shift from low-end services to higher-end research and analytical services to the clients (Rastogi: 202). The services in this sector have assumed greater depth with process re-engineering across the value chain, increased delivery of analytic and knowledge-based services (NASSCOM 2011: 5). This phenomenal rise started sometimes around mid-2000s with the global requirements of skill upgradation and technological innovation. KPOs are still

47. Anthony P. D'Costa (2004), "The Indian Software Industry in the Global Division of Labor", in Anthony P. D'Costa and E. Sridharan, ed., *India in the Global Software Industry: Innovation, Firm Strategies, and Development*, New York: Palgrave Macmillan, p. 10.

at a nascent stage of development and its future prospects will primarily depend on demand-supply equations for high-end services in US. Amidst these developments, the service providers still face turmoil in view of greater competition from the other countries with high-value offerings in the global market. The Indian companies are yet to diversify their offerings and adopt new business models for sustenance.

Competition in the International Market

The Indian software industry is facing high competition in the global market for IT and software services/products from not only developed nations like the US, UK, Germany, France and Japan but also a large number of Asian countries like Israel, Philippines, China, Singapore, Indonesia, and South Korea.

Nollen and Siddharthan (2008), in their comparative study of the growth of software and hardware industries in India and China, infer that Indian software exports are concentrated on customized services (more than 90%) which has a low-value addition component, while China specializes on packaged software that displays greater innovative skill and capacity[48] (Nollen and Siddharthan 2008: 19). Similarly, D'Costa (2004) in his comparative analysis of the ICT[49] (Information and Communication Technology) segment in various countries finds that India stood low in the global share of ICT production (D'Costa 2004; 5). *The Strategic Review* published by NASSCOM also observes that, "The Indian software industry faces stiff competition from other countries in Asia like Philippines, China and Indonesia whose governments have been on the forefront to encourage software and services exports. It

48. Stanley Nollen and N.S. Siddharthan (2008), "Software and Hardware Firms in India and China: How they differ?" in S.R. Hashim and N.S. Siddharthan, (ed.), *High-tech Industries, Employment, and Global Competitiveness*, New Delhi: Routledge, p. 19.
49. ICT goods are a product of the convergence of hardware and software. These include electronic data processing equipment, office equipment, controls and instruments, communication equipment, telecommunications, consumer electronics, and components that go into this hardware.

predicts that these countries may overtake India as the preferred skill-surplus countries"[50] (NASSCOM 2001: 40).

Competitive pressure on the IT-BPO companies in India has been a critical concern since the Y2K bug of the year 2000. It has led to a serious re-thinking about revising the existing strategies of export-led growth and find new ways to expand business in other parts of the world. Parliamentary debates during the earlier decade highlighted the need and possibility to explore prospective markets for IT services in developing countries without disturbing the traditional client base in Europe and US. In one of the Lok Sabha sessions Shri B.J. Panda asked whether the government was aware of the problems being faced by the Indian Information Technology Services in expanding their market in developing countries. In response to this question the Minister of IT stated that,

> "The developing countries were themselves following the strategy of building up their own capability in various sectors of IT. Market opportunities for Indian enterprises in the sector were therefore limited. Indian enterprises in the export market are concentrated on developed countries. Since the rate of growth was more than 50% per annum there was little incentive to explore markets in developing countries where the demand was comparatively small and largely confined to the government sector."[51] (*Thirteenth Lok Sabha Debates* 1999-2004: 125)

The larger question is that IT trade particularly with United States has political implications as it appears to be one of the core issues in the foreign policy agenda of both countries. The client companies in US with strong political links with the members of House of Representatives during Bush's regime lobbied for outsourcing-friendly policies that favoured the Indian firms. But with politicization of the matter and Democrat government's reluctance to liberalize rules and facilitate outsourcing and

50. *Strategic Review 2001*, New Delhi: NASSCOM, p. 40.
51. *Lok Sabha Debate*, Eighteenth Session (Thirteenth Lok Sabha), vol. 20, no. 3, New Delhi: Lok Sabha Secretariat, p. 125.

recently President Trump's campaign of 'American First' a point that will be discussed in greater details in the next chapter, there arises a need to look for prospective markets in other parts of the world. As observed, visa issues and non-tariff trade barriers may prove to be a threat for the software exports in future[52] (NASSCOM 2001: 49).

Brain Drain

Globalization has facilitated flow of both capital and labour across the globe. In this series, the movement of IT professionals has been the most visible outcome. Countries like China, India, Sri Lanka, and Philippines have witnessed large scale migration of their skilled professionals and engineers to US and other western countries in recent years. This phenomenon is referred to as 'brain drain.' Brain Drain generally takes place in upcoming fields of science and technology like IT, biotechnology, information science, computer hardware, space science, hardware engineering, and so on. The developing countries have over the years displayed a comparative advantage in the service sector. With their talented and highly skilled pool of engineers and computer professionals these countries are now having an edge over developed nations in the service sector.

The phenomenon of brain drain has become very common amongst software and IT professionals in India. These engineers after receiving their engineering and management degrees from the ivy league institutions like IITs (Indian Institute of Technology) and IIMs (Indian Institute of Management) migrate to developed countries like the US, UK, Germany, Japan, Singapore, Canada, and Australia in search of better job opportunities and high salaries. The 'new global economy' termed as the 'knowledge industry' demanding both technical and linguistic skills has worked best for the highly ambitious youth who find IT as an alternative job opportunity to earn a decent living. The preference for IT has a cultural cause too. The western lifestyle that comes with new modes of work culture and social interaction like global networking, late-night

52. *Strategic Review 2001*, New Delhi: NASSCOM, p. 49.

working hours, round-the-clock services, social partying etc. is best found in the service industry and most preferred by the middle class youth. These preferences have led to large-scale out-migration of the youth. In last 10-15 years Indian engineers have assumed a sizeable presence in the Silicon Valley, the global hub of IT professionals in US. As per the estimates, by the year 2000 Indian engineers were recruited in around 972 Silicon Valley-based technology companies that accounted for nearly $5 billion of total sales 25811 jobs (Saxenian 2004: 181).

The trend has however deprived the local firms of the best talents. On the contrary, the skilled labour in India has contributed extensively to the strengthening of the US economy. As Vidhu Verma points out that,

> "The main charge against the IT sector is that the software boom has exacerbated the brain drain. Programmers in India are increasingly aware of the global demand for their skills and the substantially higher compensation available in more developed economies. Many thus aspire to work for foreign companies not only for high wages but to be transferred overseas."[53] (Verma: 480)

However, recently a trend towards 'reverse brain drain' is witnessed in China and other South-East Asian countries like Taiwan and South Korea. Reverse brain drain refers to a phenomenon where the migrants after spending number of years in foreign countries return back home for equally promising opportunities available in their home country. After returning, they have contributed extensively towards building the technological infrastructure of their home country.

Saxenian (2004) explains reverse brain drain by comparing the nature of transnational networks in Taiwan, China and India. Exploring the inter-linkages between the Silicon Valley in the US and the domestic IT industry in China, India and Taiwan, Saxenian observes that the transnational ties of the Silicon Valley IT professionals with their respective domestic economies has

53. Vidhu Verma, "Globalization and the State in India", in Kameshwar Chowdhary, ed., *Globalization, Governance Reforms and Development in India*, New Delhi: Sage Publications, p. 480.

been far more intricate in case of China and Taiwan than India. She observes that while the engagement of Indian professionals with their home economy has strengthened in last few years, they are still disinclined to return to India permanently[54] (Saxenian 2004: 182).

The strengthening of transnational ties in case of China and Taiwan has been accredited to the role of the respective governments in promoting technical and business exchanges that according to Saxenian has been lacking in India. The Chinese state took a number of initiatives in the 1990s to improve and enhance external communication with the overseas Chinese in the Silicon Valley. This involved organizing series of events and programmes in the US for the overseas Chinese academia and industry representatives. The Ministry of Education in China initiated the 'Chunhui Programme' whereby short-term trips were financed for the overseas Chinese to participate in technology-associated activities. The Silicon Valley Chinese software professionals and engineers have participated in such programmes in large numbers. Efforts of the government other than those mentioned are also worth noting. Saxenian observes that many municipal governments in China have established 'Returning Students Venture Parks' within the Development Zones of High and New Technology Enterprise which are exclusively meant for the enterprises run by returnees. In these parks special provisions are extended to the returnees such as tax incentives, infrastructural facilities, and simplified bureaucratic procedures[55] (Saxenian 2004: 180). Taking complete advantage of such incentives and facilities overseas Chinese have returned back to their native place and have contributed extensively to the development of their local industry.

Concrete initiatives from the government to facilitate reverse brain drain are still missing in India. Though, recently some

54. AnnaLee Saxenian (2004), "The Silicon Valley Connection: Transnational Networks and Regional Development in Taiwan, China and India" in Anthony P. D'Costa and E. Sridharan, (ed.), *India in the Global Software Industry: Innovation, Firm Strategies and Development*, New York: Palgrave Macmillan, p. 182.
55. *Ibid.*, p. 180.

conferences and award ceremonies like the 'Pravasi Bhartiya Diwas' were organized at the governmental level to engage with the NRIs (non-residential Indians) and the NRI investments have also increased in the recent past, no specific measures were taken by the government to encourage the return of overseas software engineers/professionals to India. Nevertheless, NRI investments in states like Gujarat for building infrastructure and industry has produced new avenues for economic growth and development.

However, certain studies have shown a trend towards reverse brain drain amongst IT and management professionals in US and western countries. A sample survey carried out by Harvard Business School located factors that motivated NRI Indians to return back to their home country and found that they were mainly for better business prospects in India, and not really due to any governmental support. Some of the observations of the sample survey are as follows:

1. While only 10% of the Indians held senior management positions in US, around 44% acquired jobs at that level in India.
2. 61% of Indians found better opportunities for professional advancement in India.
3. 79% of respondents wanted return home because of greater demand for skills in the country. So, they showed keen interest in utilizing their skills for the business start-ups in India.
4. Most of the respondents feared that US economy will lack global growth rates in near future. This is possibly because of the recurrent economic slowdown in US during recent years. (www.profit.ndtv.com)

Modi's Make in India Campaign

A powerful drive to orient NRIs towards investing in India was initiated under Prime Minister Narendra Modi's 'Make in India' campaign. The underlying idea of Make in India is to strengthen transnational ties with Indian Diaspora. As Mukherji points out,

> "The fundamental objective was to give additional push to privatization and global engagement so as to create an investor-friendly environment and turn the economy into global manufacturing powerhouse. The initiative was propelled by the objective of encouraging Indian businessmen to invest in India rather than shifting their business abroad." (Mukherji, 2017: 95)

Make in India is an initiative to foster confidence in investors about the business opportunities that India offers. India's declining growth in the background of the 2008 global recession had shaken the confidence of foreign investors and Indian Diaspora. The Make in India is all set to clear the apprehensions and highlight the unique business opportunities the Indian economy offers to the world. The campaign was launched with high optimism in September 2014 with the objectives of, "facilitating investment, fostering innovation, enhancing skill development and protecting intellectual property."

PM Modi took personal initiative in popularizing the programme abroad. This was an out-of-the-box style of connecting with Indian Diaspora especially the business and the technocratic community. To get started on the campaign, this was a unique way of political communication where a leader through his charismatic appeal and mass following draws public attention in a manner that was never attempted before. For the first time, publicly connecting with NRIs in pursuit of cultural and business ties formed a core component of the Prime Minister's diplomatic visit. During his trips to foreign nations, he appealed to the NRI businessmen therein to invest in India. He made emotional appeals to the NRI audience reminding them of the richness of Indian culture and heritage and persuaded them to work towards the economic upliftment of their country. While addressing the gathering of Indian community at New York's Madison Square during his 2014 US visit he said that, "If you want human resources and low-cost production, then India is your destination. I invite you to the Make in India initiative."[56]

56. www.ndtv.com

The Australian trip to advertise the two grand programmes Make in India and Jan Dhan Yojana was yet another initiative to draw NRIs towards investment in India. In this regard, Mukherji (2017) observes that,

> "The Australian trip was even more appealing as Modi was accompanied by a business delegation from India that comprised the CEOs of topmost companies like Mahindra and Infosys. Modi was publicly lauded for his initiatives to promote private investment and looked up to Australia as a major business destination for India once the Make in India campaign succeeds." (Mukherji 2017)

These public appeals went way beyond the formal strategies of China to establish transnational ties with their Diaspora. The personal touch given to the association through PM's direct appeal without a visible institutional platform provided for greater acceptability of the innovative programmes. The other countries that served as planks for Make in India campaign were Germany, Canada and the UK.

Other than this informal way of launching the programme, an institutional structures to promote it has also been created. The Department of Industrial Policy and Promotion has been entrusted with the overall responsibility of implementing and monitoring the programme. It has developed a help desk and a website where all information related with policies and initiatives and sector-specific details are provided. The site architecture is compatible with mobile screen and the details are clearly laid out. An 'Investment Facilitation Cell' was also created in providing pre-investment and after-care support to the investors. It helps the investors in getting clearance for their business projects and makes the system of administration user-friendly and hassle-free.

Of the 25 sectors identified, IT-BPM is a critical one. The government has clearly laid out incentives for investing in the sector. These are as follows:

1. The Indian IT-BPM industry occupies 56% share of global outsourcing.
2. Fast-expanding infrastructure to support the industry.
3. Business-friendly policies and programmes of the government.
4. India offers a large pool of skilled manpower.[57]

These advantages provide unique opportunities for investment in the IT-BPM industry. Some of the concrete measures to extend financial support to the investors are: tax on royalty and technical fee for NRI investors reduced from 25% to 10%, the National Optical Fibre Network Programme, supporting technology-driven start-ups, and 100% FDI allowed through the automatic route.

The professionals of Indian origin at Silicon Valley have been specially drawn towards the Start-Up India programme which forms a part of Make in India initiative. It was launched in January 2016 with the aim of empowering start-ups to flourish through innovative practices. The programme was primarily directed towards attracting promising technocratic entrepreneurship to social sectors like health, education, infrastructure-building, and agriculture. It inspires young professionals to invest in these sectors and therefore contribute towards achieving sustainable economic growth. While addressing the US India Business Council at San Francisco Union Minister of Road, Transport, Highways and Shipping Nitin Gadkari appealed to the Indian engineers at Silicon Valley to join the start-up programme and contribute their bit the Make in India initiative. Again in his address to the Global Indian Technology Professionals Association Conference he evoked the young IT professionals to bring in their innovation towards building key sectors of economy particularly road transport, highways, shipping and road safety programmes. He assured the Indian entrepreneurs of the ease of doing business in India by clearing the apprehension of bureaucratic menace and infrastructural bottlenecks. The minister also

57. http://www.makeinindia.com/sector/it-and-bpm

informed the entrepreneurs about the growing opportunities in the agricultural sector and the innovations that can help boost productivity in the sector. The minister reported the IIT and IIM graduates working in Silicon Valley expressed high optimism about the success story of their home country.[58]

Indeed, the emerging opportunities and constant business expansion and diversification in India has facilitated reverse brain drain especially after the global economic slowdown in 2008. But the government is yet to devise institutional mechanisms like those in China and Taiwan that would trigger the process.

Imbalance between Export and Domestic Segments

Export-oriented development emerged as the core economic agenda of the government since the adoption of SAP in 1991. Moreover, the IT and software sector has always taken a lead on this count. As a result exports have surged; but little effort was taken to penetrate the domestic market. The expansion of the export segment in IT and software has therefore not been complimented by a corresponding growth in the domestic market. The issue of imbalance appears even more precarious in view of growing need of IT in the development of several social and economic sectors. Software industry has therefore cosmic links in the economy. Its applications to develop manufacturing, healthcare, education, banking and more so agricultural sectors is undeniable. The Table 6 below shows revenues generated from investment in the domestic market of various segments of the computer industry from 1997 to 2002.

Table 6: Revenues from investment in the domestic market (in ₹ crore)

	1997-98	1998-99	1999-2000	2000-01	2001-02
Hardware Services	451	564	725	991	1222
Software and ITES	3827	5242	5929	8240	9752

(contd...)

58. *Indian Express*, 18 July, 2016, San Francisco, USA.

Packages	1956	2246	1620	1944	1900
Custom Software	569	825	1145	1603	1924
Turnkey Projects	629	944	1255	1650	1815
IT Consultancy	305	456	547	725	979
ITES	368	681	1192	1198	2784

Source: *Strategic Review 2003*, NASSCOM: 45[59]

Inference: The data given in Table 6 clearly indicates that there has been a marginal increase in the share of the software industry in the domestic market. Moreover, the rate of increase has not been consistent. While there was a consistent growth from 1997-98 to 1999-2000, the rate of growth was marginal from 1999-2000 to 2000-01. Further, the growth rates have not been uniform across different segments of software and services. For instance, in the packages segment the revenue share has decreased from ₹ 1944 crores in 2000-01 to ₹ 1900 crores in 2001-02. It is observed that the domestic market accounts for only 10%-30% of revenues in all segments.

The recent growth trends also signify the subjugation of the domestic market. This is clearly illustrated by the data on revenues generated by the IT-ITES industry through export and domestic segments from 2009-2014 given below in Table 7.

Table 7: IT-ITES revenue trends ($US billion)

Year/ Description	2009-10	2010-11	2011-12	2012-13	2013-14	CAGR% (2009-14)
Exports	49.7	59.0	68.8	76.1	86.0	12.80
Domestic	14.3	17.3	19.0	19.2	19.0	8.22
Total	64.0	76.3	87.8	95.2	105.0	11.88

Source: NASSCOM data as cited in Deity (Department of Electronics and Information Technology website)

59. *Strategic Review 2003*, New Delhi: NASSCOM, p. 45.

The figures in Table 7 show a heightening gap between the revenues generated by the IT-ITES industry in export and domestic segments. The business model favouring export-led growth remains dominant despite efforts taken to re-orient ICT towards local development, a topic that will be discussed in the next section.

Measures to support export-oriented firms have been the core agenda of government policy for the IT sector. As firms availing the facilities provided by STP, SEZ and other schemes did remarkably well on the export front, it provided yet another reason for the government to extend the incentives. But growing concerns over the global economic slowdown and the need to improve public delivery systems at the local level led the government revise its position on the policy and business strategies for the IT-ITES industry. It became imperative to re-orient the industry towards local needs and demands than just concentrating on the global market. In this regard AnnaLee Saxenian suggests that the government must ensure a level-playing field between domestic and export-oriented firms so that the private entrepreneurs can also contribute to the development of the domestic market for software[60] (Saxenian 2004: 184). E-Governance has been a fall-out of this new thinking.

SECTION 4: ICT FOR DEVELOPMENT—E-GOVERNANCE

Use of ICT appears absolutely crucial for meeting the developmental goals envisaged by the government in its plans and policy agenda. With these thinking it became imperative to re-orient the industry towards offering their services for development of the national economy. This further required revision of programmes and schemes that supported outward-orientation and co-opt private firms in the national and local-level developmental projects. Second, government's direct intervention to promote public accessibility to ICT facilities

60. AnnaLee Saxenian (2004), "The Silicon Valley Connection: Transnational Networks and Regional Development in Taiwan, China and India" in Anthony P. D'Costa and E. Sridharan, ed., *India in the Global Software Industry: Innovation, Firm Strategies and Development*, New York: Palgrave Macmillan, p. 184.

became an essential condition for e-governance. It envisaged a governance network in which the government would partner with private firms to carry out its large-scale development projects.

The intensification of globalization necessitated outward-oriented policies and encouraged international trade at the behest of indigenous development. In view of the global economic meltdown the need of the hour was to backtrack from globalization and look towards opportunities within the economy. As Mascarenhas comments, "While Indian software developers have put India on the IT world map, they have unwittingly become the target of the critics who question the undue emphasis given by the government to the export of software"[61] (Mascarenhas: 171). The initial growth strategy envisaged for the industry failed to recognize the need to channel ICT for local developmental purposes. It did not emerge as a commodity of mass utility although its potential to transform human lives was tremendous. For a long time it remained a prerogative of the elites and found its utility in the international market. Therefore, ICT products were largely exported with the primary aim of triggering economic growth.

IT has the potential to transform the lives of millions who face the brunt of destitution and impoverishment due to lack of socio-economic opportunities in public life. New technological innovations are of immense relevance for restructuring the social sectors like health, education, legal aid, banking making them conveniently accessible to the masses. It also helps in removing the urban-rural divide by providing proper connectivity in rural areas. In this regard, Bill Gates speaking at a seminar on 'Digital Divide' annotates that,

> "There is an urgent need to examine the catalytic and enabling role to be played by the government in ensuring that IT provides new opportunities for the 40% of the people who are living below poverty line, so that they may move about it."[62] (Sood: 4134)

61. Mascarenhas, *op. cit.*, p. 171.
62. Bill Gate's Speech in a Seminar on Digital Divide (http://www.microsoft.com/billgates/speeches/2000/10-18digitaldividends.

Application of IT and software thus facilitates the delivery of public services. It ensures greater transparency and accountability on the part of administration in implementing welfare policies. This is referred to as e-governance.

To meet the developmental goals and improving accessibility of people to public facilities with the use of tools and techniques of ICT, the government launched the 'NeGP (National E-Governance Plan)'. Its underlying aim is to, "Make all government services accessible to the common man in his locality through common service delivery outlets and ensure efficiency, transparency and reliability of such services at affordable costs to realize the basic needs of the common man."[63] Under NeGP the government aims at providing a whole range of public services online with easy accessibility and greater transparency.

The NeGP has a three-tier structure which is as follows:

1. Common Service Centres: These are front-end points for providing services in a transparent manner at an accessible location and a reasonable cost.
2. State-wide Area Networks: These provide for electronically-shared information between various government agencies and government and citizens.
3. 27 Mission Mode Projects: These will identify high priority areas of public services and will implement them electronically. This scheme will be based on a definite schedule for implementation and carried out by project-implementation and process-engineering teams.

The NeGP is an integrated approach towards achieving the goals of e-governance as multiple Line ministries and departments in the Central government are involved in its implementation. It involves orderly coordination between all agencies, organizations and institutions that are linked with

---

asp) cited in Aditya Sood's, "How to Wire Rural India: Problems and Possibilities of Digital Development", *Economic and Political Weekly*, vol. 36, no. 43 (October 22-November 2, 2001), p. 4134.

63. National E-Governance Plan..., Department of Information Technology, Ministry of Information and Communication Technology, Government of India.

the programme. Being the nodal agency for NeGP, DeitY is meant to create a systematic technological infrastructure and coordinating mechanisms through CSCs, MMPs and state-wide networks. It lays broad guidelines, provides technical support and undertakes R&D in collaboration with other agencies and institutions. The state-level MMPs are the responsibility of the state governments which carries out its implementation under the broad guidance of line ministries in the central government. The organizational mechanism for carrying out systematic implementation of the plans and programme under NeGP is therefore well established.

Involvement of private entrepreneurs has been critical to the success of some grand e-governance projects. One such significant project was the UID (Unique Identity Project) launched by the central government under the leadership of Nandan Nilekani, the co-founder of Infosys. The UID grants an identity number to every citizen for getting the benefits of welfare services provided by the government. Lack of proper identity proof created difficulties in identifying the real target groups under PDS and MNRGES schemes. UID seeks both general and specific information from the applicants and relieves people from the onus of filling complicated forms. Its underlying aim is to make the administration and implementation of welfare schemes open and transparent. Highlighting the necessity and significance of UID, Nandan Nilekani states that,

> "The urgent need to make the social programmes more effective and ensure inclusive growth has been a big impetus behind the UID project. The lack of a reliable identity number for residents has played a significant part in weakening our welfare programmes, however well-funded and well-intentioned they have been."[64] (Nilekani 2011: 195)

The other big innovation of e-governance is the establishment of kiosks. Kiosks are booths or computer terminals that offer a

64. Nandan Nilekani (2011), "The Potential of the Unique Identity Number in India" in R.K. Shyamasundar and M.A. Pai, ed., *Homi Bhabha and the Computer Revolution*, New Delhi: Oxford University, p. 195.

range of government facilities online. Kiosks operate through CSCs established throughout the country to provide internet enabled ICT access points. Under this plan, the CSC has collaborated with several public sector banks operating in rural and semi-urban areas to create 'village-level entrepreneurs' to run the kiosks as banking correspondents (www.egovreach.in a NASSCOM initiative). NASSCOM is directly involved in this collaborative venture between DeitY and other public and private agencies. The CSC-kiosks scheme goes a long way in facilitating public accessibility. The governance architecture of such programmes depicts a transformed nature of political economy in which the emerging state-capital alliance is informed by the goals of public welfare, equity and people's participation in the development process. It marks a shift from the lop-sided, growth-centric industrial strategy in which the same alliance worked towards the single agenda of export-promotion.

Certain state governments have taken a lead in adopting special measures to collaborate with the IT industry in realizing the developmental goals. The booming IT industry in these states provided enough ground for involving private agencies in implementing the grand e-governance schemes initiated from time to time. In other words, master states in e-governance like Andhra Pradesh and Karnataka took a stride ahead of the Central Government.

Andhra Pradesh was the first state to adopt e-governance for improving service delivery in a variety of sectors. It provided a footprint for NeGP adopted by the Central Government in 2006. Some of the e-governance projects initiated by the AP government include eSeva, eProcurement, eSuvidha (complete application for municipalities), financial accounting system for Gram panchayats, Computer Aided Registration of Documents and Citizen Friendly Services of Transport.[65] In order to achieve its e-governance initiatives the government has sought to establish APSWAN (AP State Wide Area Network) connecting state headquarters, district headquarters, Mandals and village

65. http://apit.ap.gov.in/index.php/e-gov/e-gov-projects, Official website of Information Technology and Communications Department, Government of Andhra Pradesh.

panchayats all over the state for all government applications of voice, data and video services.[66] Another innovation to curb red-tapeism and facilitate the clearance of files in administrative departments with the use of IT is the KM-ATOM File Management System. Andhra Pradesh has also been one of the first states to have initiated its e-governance programmes under the PPP framework. E-Seva, as mentioned earlier is a state-established private-run centre. It was later extended through 3 kiosks namely Rural eSeva, Rural Service Delivery Points, and Rajiv Internet Village Centres.[67]

The Karnataka government has also been at the forefront in adopting e-governance programmes. Holding the distinction of having the Silicon Plateau of India in its capital city, it has travelled a long way in harnessing the talent and skills of its human resources in promoting rapid socio-economic development. The IT Policy 1997 of the Government of Karnataka clearly states in its objectives that IT will be used as an instrument to eradicate poverty, increase employment and improve governance. Going by its stated objective the government has taken a number of steps to computerize Zila Panchayats by introducing MIS (Management Information System). Some of the major initiatives of the Karnataka government include *Mukhya Vahini* for preparing a comprehensive database of the decisions taken in local bodies; *Bhoomi* for computerizing all the land records of the villages; *Khajane* for computerization of treasuries; *Therige* for computerizing several operations of the Commercial Tax Department; complete computerization of the motor branch of the Insurance Department; *Reshme* for computerizing all transaction of silk business; agricultural price formations; computerized data on registration of candidates

66. http://www.apinvest.co.in/inside/ict_policy_2010_15.pdf, *Press Release on ICT Policy 2010-2015*, Information Technology and Communications Department, Government of Andhra Pradesh, p. 10.
67. http://tier.cs.berkeley.edu/docs/Renee-ppp-ictd2007.pdf, Reene Kurian and Isha Ray, "Public-Private Partnerships and Information Technology for Development in India", *Proceedings of the 2nd IEEE/ACM International Conference ICTD 2007.*

for employment, plans for computerizing RTO offices; and permanent registration of 2.5 lakhs small-scale industries.[68] The other great innovation of Karnataka government is the establishment of kiosks all over the city for payment of water, electricity, telephone and all other bills in a common centre.

While certain states have move ahead with celerity to implement their ambitious e-governance initiatives, the National-e-governance plan is still at an incipient stage to show the desired results. Growing regional disparities call for greater attention to states that have lagged behind in achieving the developmental goals. Second, the issue of digital divide, the gap between urban and rural in technology accessibility, which is now being taken up seriously requires a concerted efforts on the part of the government and the corporate sector. The penetration of IT in rural hinterlands necessitates systematic training in ICT for local administration and Panchayats. This will improve the monitoring of welfare schemes and ensure overall transparency in public works at the local level.

It is observed that the e-governance plans of the government through PPP have been lagging behind because of the absence of the participation of the SMEs in the software and IT sector. While the role of SMEs in software development has increased over the years, their confinement to trade with United States has blurred the possibilities of their partnership with the government and large companies in the national developmental efforts. In their perspective, the lack of will is due to excessive bureaucratization in business with the public sector.[69] The PPP in e-governance has thus remained restricted to some of the big companies like TCS, Accenture, Infosys and Wipro. The potential of SMEs still remain untapped in e-governance programmes of the government.

Lastly, the e-governance policies have mostly benefited the well-off sections in both rural and urban areas. According to Mascarenhas,

68. http://www.bangaloreitbt.in/informationtechnology.html, *IT Policy*, Official website of Department of IT, BT and S&T, Government of Karnataka.
69. Interview with a manager of a Noida-based software company.

> "E-government in India faces an uphill task to reach interactivity and actual delivery of services with evidence suggesting that it is only reaching the economically and educationally well-off who are accessing these services."[70] (Mascarenhas: 152)

On similar lines Narayan Murthy observes that,

> "Millions of Indian still live in poverty completely shut from the benefits of the IT Age. The internet access in India is primarily available in the twenty-two largest cities and about 52 million Indians connected to internet, but the number is extremely small than the total population."[71] (Narayan Murthy 2011: 153)

E-governance could thus be meaningfully implemented only when adequate attention is paid to the IT education of the users amongst marginalized communities. Unavailability of information in vernacular languages is yet another big challenge. There is reluctance to develop software in local languages due to high rate of the software packages. But a recent programme of MHRD 'Lok Vanni' is an important step to digitalize local languages.

Shortfalls in the implementation of e-governance thus need to be addressed on a wholistic and integrated basis. Schemes of e-governance must have a local context otherwise difficulties in its social acceptability may emerge at the grassroot level. Identifying the contradictions in the motives of good governance, Niraja Gopal annotates that, "In attempting to make the project of good governance more sensitive to the particularities in the form of cultural differences, it fails to question whether cultural specificity also demands different ways of conceptualizing development" (Gopal 2013: 202). However despite difficulties in the local contextualization of e-governance, the project seems to invoke the private industry to share the social responsibilities

---

70. Mascarenhas, *op. cit.*, p. 152.
71. N.R. Narayan Murthy (2011), "The Indian Software Industry: Present, Past and Future", in R.K. Shyamsundar and M.A. Pai, ed., *Homi Bhabha and the Computer Revolution*, New Delhi: Oxford University Press, p. 153.

of the government and offer their skills and best practices to achieve the goals of inclusive development. And with this the new direction that the IT policy takes combines the agenda of export-promotion with social welfare.

Digital India

Digital India launched by the recent government marks a paradigm shift in the e-governance initiative of the government. The grand programme was initiated with the realization that a more comprehensive approach was required to transform India into a knowledge economy and to promote greater interoperability by improving the architecture and infrastructure of e-governance. The first ambitious programme introduced under Digital India is the e-kranti programme that marks a shift in the approach of government from translation of goals to comprehensive transformation. The key principles of e-kranti have been enumerated as follows: "Integrated services from individual services, government process re-engineering in every MMP, ICT infrastructure, cloud by default, mobile first, fast-tracking approvals, mandating standards and protocols, language localization, National GIS, security and electronic data preservation."[72]

To manage the programme, a special administrative structure has been created. It consists of three organs which are as follows:

1. Monitoring Committee on Digital India to be headed by the Prime Minister.
2. Digital Advisory Group headed by Minister of Communications and IT.
3. An Apex Committee headed by the Cabinet Secretary.

The administrative structure involving the Prime Minister, Minister of IT and the Cabinet Secretary indicates high order of management and supervision for the grand scheme. The monitoring committee would also include other cabinet ministers in its fold from time to time. Secondly, Ministry of IT would coordinate with state governments and union territories in implementing the MMPs envisaged under the plan.

72. http://www.digitalindia.gov.in/content/introduction.

Therefore, the administration of the scheme is said to involve the entire federal machinery. In addition, the government would be in consultation with non-state actors and institutions like the industry, civil society organization, and above all citizens while implementing the programme. Being a citizen-centric IT programme it envisages participatory governance and collective involvement of all stakeholders. It has set a phased-wise implementation of the project setting a target of 3 years for the completion of the major schemes. The government is thus set to expedite the implementation process by systematically integrating the various components of the programme.

The corporate sector has shown acumen in making desirable contribution to Digital India. Hewlett-Packard's CoE (Centre of Excellence) initiative that aligns with Digital India is a significant step in this direction. CoE as a platform to bring about digital transformation in India was launched by the company on 8 March, 2017. It was inaugurated by P.P. Chaudhary, the Union Minister of Electronics and Information Technology along with the Union Minister of Law and Justice. As a part of the Digital India programme, CoE tends to provide IT solutions and support for indigenous sectors like healthcare, education, BSFI and manufacturing. Some of the innovative practices under its future plans include IT solutions for "better security and surveillance, healthcare and mobility with digital ICT labs, e-health centres and telemedicine and education with digital classrooms" (*The Economic Times*, 8 March 2017).

Most recently, the government has invited private tenders for its Digital India projects under RFP (request for proposal). It is a bid to ease the process of procurement which in the industry's view has been an irritant for the industry in undertaking PPP projects. The RFP moved by the Ministry of Electronics and Information Technology is a response to the long-standing demand of the industry of relaxing the procurement process. It is reported that the new model of procurement emerges after extensive discussion with corporate bodies like NASSCOM and MAIT and American Chamber of Commerce in India. (*The Economic Times*, 3 May 2017)

Clearly, Digital India brings forth a kind of state-capital alliance that is informed by the goal of developmentalism. It sets an example of a state-initiated programme that entails active involvement of corporate bodies and the collaboration works towards finding IT solutions to promote citizen's welfare. It marks a transformation in the approach of government and corporate sector that perceives development not only in terms of export growth but as the ability of the state to empower citizens through digital transformation. In this venture the state collaborates with corporate sector in which the latter finds the collaboration useful both in terms of compensating for the loss of business in the global market due to recession or rise in protectionism and to identify themselves better with the national goals of social security, welfare and development.

Conclusion

The initiation of liberalization of the software industry in the 1980s finally culminated into its global integration since early-1990s. But as shown, the transformative political economy of the early-1990s with the adoption of New Economic Policy with a strong thrust for export-promotion worked best for the growth of the emerging IT/software industry. Policies supporting global integration of the IT sector were met with no opposition. In addition, the emergence of NASSCOM as the chief industrial body for software and services industry produced institutional changes that not only facilitated exports but opened a new chapter of state-capital collaboration in the context of globalization.

Though bureaucratic interests never impeded the process of liberalization and institutional support for the industry, the existence of the same in auxiliary sectors posed newer challenges. The rift between the DoE and DoT is a case in hand. The DoE along with NASSCOM discredited the monopoly of MTNL supported by DoT and persuaded the government to engineer competition in the telecom market. The uphill task of providing round-the-clock services required high-speed internet connectivity. Lack of competition hampered the availability of high-speed, low cost data communication links at STPs.

The DoE and NASSCOM realized that ending the monopoly of MTNL and its regulatory institution DoT could serve as the only alternative to the problem. Meanwhile, the DoE undertook the initiative of providing data links to the software firms in the STPs on its own by collaborating with foreign firms. This immensely helped software firms shift from onsite to offshore services and thereby provide qualitative and timely services to the offshore clients. As the *Annual Report 2005-06* of the Ministry of Communications & Information Technology observes that,

> "Consequent shift (in case of telecom industry) has been from monopoly of government as service provider to private entry in telecom to promote competition and establishing a neutral regulatory agency. The essence of the convergence spirit and the vitality of changes have led to lowering of tariffs, plentiful availability of bandwidth at increasingly lower cost, competition and growth in technology."[73]

The growth story of the IT industry could well be explained in terms of the developmental alliance between DeitY/DoE and NASSCOM. The creation of STPs in the early-1990s was one of the revolutionary steps that resulted from this collaboration. STPs facilitated investments in the software sector and opened a gateway for a variety of SMEs that intended to export. Therefore, the creation of STPs could be cited as a 'new institutional innovation' on the part of the government to promote private investment. The software firms have taken full advantage of the facilities being provided at STPs. The number of firms registered with the STPs has risen sharply.

However, the institutional support from STPs came to a standstill with the termination of tax exemptions in April 2011. The decision and reluctance shown by ministries of finance and commerce was met with opposition from NASSCOM with the backdoor support of the IT ministry. NASSCOM on behalf of

73. *Annual Report 2005-06*, Department of Information Technology, Ministry of Communications and Information Technology, Government of India, pp. 6-7.

the industry made vociferous claims for the extension of tax holidays upto 5 years. Recognizing the financial implications of this measure, finance and commerce ministries expressed reservations over the period of extension of tax holidays within the STPs. Ministry of Communications and IT has assumed a balanced approach in this regard by suggesting the extension in a phased manner. However, as observed NASSCOM repeatedly pressurized the Minister of State for IT, A. Raja to lobby with the other ministries in fulfilling the demand of the software and services industry at large. Moderating export incentives and simultaneously opening business opportunities for the companies in the domestic market was a two-pronged strategy of the government:

1. To continue supporting exports but with balanced incentives
2. To involve private sector in local developmental programmes through PPP.

This model definitely marked a departure from the previous position of the government that was unconventionally tilted towards export-promotion. The mission was carried forward and worked upon more actively by the NDA government as it instituted the task force that finally culminated into the creation of the IT ministry. The NDA regime initiated dramatic changes in the policy framework for the emerging IT-ITES industry in order to acclimatize the industry with changing trends in global market. This was achieved through the establishment of 'National Information Technology Task Force' in 1998 and the consequent advancement of the IT-Action Plan that was presented in three parts. These reports gave a number of recommendations on a variety of issues like taxation, IT security, software piracy, development of human resources, improving infrastructural facilities and further simplification of bureaucratic procedures. NDA's approach to globalization and economic integration bolstered export-oriented sectors like IT so as to make the best of the new global economic order characterized by growing opportunities for trade with United States, Canada and Europe in ICT. To meet the global standards of technology upgradation and security concerns, the government felt that it was necessary to establish a condign legal regime that would not only address the existing administrative bottlenecks but also facilitate prospective entrepreneurs by creating a separate ministry for IT.

The singlemost concern that preoccupied most of the policy deliberation at the international level during late-1990s was unchecked cyber crime and software piracy. To establish a legal framework in accordance with the provisions of the WTO, the IT Bill 2000 incorporated new measures to secure IPR (intellectual property rights) and check software piracy. Under this legal dispensation, new institutions were created to ensure a secured IT environment and controlling hacking. Interestingly, cyber security as an area of concern has assumed the attention not only of the government and the local software firms but also international agencies and other countries that are willing to collaborate with the concerned government bodies and private agencies in the security mission. But most importantly, it would be appropriate to annotate that the cyber security law has been a fall-out of compulsions to confirm to the global standards and norms of software policy. It was yet another step to affirm India's commitment towards the norms and ventures of economic globalization.

The emergence of NASSCOM as an umbrella organization for the software and services industry in India was an important breakthrough in the field of software development. NASSCOM maintained a cooperative relationship with the DoE, and later Ministry of IT to promote the development of software and services industry, particularly in the area of exports. Some of the positive fall-out of this collective endeavour was the STP scheme and other forms of institutional support like DTA, EPZ, and SEZ. NASSCOM's involvement at different levels of government and administration has audaciously worked towards building the state support for the industry with the sole aim of enhancing its global image. NASSCOM and the newly-established ministry have collectively lobbied with other ministries and regulatory agencies to push for investment-friendly policies and globalization of the industry in all possible ways.

The collaboration has primarily focused its attention towards making inroads into the global market but done little to perceive or work upon impending challenges resulting from globalization. While the global market for ICT produced welcome opportunities for the prospective export-oriented firms, it resulted in new forms of contradictions and predicaments. To begin with, the shift from onsite to offshore services tended to be a slow-moving process and that outsourcing comes under severe strain due to rising political dissensions over outsourcing-friendly policies in United States; a point that will be taken up in the next chapter. The software firms in India, particularly the SMEs, still confine themselves to routine tasks like coding, debugging, and so on which have a low-value added content. Large turnkey projects involving higher skills and values are mostly undertaken by a few top-level software companies like TCS, Wipro, Infosys, Satyam Computers, and so on. Success of big companies shifting towards high-end services only presents half-hearted achievements of the industry. A large number of SMEs ensure their presence only through low-end services and are unwilling to move up the value chain. It has been found that the top 5 exporters for the year 1999-2000 accounted for nearly 10.6% of the total software exports.

Table 8: Export revenues of the top 11 software companies in India for the FY 1999-2000 (in ₹ crores)

Rank	Company	Exports
1.	TCS	1820.35
2.	Wipro Technologies	1044.12
3.	Infosys Tech. Ltd.	869.70
4.	Satyam Computer Services Ltd.	662.93
5.	HCL Tech Ltd.	551.79
6.	NIIT Ltd.	551.79
7.	Silverline Tech Ltd.	434.83

(contd...)

8.	Cognizant Tech. Solutions	414.27
9.	Pentamedia Graphics Ltd.	389.03
10.	Pentasoft Tech. Ltd.	353.01
11.	Patni Computers Systems Ltd.	295.51

Source: *Strategic Review 2001,* NASSCOM: 28[74]

Another major loophole with the business strategies of private companies is the inability or rather unwillingness to tap the opportunities in the local market. For a long time, even the government bodies fell short of recognizing the potential business opportunities for the industry within the country. This is in contrast with the developmental strategy in China, Taiwan, South Korea, and Japan where governments in collaboration with their local entrepreneurs and NRIs have undertaken local development projects. Although NRI investments in local developmental projects have been gaining currency even in India and is most likely to expedite in the present scenario, the involvement of technocratic entrepreneurs still remains a distant possibility.

Paucity of skilled human resources is yet another major challenge confronting the industry in present times. The situation becomes even more precarious as a large mass of engineering graduates migrate to US, Canada and European countries in search for better job opportunities. The trend towards reverse brain drain as is the case in China, South Korea and Taiwan goes untapped in India. As a result, the growth story remains invariably lop-sided with high rates of attrition due to disincentives in Indian firms on one hand, and large-scale migration in view of better job prospects on the other. But perspective towards Indian business seems to be changing in recent times with greater investment prospects and assurance of quality infrastructure under programmes like Digital India, Make in India and Start-Up India. How much of this influences the transnational orientations of technocratic entrepreneurs in US and other western countries is still a matter of speculation.

74. *Strategic Review 2001*, New Delhi: NASSCOM, p. 28.

The overall scenario of the sectoral growth has been one that appears to be a mixed baggage of strengths and weaknesses. The opportunities for business expansion accrued from the widening market base for ICT in US, Canada and European countries. But the institutional support that came from DoE and later Ministry of IT was an enabling factor. Government support seemed crucial to tap the offerings of the global market amidst concerted efforts of NASSCOM to lobby with different ministries and departments from time to time to set the order of the day.[75] The MIT however remained a close ally of NASSCOM in the process and subsequently the industrial body came to be involved directly in the policy agenda of the government. The two bodies have also moved together in pursuing the larger developmental agenda envisioned by the government more recently in the form of e-governance and ICT for local development but have remained unfettered in their fundamental business strategy of export-promotion. The pressures of globalization, both economic and political, are seen to be a passing phase and would attain normalcy in due course of time. So, the larger question still remains is whether e-governance as a new model of business using technological innovations a recess from the core growth strategy of export-promotion or the two models of development could co-exist for times to come. More importantly, a policy shift is definitely visible with indigenous development and good governance gradually emerging as the major political agenda of the government; but it is also true that globalization-driven business remains the core policy agenda for IT and software.

❐

75. V. Rajiv Rastogi, "Indian Electronics and IT Industry Production Profile: 2004", Electronics *Information and Planning*, June 2005, vol. 32, nos. 9-10, p. 202.

Chapter 5

Critical Areas of Software Policy and Regulation: Corporate Perspectives and Challenges Ahead

The software companies in India have grown rapidly over a period of two decades. While at the initial stages of development, business was confined to large players like TCS, Wipro, Infosys and Satyam, with passage of time SMEs have emerged as major drivers of growth. Today, they occupy a significant position in the export business. Alongside, rapidly advancing BPO and KPO segments has provided an additional strength to the service industry. However, export performance is only one of the many development indicators to provide an overarching picture. Growth represents only one important facet of development. To assess development, an overarching framework of assessment may be useful. Any assessment of development must involve the aspects of 'development of' and 'development in' the industry. Estimation of productivity will therefore entail the nature of internal work environment as well as work processes and business output. Internal components of development include labor productivity, in-house R&D (research and development) and working conditions, nature of work processes, ability and freedom to apply one's creativity in the work processes, and the overall capabilities and training of human resources. Externalities focusing mainly on work output include export growth, quality of products and services, foreign collaborations, and performance in the domestic market. To strengthen both internalities and externalities, the collective intervention of corporate players and government is necessary. To begin with, the vision of technocratic entrepreneurs has been critical in shaping the developmental path for the software industry. The strategy that they follow, the way they address and meet the challenges to development largely emerges from their vision of development or the way they perceive development. Contrary to the belief about insularity and social insensitivity of the capitalist class, the technocratic leaders of the IT sector have exhibited a panoramic vision of technology and development. This, however, may contrast with the qualified vision of smaller players who still find it difficult to address the externalities and are apathetic towards work process and environment in their organization.

This chapter captures corporate perceptions on government policies, challenges of globalization and strategies to withstand global pressures. To explore the internality especially the internal work environment, the views of young professionals were taken. Field surveys were conducted in software companies and firms at New Delhi, Bengaluru, Gurugram, Noida and Pune. The survey involved informal conversations with software professionals in large software companies as well as SMEs in Pune to get their inputs on work culture in the software industry. This exercise was carried out through non-participant observation method. The other round of interviews collected information on R&D, innovative capabilities, production and investment trends, export destinations, government support, institutional support, human resource development and foreign collaborations. It also involved formal interviews with senior managers of the software companies. Organizations of different forms and sizes were selected like the large ones, the SMEs, multinationals and those that were situated in the STPs. The underlying objective was to account for variations and commonalities in views, if any, of organizations that may otherwise be structurally different. Firms were selected from major cities like Pune, Noida, Gurugram, New Delhi and Bengaluru. The interviews involved face-to-face interaction in some cases and communication through e-mail in others. Electronics communication was used in case of unavailability of the interviewee. The interviews in Bengaluru were mostly conducted through e-mail.

The diverse perspectives on the programmes and policies of the government and the specific strategies to overcome the challenges facing the industry on the policy front could more clearly be understood in the background of the vision, goals and objectives of the leading entrepreneurs in the industry who have assumed both national as well as global credentials for their technocratic innovations. The software entrepreneurs represent a new generation of businessmen who have utilized their technical expertise not only to move up the value chain and correspond to the high-end side of the service industry but have invented new business models for information services to set their mark in the global market. Secondly, they have been on the forefront to realize the goals of corporate social responsibility by partnering with government agencies to meet the desired social goals of development. In other words, their long-term vision of a progressive society takes them far beyond the agenda of export-led production and makes them new partners of the government in its inclusive development programmes.

Visions of IT Leaders—The New Entrepreneurship

The IT industry has achieved its momentous growth as a result of the future vision of its great leaders like Aziz Premji, Narayan Murthy, Nandan Nilekani, Subroto Bagchi, and many others. Qualifying engineering from prestigious institutions like IITs, IISc, and other pioneering engineering colleges of India, they established some of the leading software companies of the country. This happened in a political environment when the government was all ready to renounce its previous anti-business attitude. These entrepreneurs hailing from middle class families with no business background embarked upon an area of business activity that neither required high-capital investment nor a large piece of land for establishing factories. They simply required an office space with computer system and internet connection to provide information and business services to organizations all across the globe. This newly explored comparative advantage of Indian business could lead to a paradigm shift in Indian economy. It had twin advantages of glorifying the image of India as a technocratic superpower and at the same time radically transforming the society by facilitating inclusive development. Although, the technocratic leaders remained committed to the former goal in the beginning, they subsequently realized the importance of the latter and re-oriented themselves to the social needs of development.

To begin with, the software entrepreneurship that emerged in the late-1970s began their business journey with the export agenda. In this venture, they received full support of the government which itself was undergoing through a phase of ideological transformation by getting oriented towards liberalization and globalization. With growing demand for software in the global market and the emerging assistance from the top-notch political leadership and bureaucracy, new software companies emerged in the early-1980s. Infosys was established on July 1981 while Wipro Information Technology Ltd. came into being in the same year. TCS, being an offspring of Tata Group of Companies, was an already-established software company by then. The three companies that assume the topmost position in India's IT industry and global branding in diverse technological applications have also worked on several developmental projects within the country. In this regard, they have recently taken concerted efforts at the individual level or in partnership with the Central and state governments in strengthening social sectors. Their efforts to build a new India free of social and economic distress is based on their panoramic vision and endeavour to democratize technology by bringing it closer to masses and transform the life of millions. Such socially informed purposes distinguish them from the general breed of entrepreneurs and assist them to make desirable contributions towards national policies and programmes envisaged by the government.

Aziz Premji Foundation, a social initiative of Wipro, has taken a lead in revolutionizing quality education at the grassroot level. Its primary objective of "contributing to achieve quality universal education to facilitate a just, equitable, humane and sustainable society"[1] has given it the strength and rigour to work actively towards the upliftment of underprivileged groups in the society. The organization has taken significant measures to improve both accessibility and quality of education. It has been involved in capacity building programmes at the grassroot level. Currently, it operates in about 8 states with nearly 3,50,000 schools imparting quality education in peripheral regions. In the year 2011, the organization planned to start around 1300 schools, two per district, in the identified states. Such schools were to provide education in local language and free of cost and would be affiliated with the state board. They would also take due care of the health and nutrition of children during school hours and mainly serve children in areas that lagged affordable schools and colleges (*Times of India*; 30 October 2011). But, most importantly the thrust of the programme would be to impart quality education so that the children were able to withstand the competitive pressures of the job market. Emphasizing on the quality aspect, Aziz Premji in a speech delivered remarked, "To build universal perspective on quality education, it is important to understand quality, not in the context of varied individual desire, but in the context of the kind of society India inspires to be."[2]

N.R. Murthy, is yet another visionary who gave a new orientation to technocratic thinking in India. His professional experiences and ventures made him demonstrate the virtues of what he called as 'compassionate capitalism'; an idea that underscored the moral underpinnings of corporate governance. He insisted on shedding the 'black skin-white mass' image of elites so that they could comprehend social realities in a better way and contribute towards equitable and inclusive growth (Murthy 2009: 17).

N.R. Narayan Murthy highlighted the dichotomy of the two faces of Indian society, one that make the best out of the

1. http://www.azimpremjifoundation.org/home.html, website of Aziz Premji Foundation.
2. http://www.azimpremjifoundation.org/speeches.html, Speech delivered by Aziz Premji, Chairman, Wipro Corporation, *Business Today*, Anniversary Issue, January 2006.

achievements of science and technology and the other that remains in the margins. The rising GDP has not led to corresponding improvements in the economic lives of the people. Underscoring this enigma of Indian economy, Narayan Murthy observes that,

> "The progress in higher education and in science and technology has not been sufficient to take 350 million Indians out of illiteracy. It is difficult to imagine that 318 million people do not have access to safe drinking water and 250 million people do not have access to basic medical care."[3] (Murthy 2009: 10)

Corruption and mismanagement are cited as the roots of underdevelopment. For him, political freedom has not translated into economic freedom. In Murthy's view, the only way to escape poverty is entrepreneurship. Misguided socialism exhorting License Raj had impeded creative entrepreneurship and only resulted in lack of public accountability. But, a new lease of life was given to the Indian economy in 1991. In Murthy's view the year marks the beginning of a prosperous future for India and for the success of software industry.

Narayan Murthy's approach to economy and polity is undoubtedly liberal. While appreciating the robust growth of export business, he identified serious restrictiveness in India's trade policy. Citing economist Raguram Rajan, it is noted that India's score is eight of ten in the IMF's trade restrictive index (Murthy 2009: 38). The ambivalence in political and administrative thinking is seen to continue and create difficulties in pursuing liberalization. Private companies still find it precarious to pursue ambitious goals on the export front despite signs of success. The ambivalence however arises not of any domestic political constrains but uncertainties of globalization and external shocks and fluctuations. Murthy corroborates an open trade regime one that would not only abandon licensing but also create avenues for FDI. He exemplifies FDI in IT, automobile and BPO sector to suggest how it could not only trigger growth but also establish quality standards in the industry.

3. N.R. Narayan Murthy (2009), *A Better India A Better World*, Penguin Books, pp. xiii (18).

Applauding the tremendous progress made by the Indian software industry in a short period of time, Narayan Murthy feels that the industry faces serious challenges to seize the global and local opportunities. In his view, industry faces several constraints on both domestic and international fronts (Murthy 2011: 153). They have been identified as follows:

1. Poor infrastructure—roads, railways, airports, and more importantly, electric supply
2. Confinement to just 9 Tier-I cities and reluctance to enter Tier-II cities due to poor infrastructure, accessibility and paucity of skill and talent
3. Corruption
4. Lack of internet access
5. The general economic conditions unsuited for IT expansion
6. Political opposition to outsourcing in major export markets.

Nevertheless, despite these constraints the industry has witnessed tremendous expansion in the last two decades with its high-valued offerings and best practices. The industry, for instance, has gradually graduated from application development and maintenance to product development. To cite an example, the product *Bancs2000* was introduced by Infosys for meeting the commercial requirements of large banks. The product was re-introduced as *Finacle* in July 2000 that offered multiple operations for banks all across the globe (Murthy 2011: 160-61).

Murthy's views and perspectives of economic policies and the overall assessment of IT industry's performance appears to be full of optimism. His positions on liberalization and globalization closely approximates with Jagdish Bhagwati's advocacy of benign capitalism. Murthy firmly believes that while third generation reforms are required to eliminate the remnants of Licensing Raj, the corporate sector must contribute towards national programmes for inclusive growth in the country. For this, the government is seen to be lagging in leveraging the power of IT on a large scale. However, on a sanguine note Murthy's observes that,

> "Countries like India, Brazil and China have moved rapidly to install large-scale application systems in IT for tax management, e-governance, management of power generation and distribution, healthcare, food distribution, security, defence and other vital functions of the government." (Murthy 2011: 168)

Thus, Murthy appreciates the political will of policy-makers in leveraging IT for improving administration and governance. At the same time, he evokes the corporate players to seize opportunities extended to them by the government in its developmental projects.

Altogether, the socially-informed goals of the technocratic entrepreneurs and the technocratic-cum-business vision of the political leadership seem to be converging with each other. The leading technocratic entrepreneurs carry a vision and mission that goes beyond business parochialism of the past. Second, they hold on to an ideology that undermines the earlier notion of state-capital dichotomy and appreciates state-capital alliance as necessary for promoting economic growth and social transformation. They cherish the collective efforts of the government and IT industry to build the superpower image of India at the global level. At the same time, they recognize the deplorable economic conditions within the country and along with the government commit themselves to the goals of inclusive development. Nandan Nilekani's UID project, as discussed earlier, is a testimony to this progressive agenda. Nevertheless, their advocacy for greater liberalization and FDI forms the core agenda of their economic thinking. And therefore export-led growth still remains the fundamental business strategy of the IT companies.

In this background of the socio-economic vision of IT entrepreneurs, the next section would understand business perspectives on the challenges, both internal and external, faced by the industry and possible alternatives. The respondents include employees from both small and big companies as per the availability. Intensive interviews with managers in some cases helped in exploring new dimensions about globalization and its impact on the IT industry. The lop-sided development of the industry can be understood in the context of both internal deficiencies and external constraints. Internal deficiencies will mainly account for the unfavourable work environment within the organization and shortfall in in-house R&D. External constrains would include the study of market scenario, policy bottlenecks, rising protectionism in US and human resource issues.

Work Culture in IT Companies[4]

The major labor force of the software companies comprises the software engineers, BPO workers, and other professionals involved in IT-related tasks. Since the nature of work involved in IT and software sector is purely technical, the industry demands greater skill, innovation and technical capabilities amongst workers. Although the workers need greater autonomy or flexibility in work processes as compared to the conventional manufacturing industries, due to increasing routinization of tasks within the sector the trend seems to be shifting towards greater control of management over work processes. As Upadhaya and Vasavi point out that, "Most accounts of software work in India emphasize the routinized and mechanical nature of much of it, coupled with high levels of stress caused by unrealistic project deadlines and consequent long working hours" (Upadhya and Vasavi, 2008: 29).

The nature of management control that is witnessed in the ITES (Information Technology Enabled Services) industry subscribes to the practices of Taylor's scientific management. The theory proposes stringent management control over its employees through panoptic systems of monitoring and surveillance. Another scholar Carla Freeman has observed that, "Informatics workers are subjected to the gaze of computer, the gaze of supervisor, the manager, the fellow production worker,

4. The information given is based on informal conversations with the professionals in IT companies at Pune. The non-participant observation method was being employed.

and finally the internal gaze of the self" (quoted in Upadhya and Vasavi 2008: 30). Due to performance of routine and monotonous tasks the employees tend to remain incubated in their professional sphere. They lack innovation and personal growth. The irony remains that while technology-intensive sectors like software demand greater creativity and innovation on the part of the worker, they tend to remain incubated in their regular and repetitive tasks as observed in typically bureaucratic organizations.

The Factory Act 1948 does not apply in case of labour in case of software industry which clearly indicates that there are no legal safeguards against the exploitation of workers in the software industry. It is a deregulated or rather unregulated sector as far as labour is concerned.

The terms and conditions of work in software and IT Companies are also less flexible as compared to other industrial sectors. The hiring-firing phenomenon is very common in this sector. The sacking of a large number of software professionals in some of the large companies like TCS during 2008 recession is a clear indication of the job insecurities faced by the employees in software companies. The uncertainties associated with globalization could be a plausible cause. The impact of global economic recession was widely felt in the Indian software and IT industry. Loss of business in the external market particularly US caused a sudden drop in the profit margins of the local companies. The loss was compensated by downsizing staff. The second factor which has heightened the insecurity of employees is the absence of trade unionism. Lack of association for channelling work-related grievances has further added to the vulnerability of software employees. The tyranny of managers continues while there remains no political space to oppose them.

In order to find out the contradictions inherent in the work culture, a short field survey based on the methodology of non-participant observation was conducted in some software companies in Pune. Informal conversations with professionals in such companies provided mixed responses about the level of satisfaction of the workers on several counts. To begin with, the professionals expressed high satisfaction with the infrastructure provided by the organization. The appreciation was especially for the exotic design of their office, uninterrupted power supply, round-the-clock high-speed internet facility, pick and drop facilities, lunch and snacks facilities, recreation facilities like gymnasium, medical reimbursements and others.

In few top-performing software companies, majority of workers showed high degree of satisfaction for the emoluments received. In their opinion, the companies provided decent salaries to the software professionals that ensured them a comfortable standard of living. Furthermore, it was found that the respondents who mostly belonged to middle class families and hailed from states like UP and Bihar said that getting into a software company was surely the only way of surviving in big cities. In the course of conversation, one of the respondents said that, "Getting employed in a software firm after completing an engineering or a professional degree in IT and software was one of the shortest route to earn a decent living." He added that the most of his school mates followed this job route and after only few years of struggle and hardwork they got placed in some of the big Indian software companies like TCS (Tata Consultancy Services), Wipro, Infosys, Accenture, Satyam, and many others.

In the middle-range software companies, the professionals expressed strong resentment over salaries received. Most of the respondents in this segment of the industry found their salaries to be insufficient in meeting the escalating living costs in big cities. The salaries, according to them, were not tantamount to the hours and nature of work performed. The perquisites were also less than what was provided in the large companies. However, basic facilities like transport and lunch were provided to them. This group of software professionals was hopeful of moving up the ladder and getting absorbed in large companies. They also showed great interest in moving abroad, particularly United States for growth prospects and better salary. However, they faced a deep sense of insecurity during recession as attrition rates in most of the companies were high and there was lack of new opportunities.

The common concern for all software professionals in all organizations was their disenchantment with the working conditions and the exploitative character of the management team/project coordinator/team leader. The employees in large and medium-sized enterprises, including domestic and multinational companies, revealed that exploitation within the organization by team leaders and managers assume several forms. The panoptic surveillance of their managers had subdued their creative potential. For them, innovation was the key to success in a knowledge-based industry like IT and software and creativity, the working principle. Once this is destroyed, organizations become untenable. In their view, their organizations had left little space for worker's creativity under managerial tyranny.

While the work processes may appear innovative, the work culture remains rooted in the most classical forms of bureaucracy. The power and prestige typical of bureaucratic organizations is thus attached to the rank and file of the members than professional competence. The element of autonomy, as told, was completely missing. The professionals were meant to perform their tasks strictly under the terms and conditions of the project set by the team leader or the top management. The nature and quality of work was labelled as 'routined/hackneyed', lacking innovation and rigor.

Another area of serious concern that appeared during the course of interviews was long working hours in almost all organizations surveyed. Majority of respondents complained about long working hours sometimes stretching over 14-18 hours. In addition to this, the holidays were found to be meaningless as most of the Sundays or other leaves required attendance of the workers on the pretext of the urgency of projects. The female professionals, in particular avowedly opposed the long working hour policy of their companies on the ground of security concerns and additional domestic responsibilities. Few of them shared their experiences of job and family pressures.

The third area in which opinion was sought from the software professionals was the extent of communication across different levels of hierarchy in the organization. It was well documented that top management officials hardly find time to interact with their employees particularly those who are involved in operational responsibilities. Also, it was observed that there were no effective channels of communication between the employees and management. The professionals had limited interaction with the project coordinator or the team leader. However, in most cases the interaction was unidirectional assuming the form of unity of command. The concept of participative leadership seemed to be missing.

Finally, most of the respondents believed that it was unfortunate that labour laws were not applicable to the software sector. Considering the remarkable growth of the Indian software industry they held the view that the government must intervene in the software sector and frame laws and regulations that improved the working condition of the employees. It is necessary to recognize that software sector is one of the youngest industrial sectors in India but has witnessed tremendous expansion in a short period of time. However, its expansion under globalization has produced both conventional and new forms of exploitation faced by the software professionals.

Technology Capabilities and R&D (Research and Development)

Research and Development received a significant thrust with the advent of liberalization in the 1980s. K. Narayanan states that there is a positive correlation between export performance and R&D intensity and import of technology. Adaptability to the latest technology is a precondition for the growth of the industries. Therefore, domestic R&D required adaptation of borrowed technology and develop new technologies. The R&D activities in the software industry include prototyping, requirement analysis and product conceptualization. Furthermore, domestic R&D necessitates foreign collaborations for technology transfer. However, blindly applying borrowed technology does not necessarily lead to innovation. Innovation demands high levels of technical skill and best management practices on the part of domestic producers. This is more of a requirement in the emerging knowledge industry like IT where innovation is the mainstay of its growth.

The background of scientific development in India is promising. R&D efforts were taken decisively with the creation of premier science and research institutes by Jawaharlal Nehru. The R&D efforts of government therefore date back to the creation of high-order scientific institutions in the 1950s. The Council of Scientific and Industrial Research was the nodal agency for several research institutions and laboratories across the country. The S&T institutions established during the yesteryears of independence provided a foundation for advanced research and development. Unfortunately, the R&D benefits have not percolated down to the industry and have not produced institutional complementarities in industries to this direction. Also, the challenge remains in filling the gap between the knowledge generated by such S&T (science and technology) institutions and application of such knowledge in technology-intensive industrial sectors like software, telecommunications and biotechnology. As Mascarenhas observes that, "In India, with the exception of IISc (Indian Institute of Science), which has had extensive interaction with industry over the years, the link between the many institutions undertaking research in S&T and producers has been notably week" (Mascarenhas 2010: 30). The synergy between the research institutions, business and government in the area of knowledge creation and transfer is thus missing. This absence of linkage has resulted in the failure of developing indigenous technology.

There has been very little effort on the part of software firms in apportioning a substantial part of their investment in in-house R&D. Even the large software companies invest less than 10% of their sales on R&D. Trg. & Dev. (Training and Development) has emerged as one of the areas that involve expenditures on R&D. One of the senior officials in Wipro Technologies commented that, "Indian organizations are now covering entire gamut of software activities. We have come a long way. However, product management and R&D is an area where Indian organizations are still lagging."[5] Medium-sized companies and the small software companies, the starters, because of resource crunch spent less than 5% of their sales on R&D. Since their job was mainly of 'consultancy type' they were mostly involved in providing IT support services, software testing, development and maintenance and UI design. R&D works were limited to the type of business undertaken. R&D for product development thus required what was referred to as 'domain knowledge.'[6] For instance, if the product was meant for its utility in banking then domain knowledge would involve knowledge in banking to develop the required function. Additionally, the R&D works were primarily undertaken by large companies like IBM, TCS, Cisco and others. However, even the big companies mainly concentrated on support services than actual R&D.

The government support for R&D for these companies was virtually missing. The respondents were of the opinion that the government must encourage foreign collaboration in the software industry.[7] As one of the senior managers in Wipro commented that, "Foreign collaborations will help budgetary funding which is badly needed in R&D in domestic industry...foreign collaboration will also facilitate opening up of larger markets for newly researched solutions/software."[8] It was recognized that some of the major factors that inhibited investment in in-house R&D were time, costs, market need and skills. The STPs also did not provide enough R&D support as its primary purpose was to provide tax concessions and some infrastructural support for the exporting firms. Also, technology transfer was lacking in some of the large software companies because of the absence of foreign collaboration. However, certain collaborations were in the form of short-term agreements and were project-based.

5. Interview with a senior official at Wipro Technologies, Bengaluru.
6. Interview with the senior manager in Differential Solutions, a software firm located in New Delhi.
7. Interviews conducted in some large software companies in Pune.
8. Interview with a senior manager at Wipro, Bengaluru.

The software industry, mainly focusing on support services to several sectors of the economy, has primarily remained confined to hackneyed tasks. However, a gradual shift from low-skilled tasks to high-value added tasks is visible. Foreign collaborations which are short-term, project-based have not been able to promote technology transfer which is essentially required to develop R&D. Third, SMEs (small and medium enterprise) faced severe resource crunch in investing in R&D. The government incentives in this area also seemed to be inadequate.

Market for Indian Software Companies—Challenges and Opportunities

It is observed that almost 60% of the software exports goes to United States, approximately 30-35% to West Europe, Australia, New Zealand, and Canada and rest 10% to other countries. In recent times, the outsourcing business has expanded to Japan on the Eastern hemisphere.

Table 1: Percentage of software exports in major destinations for the year 2008-09

Countries	Percentage of exports
United States of America	58.42
European Union	30.50
Middle East	3.00
Singapore, Hong Kong and South Africa	2.85
Australia and New Zealand	1.70
Japan, Korea	1.20
Non-EU countries	1.10
African countries	1.00

(contd...)

Latin America	0.19
Russia and Central Asia	0.08

Source: http://www.escindia.in/ (Electronics and Computer Software Export Promotion Council official website)

The data for the year 2008-09 given in Table 1 clearly shows that India's IT business is mainly concentrated in US. In case of SMEs, almost 100% business comes from United States.[9] This clearly explains how the 2008 economic downturn in US affected India's IT industry. The impact could be explained from two contrasting standpoints:

1. Absence of employment opportunities in the Indian IT industry, salary cuts for the existing employees in the wake of economic recession.
2. Looking for solutions from a low-cost country like India during recession.

The recession clearly resulted in job losses in the IT sector and was detrimental for new aspirants. Other than this, the companies did not provide any increment or perquisites to its employees. Attrition rates even in large software companies were extremely high during the recession period.[10] In addition to this, a number of software professionals in United States lost their jobs during the recession period and had to return to India. However, the loss of opportunities and new projects was more visible in the SMEs. Many SMEs were at the brink of closure during the period.

The other viewpoint suggests that business opportunities expanded to low-cost countries like India during the recession period. The US companies were looking for cost-effective solutions and found ample opportunity in India. It was observed that as United States and other countries of Europe recovered from economic recession, Indian IT sector was flooded with new opportunities. Growth suddenly picked up with increasing

9. Interviews with SMEs at Noida and New Delhi.
10. Interview with a senior official at a large software company situated in Noida, UP.

outsourcing from United States. As a result new job opportunities were created not only in the large companies but also in the SMEs. A look at the recent geographical export trends as given in the table below substantiates this point.

Table 2: Percentage of software exports in major destinations for the year 2016

Country	Percentage of exports
United States	62%
Continental Europe	17%
United Kingdom	12%
APAC (Asia-Pacific)	8%
Others	2%

Source: http://www.nasscom.in/india-itbpm-exports (NASSCOM website)

The data show that India's IT exports remain largely concentrated in the US. There is nearly a 3.5% rise in exports from 2008 (see Table 1) to 2016. With Brexit, exports to Continental Europe have also declined and UK still remains a marginalized export venue. Interestingly, there is a visible rise in exports to Asia-Pacific nations from 2.5% (on an average) in 2008-09 (see Table 1) to nearly 8% in 2016. The rising trend is accredited to the FTA that India has signed with ASEAN and is working hard towards strengthening multilateral ties with Asia-Pacific nations under the newly-envisioned Act East policy. Recently, Japanese companies are outsourcing a great deal of business to Indian software companies. It was predicted that the business will expand in coming years. This is in the wake of the recent earthquake resulting in a severe economic downturn in Japan. Japanese companies will look for cost-effective solution and will therefore approach low-cost countries like India and Philippines.

There is a plausible belief that India faces stiff competition from emerging IT players in Asia like China and Philippines.

There are mainly three views in this regard which are as follows:

1. China seen as a future competitor
2. China not seen as a future competitor
3. China seen as an ally in software business.

The first view holds the assumption that China will pose a serious challenge to the Indian software industry in near future. It is slowly emerging as a cost-effective destination for doing software business. China had already shown its capability in the production of software packages and products, but is now venturing into ITES and BPO business. It is also shown in chapter 3 that Chinese investment in R&D is much higher than that of India. The Chinese government has also taken several initiatives to promote a balanced development of its hardware and software segments. China is trying to overcome its major bottleneck that is lack of English knowledge, an essential qualification for IT-BPO services, by opening or funding several English-language training schools and institutions. The underlying aim is to create a pool of technically-skilled, English-proficient software professionals in near future.

The other view does not perceive China as a future competitor to India. Indian software professionals having a comparative advantage over Chinese counterparts in their proficiency in English language and cost-arbitrage still feel that the Indian IT and software assumes a dominant position in the service sector. Although several institutes and organizations has started courses to promote training in functional English amongst software/BPO professionals the results are still bleak for China. For instance, it is observed that an estimated 30,000 organizations or companies offer private English classes in the country (*Guardian Weekly*; 13 July 2010). John Falon, the chief executive of Pearson International Education Business also noted that, "With the development of Chinese economy and further opening up, there has been a hugely expanding group of people learning English here in recent years. The English education and training market in China enjoys very significant growth opportunities and will maintain the fast development momentum" (*China Daily*; 25 May 2012).

The third stance looks at China as a future ally than a competitor. It holds the assumption that instead of posing a challenge to each other in the software business, India and China will strengthen their trade relations in IT and software. Business in IT would involve complementarities. The Chinese market provides immense opportunity to Indian software companies. A number of projects of the large companies are already in pipeline. Many large companies like Infosys and TCS have opened their branch office in China. Also, the Indian domestic market itself provides immense business opportunities to Chinese software companies. High-end technologies in China could help Indian companies learn and adopt them.

The public sector itself offers immense opportunities to the local software companies with its ambitious e-governance schemes and programmes. A large number of government projects involving wide-scale application of IT and software services is underway. In this regard the senior manager of one of the reputed IT company commented that, "The government needs to strengthen its PPP strategy. Projects of worth ₹ 1800 crores are lying with the government which is yet to be picked up by the IT industry, e-governance being one of them."[11] He further observed that one of the main impediments before PPP in IT is that the bureaucratic system is still very rigid and discouraging. Administrative clearance involves multichannel scrutiny and in many cases the private partners fail to get the approvals. It was felt that the government must take positive steps to make the system flexible to facilitate its partnership with the private industry in the field of IT and software technology. Recently formulated programmes like Digital India, Start-Up India and Make in India will see a lot of PPP projects coming up in near future providing greater flexibility to PPP. For example, the TRAI has recommended a PPP model for the BharaNet project under Digital India set to provide broadband connectivity across 25,000 village Panchayats. The private stakeholder will be especially involved in maintenance, marketing and infrastructural usage.

11. Interview with a senior manager at a reputed IT company in Noida, UP.

Overall, the business opportunities for the Indian IT companies are immense in both domestic and international market. In the latter, a resurgence of protectionist policies in US and West European countries has raised new concerns about the future prospects for the Indian IT industry in such markets. However, the fact remains that even after the imposition of certain restrictions by the foreign governments the Indian companies receive maximum business from these countries, particularly US. Therefore, the dependence on US for the sustenance of the industry remains undisturbed. In fact, many software companies view the protectionist policies of the US government as passing phase.

Governmental Support through STPs and SEZs

Government support has been a crucial factor behind the rapid growth of the software and IT industry. The creation of STPs has been particularly beneficial for the emerging SMEs which are export-oriented. They are provided infrastructural facilities like continuous power supply, telecommunication links, internet facilities, and so on. Additionally, the export-oriented firms enjoy tax holidays within the STPs. The prime beneficiaries of the STPs are the SMEs and multinational companies.

The IT industry has various data protection and business continuity needs. STPI provides customized solutions for the customers. This includes remote backup services, remote disk backup, enhanced back up, managed vaulting services, remote NAS services, remote server services, and customized services[12] (STPI official website). Second, the STPI provides incubation services to the SMEs in addition to Internet facilities like Soft Link, Soft Point, and Service Destination. These facilities are widely availed by the IT firms to increase their productive capacities.

However, the cost of internet facility was found to be high due to monopoly of internet providers in the STPs. Also, the speed of internet was shaky although the supply was continuous.

---

12. Official website of STPI, http://www.stpi.in/index1.php?langid=1&level=1&sublinkid=179&lid=271

In this regard, it was commented that the internet facility provided by such technology parks in China and several West European countries was far more efficient and cost-effective.[13] Data communication links were seen as the backbone of the IT industry. Therefore, it was suggested that the government must pay adequate attention to the provision of speedy, cost-effective internet links.

The STPs are specifically meant to support export-oriented firms. The policy preoccupation with export-led growth has led to a neglect of domestic sectors. This appears as a major cause of uneven development of IT sector. China, on the other hand has focused evenly on both export and domestic segments. As R.C. Mascarenhas points out that, "The short-sightedness (of the private companies) ignores the importance of the sound domestic markets as a springboard for exports…the denial of special government support in the form of incentives and tax subsidies to domestic users of ICT (information and communication technology) have certainly not helped the situation"[14] (Mascarenhas 2010: 159).

To re-orient the industry towards domestic sectors, the government subsequently decided to moderate the incentives for exports. Toeing this line, tax exemptions given to exporters under STPI were removed in the FY 2008-09. This measure was undertaken in the wake of the completion of the five-year term. In the Budget of 2008, the finance ministry decided non-extension of Section 10A/STPI tax holiday. However, with increasing pressure from NASSCOM the government finally decided to extend the tax holiday by one year till 30 March 2010. A number of official parleys took place between NASSCOM (National Association of Software and Service Companies), Ministry of IT, Ministry of Finance, Ministry of Commerce and Industry, and the PMO (Prime Minister's Office). In response to this positive move by the government, NASSCOM in one of its statement said that,

13. Interview with one of the owners of a software firm of a small size at Pune.
14. R.C. Mascarenhas, *India's Silicon Plateau, op. cit.*, 159.

> "The decision is particularly beneficial for BPO (business process outsourcing) companies and the small and medium segment that have been greatly impacted by the rupee appreciation, inflation and signs of slowdown in the US economy...the benefit will also give it time to come up with other workable and acceptable options for the future."[15] (*The Hindu*, 30 April 2008)

Concerned about the impact of government policies on STPI, NASSCOM reports that, "The tax exemption on STPI ends in April 2011. With no extension in the Budget, companies established in software parks will have to pay a corporate tax of 30%."[16] In order to overcome this predicament, NASSCOM asked for a 2-year extension on STPI. It also predicted that if this does not happen then the SMEs will be forced to move to SEZs (special economic zone) or even to other countries like China, Philippines, Egypt and Africa that provide better tax benefits. However, the tax exemptions were extended by one year which meant that the STPI, which offered tax exemptions under Sections 10A and 10B of the Income Tax Act was effective upto 31 March 2011. But, the Minimum Alternate Tax was imposed on the IT industry. NASSCOM President Som Mittal stated the implications of the non-extension of tax benefits (*Hindustan Times*, 6 February 2011).[17] These are as follows:

1. Larger companies for whom the STPI benefits are over have moved and will be forced to move to the SEZs.
2. The tax rates for Indian IT companies will go upto 25-30% from the current level of 20%.
3. The profits margins of the SMEs will come down by 10-15%.

Finally, the Union Budget 2011 stopped the extension of tax holidays in STPI. The signs of reluctance were well expressed in some of the earlier statements of the government. The then

15. *The Hindu*, 30 April 2008.
16. http://www.moneycontrol.com/news/business/nasscom-seeks-two-year-extensionstpi-schem e_444504.html
17. *Hindustan Times*, 6 February 2011.

Minister of State for Commerce and Industry Shri Jyotiraditya Scindia said that,

> "Tax benefits under STPI and export-oriented unit schemes are not likely to be extended beyond March this year...there is a sunset clause, the Finance Minister announced in his last budget that this would be the final year (of STPI and EOU scheme)."[18] (*The Economic Times* 22 February 2011)

While the larger companies expressed half-hearted satisfaction towards the non-extension of the STPI term and an increase in the minimum alternate tax from 18% to 18.5%, the SMEs will bear the brunt. In response to the new measures taken for STPI, the TCS Chief Financial Officer and the Executive Director S. Mahalingam commented that,

> "Overall, it is a good budget, but the finance ministry could have given more focus on the IT sector. There is nothing new for the IT sector in the Budget proposal, apart from reduction in the tax from foreign subsidiaries of the Indian companies...it is disappointing that the Budget has not extended the STPI benefits, but it will not affect the sector to a great extent."[19] (*The Economic Times*, 28 February 2011)

The SMEs, which were primarily seeking the benefits of STPI, were deeply concerned with the implications of non-extension of the term.

On the other side, the SEZs as compared to STPs provided a mix of business and therefore did not extend any specific benefits to the software companies. As a result, the companies were less interested in making any new investments in the SEZs. Second, while the STPs provided single-window clearance, the SEZs involve multi-channel scrutiny in getting clearances particularly in case of imports. Therefore, in SEZs there was lesser sensitivity towards the needs of the IT sector. Third, a number of benefits like relaxation of duties on hardware imports, provision of setting up new units for part upgradation, excise exemptions

18. *The Economic Times*, 22 February 2011.
19. *The Economic Times*, 28 February 2011.

for purchasing local equipments like air conditioners provided by the STPs were not available with SEZs. Fourth, in SEZs if a firm decided to set up two units in the same building then they would be treated as two separate units and will be subject to rules and regulations differently. The discount or rebates on exports will therefore be counted differently. Such rules and regulations were not applicable in case of STPs.[20] A senior manager of a reputed software company commented that there was a lack of consistency between STPs and SEZs in terms of the benefits provided by them. The companies were faced with a contradictory situation as on one hand the STP benefits were taken away in the subsequent budgets since the lapse of the five-year term in FY 2008/09, and on the other hand the SEZs were laden with myriad restrictions and did not provide any special package for the software companies.

The SEZ and STP comparison clearly suggests that the former in addition to providing certain benefits has imposed new regulatory measures on the export-oriented IT companies. The elimination of tax benefits under Sections 10A and 10B of the Income Tax Act and imposition of minimum alternate tax on the IT sector are signs of new regulatory mechanisms employed by the government. Furthermore, the increasing number of bureaucratic hurdles with multichannel scrutiny has raised new concerns among the software firms. Re-imposition of regulation and control in SEZs clearly indicates a gradual shift from liberalization to regulation.

More importantly, the withdrawal of tax benefits under STPI and initiation of e-governance programmes actively indicates a shift in the policy orientation of the government towards indigenous development. It serves as a means to attract private investments towards local developmental projects and programmes. It would however be a misnomer to suggest that the policy shifts mark a complete departure from the export-oriented strategy. This is probably a short-term response to the recessionary pressure or protectionist policies of the US and

20. Interviews with senior managers of software companies situated at an STP in Noida, UP.

European governments and may just be referred to as a passing phase, as few respondents perceive.

Politics of Outsourcing—Protectionist Measures of the US Government

Another major external constraint to business outsourcing has arisen out of protectionism in United States. The business community in India has expressed apprehensions over politicization of outsourcing in the country and its impact on the business prospects of Indian IT companies. The question that arises here is: how did the matter get politicized in US? The outsourcing of IT and software services to India has resulted in unemployment and job losses in United States in recent years. While America emerged as a global economic superpower since the termination of Second World War, its domestic economy remains troubled due to rising unemployment. Business outsourcing to low-cost countries like India, Philippines, China and Mexico particularly after the Y2K bug is often cited as the casual factor. Outsourcing did not generate much opposition before 2000, as till then, the Indians performed only some of the low-end tasks while most of the white-collar jobs went to the Americans. However, it caught the attention of the policy-makers and the software professionals in US only after a large number of high-end, IT-enabled services in banking, health, legal services, infrastructure development etc. were being outsourced to Indian companies. Subsequently, in the face of competition from their Indian and Chinese counterparts, white-collar professionals in US felt the tint of job insecurity. On one hand, the industrialists wished to expand the business of outsourcing to India by even planning to set up their own operations in India, the local software professionals began resenting the move in the face of job insecurity. As pointed out by Baily and Lawrence,

> "There is uneasiness that manufacturing and service sector jobs have been, or will be, moved abroad. Partly because of technological change and partly because of trade agreements, so the argument goes, US workers now have to compete against a huge low-wage global

> labor pool, and the sustained weaknesses in employment since 2000 is a sign that this competition is undermining the great US job machine."[21] (Baily and Lawrence 2004: 212)

America's dependence on Indian IT sector increased primarily because of the internet revolution and the capabilities of the Indian to tackle the Y2K problem. Ingnatius Chithelen observes that,

> "Sharply rising demand for labor for the internet boom and for tackling the Y2K problem led to big shortage of IT staff in the US in the late-1990s. Companies lobbied the US administration to increase the number of professional work visas granted each year so as to bring in more foreign IT staff mostly from India."[22] (Chithelen 2004: 1022)

Outsourcing to India, which has become a major source of unemployment or job cuts for US citizens, has been politicized in recent years. The outsourcing card was used by the Democrats to charge the Republicans for being apathetic towards rising unemployment in the country. The politics of outsourcing can thus be understood on two contradictory counts:

1. Lobbying by the private industrialists to increase the number of professional visas to Indians.
2. The issue of outsourcing occupying the centre stage of electoral politics placing Democrats and Republicans in a blame game.

In the previous Presidential and Congress elections, the Democrats promised to abolish tax breaks for US companies that outsource IT services to India. Therefore, the Democrats were all set to besiege Republicans on the issue of rising unemployment

---

21. Martin Neil Baily and Robert Z. Lawrence, "What Happened to the Great US Job Machine? The Role of Trade and Electronic Offshoring", *Brookings Papers on Economic Activity*, 2004, no. 2, p. 212.
22. Ignatius Chithelen, "Outsourcing to India: Causes, Reaction and Prospects", *Economic and Political Weekly*, 6 March 2004, vol. 39, no. 10, p. 1022.

resulting from outsourcing. Quite possibly, the outsourcing issue provided political mileage to the Democrats against the Republicans. However, even after the victory of Democrats in the Congress and Presidential elections the political debate continued. In this regard, the Assistant Secretary of State for South and Central Asia Robert Blake commented that,

> "Outsourcing is always a hot button issue around elections, particularly when unemployment is high. People naturally take a look at these kinds of things.... But the point I would make about our economic relations with India is that they're increasingly balanced. The kind of offshoring...that is taking place, is an economic reality around the world now and all companies have plants in China and in India to basically be able to avail themselves of whatever the opportunities are in those countries."[23] (*The Economic Times*, 27 April 2011)

The statement of the senior official clearly indicates there is no scope for backtrack from outsourcing as far the government policies are concerned as several business organizations and economic sectors in US are dependent on the Indian IT industry, particularly for business-related services. The engagement appeared particularly important in the wake of the ongoing Indo-US nuclear deal which held a strategic importance for both the countries.

Nevertheless, the social pressures to curb outsourcing and create jobs for Americans have remained intact. Policy response to such pressures has been in the form of imposing restrictions on visa for IT professionals. Long back it was reported by Sarah Nelson, consular officer at the US consulate that, "The United States will tighten visa regulations and also reduce the number of H1B visas it issues to specialists such as IT professionals, a US government official said on Tuesday.... We would like to protect US jobs"[24] (*The Times of India*, 27 August 2011).

On a similar note, the UK government has imposed several restrictions on immigration of Indians, particularly the IT

23. *The Economic Times*, 27 April 2011.
24. *The Times of India*, 27 August 2011.

professionals. The new immigration rules which were framed in order to protect the jobs of the local workers and professionals were as follows:

1. The basic requirement to enter Britain under the tier-I category of the points based immigration system was raised. Many Indian IT professionals come under tier-I category.
2. The minimum qualification and salary levels were raised from undergraduate degree and 17,000 pounds to masters' degree and 20,000 pounds respectively.[25] (*The Times of India*, 22 February 2009)

The visa restrictions on the Indian software professionals and tax-related restrictions on the US companies that seek to open up back offices in India in search of cheap, qualified and English-speaking labour will be detrimental for the IT companies. The consequences of such measures imposed by the US and UK governments was widely acknowledged in both corporate and governmental circles. In a parley between the previous Indian Commerce and Industry Minister Mr. Anand Sharma and the US Commerce Secretary Mr. Garry Locke the apprehensions over the visa restrictions by the US government hurting the IT industry was raised. However, it was ascertained by Mr. Locke that the US government was concerned of the Indian sensitivities and will not target sectors that provide a strong basis of economic partnership between India and US. Prior to this meeting the government decided to settle the issue at the level of WTO.

The US move to hike visa fees has been opposed by the Indian IT industry. To begin with, NASSCOM offered its resistance to the protectionist policies of US. It took up the matter with the government as government intervention at the diplomatic level was felt necessary. In response to such concerns the Minister of Commerce and Industry Mr. Anand Sharma said that,

> "We have raised with the US whatever NASSCOM (the Indian software body) had conveyed to me. We hope that there will not be any measures which impact the

25. *The Times of India*, 22 February 2009.

movement of professionals between the two countries, particularly our IT professionals going to the US."[26] (*The Hindu*, 7 February 2011)

On the industry side, many companies reacted sharply to restrictions on L1 Visa that permitted inter-company transfer providing a blanket cover to the organization as a whole. A number of large companies like TCS, Wipro and others require the L1 Visa. Initially, the US government granted the visa to facilitate inter-company transfer like TCS-India to TCS-US. However, the Democrat government, abiding by its commitment to check unemployment and restrict immigration has put such visa restrictions.[27]

The US Call Centre Bill is yet another source of grievance of the Indian IT companies. It aims at limiting the scope of outsourcing and create opportunities within the country. The Bill was tabled before the House of Representatives in December 2011. It was introduced by the Democrats Rep. Tim Bishop and Rep. David Mackinley of the House of Representatives. The Bill provides that any company which intends to carry out its business operation through call centres located abroad will be denied federal grants and loans. Second, if the company locates its call centres in another country without informing the same to the US Department of Labour in 120 days then a fine of $10,000 will be charged on it. The Bill was therefore a move towards protectionism as it sought to safeguard the service sector jobs in the country. The initiative is largely political in nature as it was taken to re-affirm the promise made by Democrats in their election campaigning to raise employment by prohibiting outsourcing. It acts as a bulwark against the Republican claims of promoting outsourcing which they consider it to be beneficial for the economy in the longer run.

The issues was well negotiated by the present government. One of the major agenda items of the meeting between Indian Prime Minister Narendra Modi and Barrack Obama at the

26. *The Hindu: Business Line*, 7 February 2011.
27. Interview with a senior member of Manufacturing Association of Information Technology at Gurugram, Haryana.

White House was the impact of visa restrictions implicit in the Immigration Bill and the prohibitive Call Centre Bill. The new government expressed its concern over the policy measures of the Obama government that were discriminatory, restrictive, and discouraging for prospective Indian IT companies getting most of their outsourcing business from US. The meeting between Obama and Narendra Modi at Washington however only made passing reference to the restrictive policies of US government.

Conversely, the new Republican President Donald Trump has made a sharp reversal from its earlier stance of globalization. Going back to protectionism was the new political standpoint of the Republican president in his electoral campaign. The campaigns were specially targeted against the opposition which had fallen short of its promises to restrict globalization and outsourcing. The political slogan of 'America First' used by Trump clearly manifested the party's priority for safeguarding local interests. In his speech at Monessen, Pennsylvania, Trump squarely targeted the self-centred businessmen and their political supporters. He said that, "Selfish businesses are sending American jobs overseas, and politicians have let it happen.... Our politicians have aggressively pursued a policy of globalization, moving our jobs, our wealth, and our factories to Mexico and overseas.... Ladies and Gentlemen it is time to declare our economic independence again."[28] These statements had marked a departure from his earlier claims about global unity and interdependence to bring in greater financial stability. The shift is clearly explained by the political imperative to impress upon a large section of jobless youth who went frenzied with the idea of outsourcing. It was an instrument to counter the opposition for the false promises made about creating jobs for Americans in America.

The adoption of protectionist policies has an inherent political logic. Earlier, the issue of unemployment and immigration had been a matter of serious political debate between Republicans and Democrats and outsourcing software services to low-cost countries like India, China and Philippines was cited as one of

28. http://time.com/4386332/donald-trump-trade-speech/, Sam Frizell, 29 June 2016.

the prime reasons behind job cuts in United States. Outsourcing was played as a political card by the Democrats to oppose the anti-labour stance of the Republicans during the previous Presidential and Congressial elections. The present President plays on the same politics to counter the Democrats who were held culpable for making false promises to generate employment for the local inhabitants to get votes. Trump in his speeches repeatedly warned the American companies that outsourced jobs of dire consequences. Will restrictions be imposed through concrete policy measures as the earlier government did, or some other mechanism would be devised is still a matter of speculation. But by now it is clear that, willingly or unwillingly, both parties would have to moderate it for gaining political expediency. Outsourcing is a decade-long issue of mass politics and will remain contested as long as unemployment captures the larger public imagination. Whatsoever might be the case, the protectionist policies of the US government will have an adverse impact on the growth of the software industry in India in the longer run.

Human Resources—The base of the Software Industry

The backbone of all technology-based industries like IT and software, hardware, microelectronics, telecommunications and biotechnology are its human resources. As observed, "The structural change in the information economy is that it transforms the labour market and generates demands for specific skills worldwide. The character of labour undergoes a shift from manual labour to intellectual labour."[29] The success of such economic sectors is completely dependent on the efficiency, capabilities and talent of its professionals. The development of information and communication technology, often referred to as the third industrial revolution, led to the emergence of knowledge economy demanding highly skilled, technically-sound manpower. In the wake of catching up with the developed nations of the world in the race of globalization, the

29. Rakesh Basant and Uma Rani, "Labour Market Deepening in India's IT: An Exploratory Analysis", *Economic and Political Weekly*, vol. 39, no. 50, December 11-17, 2004, p. 5317.

late-industrializing nations of the Third World like China, India, Philippines, Egypt, and many others focused on harnessing the opportunities of the new economy by strengthening their human resources. As a result, with the support of the government new institutions and research organizations were set up to produce a talented pool of engineers and technical professionals.

The Indian software industry today draws its strength from its human resources comprising highly-skilled engineers and software professionals trained in premier government institutions like IITs, IIMs, and several other reputed engineering colleges. These institutions hold the distinction of providing the best quality education and are comparable with the topmost technology and management institutes of the world. The IITs are particularly known for their academic and research credentials worldwide. The underlying objectives of IITs are as follows:

1. Carrying out original and cutting-edge research and promoting technology development.
2. Imparting training to create competent, motivated engineers and scientists.
3. Encouraging freedom of thought and inculcating human values for the environment and society.[30]

Considering the popularity of the IITs (Indian Institute of Technology) and IIMs (Indian Institute of Management) and the increasing demand of skilled engineers and professionals from the industry, the government recently took the initiative of opening new IITs and IIMs in different parts of the country. According to one of the managers of a medium-sized enterprise the trend is purely demand-driven. There are 8 new IITs located in Bhuvaneshwar, Gandhinagar, Hyderabad, Indore, Patna, Kota, Mandi and Ropar. Other than these, government has allowed new engineering colleges to come up in a big way to meet the increasing demand of the software professionals industry. Additionally, almost all universities and popular colleges have IT departments. However, from an industry's perspective, rising numbers do not indicate any qualitative change in the

30. http://www.iitk.ac.in/ (IIT Kanpur official website)

overall performance. As one of the senior managers of Wipro commented,

> "The private technical institutions and engineering colleges have been little helpful in strengthening the human resources required by the industry. Education is far removed from what is actually needed in the industry. This is one area where the government can help through proper course curriculum formulation."[31]

On the other hand, a number of those completing education from these colleges are unemployed. In this regard, another respondent commented that about 3-4 lakh talents from IT are yet to be tapped.

Despite the efforts and initiatives of the government in strengthening the human resources much required for the emerging knowledge economy, the software industry faces several other challenges today on this front. Undoubtedly, the Indian software industry holds the distinction of employing highly-skilled, English-speaking engineers and software professionals. Nevertheless, a large number of these professionals prefer to migrate to US and other countries for better job opportunities, a phenomenon referred to as brain drain. This creates a shortage of skilled manpower in the domestic industry. However, from an industry's perspective a new trend in the direction of reverse brain drain is clearly visible. A number of Indian software professionals, particularly those employed in Silicon Valley are returning back to India to join the domestic industry. In this regard, one of the senior managers of a big software company commented that, "Indian companies are trying to attract people from abroad. However, the government should accelerate the process by providing adequate incentives."[32]

In brief, the two main issues concerning human resources of the software industry from a corporate perspective are: the quality of education provided by the public and private educational institutions, especially the newer ones; and the need

31. Interview with a senior manager at Wipro, Bengaluru.
32. Interview with a senior manager of a large Software company 'Colt' located at Gurugram, Haryana.

for a positive intervention by the government to promote reverse brain drain. However, a bigger challenge before the industry in the longer run will be to upgrade its service offerings for which multi-tasking professionals have to be produced by the educational and research institutes. For this, a synergy between the existing research institutions and the industry is must. The recent thrust for industry collaboration in the Ministry of Human Resource Development is viable step in this direction. In 2014, the government established the Council for Industry and Higher Education Collaboration for identifying arenas and instruments of synergy between industry and the institutions offering higher education.[33] The larger aim is to adjust the course curriculum as per the needs of the industry so that the human resources are made viable and needful for the market economy and society as a whole.

Conclusion

In contemporary times, the software industry in India is confronted with new challenges at both domestic and global levels. The work environment and the dominance of supervisors at the organizational level have embittered the relationship between workers and managers, while the external challenges have resulted from globalization. The existing labour laws do not apply in case of software industry as it is not covered in the Factory's Act meant for regulation of industrial sectors. As a result, new forms of hierarchical relations typical of Weberian bureaucracy have been produced.

Advancement of fiscal and non-fiscal incentives is yet another significant internal issue. As observed, on one hand the tax incentives extended by the STPs have been terminated, on the other hand SEZs have imposed several restrictions in case of new investments. The corporate sector has looked at government's support for exporters with great optimism, but they feel dejected by the recent regressive actions. The SMEs, who are primarily involved in export business face the brunt of the policy backtrack in the biggest way. Their dependence on government support appeared to be much higher than the bigger

33. http://mhrd.gov.in/sites/upload_files/mhrd/files/ru_1603.pdf

companies. They find it difficult to stand on their own as they lack resources to do so.

Furthermore, there is little incentive on the part of software companies, particularly the SMEs, to upgrade their products and services. While the large companies have made some efforts in this direction, a large number of SMEs still remain confined to low-value added tasks with almost negligible investment on in-house R&D. In general, they feel de-motivated to upgrade their offerings as they lack incentives for this.

The other domestic-level challenge includes the upgradation of human resources that appears to be under severe strain with the quality of education being offered by most private engineering colleges and universities. It is felt that instead of opening several professional colleges, it is important to upgrade the teaching curriculum by introducing areas of advanced knowledge and research. The PPP involving government-private sector partnership has facilitated the extension of technical and professional courses. However, little effort is being taken in designing courses that would directly link with the professional requirements of the industry. Second the synergy between the industry and professional institution also seems to be missing. Some recent steps of the government in establishing the synergy is worth noting.

Government support will be most crucial at a time when the external challenges of global recession and the rise of protectionism in US and Western Europe, the two major export destinations for Indian IT companies, are in full swing. The industry finds itself in a double trap of external protectionism and internal loss of support. Such a dilemma makes the software professionals worse off as they find themselves in a position of acute insecurity. NASSCOM, as observed, has taken the matter of such devastating effects with the government at several political forums, but has remained largely ignorant about the issue of worker's rights in the software industry.

A number of respondents observed that the growth of the software industry has reached its saturation point especially after the global recession of 2008. Following inferences could be drawn from these observations:

1. Existence of STP-related benefits in the 1990s propelled the growth of the software industry.
2. SEZs—a government sponsored scheme for the export-oriented companies have not extended any special incentive to the software industry and have instead created new regulations.
3. Dependence on the US market has produced lop-sided growth especially during global recession.
4. External protectionism and termination of institutional incentives by the government will impact the growth of IT industry in the longer run.

To conclude, the industry that holds the distinction of being a leader in the international market is now facing serious challenges in the wake of global protectionism and policy backtrack by the government. Both internal and external constraints being severe need to be addressed at policy level. The business community is of the view that the governments of the two leading economies US and India must tackle the issue of IT trade at diplomatic level and jointly address the existing policy bottlenecks that restrict trade and inhibit outsourcing. At the same time, they expect the government to rethink its domestic policies that backtrack from the support system provided to the export-oriented firms during initial stages.

❒

Conclusion

The software industry in India has travelled a long way since its inception in the 1970s. Government intervention has been a crucial factor behind its rapid growth and sustainability. Considering the political context, it has taken various forms at different stages of its growth. Realizing the potential of the sector in the international market the government especially since the mid-1980s has provided special incentives and created new institutions for its promotion. Although political support for its promotion has been more or less consistent in contrast with other industrial sectors, there have been intermittent policy disagreements especially during the early stages of its growth. Second, the regulatory institution, DoE, which initially upheld the dominance of ECIL, the major PSE for the production of computers and electronics gradually, changed its orientation towards privatization and subsequently globalization. Therefore, private entrepreneurship received strong impetus from both bureaucracy and political leadership during its initial stages of development.

The nature of state intervention during the mid-1980s approximates very closely to the 'guardian role of state' observed for the promotion of electronics industry in South Korea. Computer software, unlike many other sectors, emerged as an export-oriented industry receiving direct attention and assistance of the policy-makers. Incentives were however complimented by some degree of performance appraisal and requirement of in-house R&D (research and development). The chief purpose was to establish an industry that was rich in its technological know-how and the technocratic entreprenuers could serve as potential players in the international market for advanced software technology. But, import liberalization for export-promotion also meant unwarranted drainage of foreign exchange. The deteriorating BoP situation was a clear indication of this economic predicament. The other difficult terrain was the radical shift from socialism to free enterprise which was politically unacceptable. Concerns were raised not only by opposition parties but also by the old guards within the Congress party. Although the liberalization of software policies did not lead to the magnitude of opposition witnessed in other sectors, it did invite some disagreements over imports required for producing software. In the face of both economic crisis and political opposition to import liberalization the government was forced to initiate policy backtracks in late-1980s clearly indicating a reversal to regulation fearing the dire consequences of uncontrolled liberalization.

Three important changes took place at the political and administrative levels that led to the emergence of private entrepreneurship in software sector in the 1980s. These are as follows:

1. Emergence of political leadership with technocratic orientation.
2. Support from the main regulatory institution DoE (Department of Electronics).
3. A general trend towards liberalization.

The political context suitable for promoting private entrepreneurship had already emerged during Mrs. Gandhi's second tenure when the government sought collaboration with the private entrepreneurs. This new association resulted from the need to abandon the hostile attitude towards private sector and seek the assistance of business enterprises in building the industry. Therefore, the government during Mrs. Gandhi's second tenure introduced several incentives for private players encouraging them to invest in new and emerging sectors like electronics and computer software. However, no radical departure was made from the past policies in fear of political repercussion. The rhetoric of socialism was well maintained by the Congress party during this time.

The main difference between the orientations of Mrs. Gandhi and her son Rajiv was that while Mrs. Gandhi was advancing liberal policies primarily for political reasons i.e. to seek the political support of private business that was ignored in the previous tenure, Rajiv's technocratic background conditioned his ideas supporting liberalization and promotion of the computer industry. In the earlier case the policy change was politically-motivated, while in the latter one they were self-motivated. In view of his technocratic vision, Rajiv Gandhi provided special incentives to sunrise industries like computer software and telecommunications realizing its potential for the overall development of the economy. For the first time, computer software was recognized as an independent industrial sector that was deemed to have enormous growth potential in future. The computer policies of 1984 and 1986 provided special packages for the promotion of software sector by encouraging private investment.

Second, the nature of bureaucracy in the DoE, the main regulatory institution for electronics and computer also underwent a significant change since the mid-1980s. N. Seshgiri, the additional secretary of DoE strongly pushed for liberalization of software policies. He served as one of the most important economic advisors to Rajiv Gandhi. Most of the prominent bureaucrats in the DoE, often referred to as 'computer boys', constituted a team of economic advisors to the Prime Minister. The DoE has lobbied with several ministries and government agencies to support private investment in the software sector. In collaboration with NASSCOM (National Association of Software and Service Companies) it has been instrumental behind the establishment of STPs (software technology park) for assisting the export-oriented firms. The joint endeavour of DoE and prospective software companies since the mid-1980s led to a promising beginning for the software industry during its initial stages of development. Most of the leading Indian software companies like Wipro, Infosys, Satyam, and so on started their business during 1980s. TCS, was probably the only software company that was established as early as 1968 primarily to serve other Tata firms and some of the public sector enterprises.

Third, a general trend towards industrial liberalization started during Mrs. Gandhi's second tenure. The new policy framework marked a shift from import substitution industrialization towards export-oriented growth. It is observed that the first firm that agreed to export software in return of the allowance to import computer hardware was TCS in 1974[1] (Heeks 1996: 69). Several five-year plans, industrial policy resolutions and government budgets incorporated liberal policy measures to encourage private investment and production. The policy shifts witnessed during the 1980s was in line with the economic interests of the new middle class that emerged in this very process of commercialization. E. Sridharan observes that, "Deregulation can be expected to command widespread support among the middle class, as regulation is identified with corruption and inefficiency"[2] (Sridharan 2004: 425). Computer business was no longer restricted to defence establishments of the government as was the case in the 1960s and 1970s. PCs (personal computers) were now popular amongst the middle class and were by then considered a luxurious household commodity. The liberalization of 1980s well supported the initiatives for private investment in the emerging software industry. In fact, it could be said that facilitation of computer software appeared to be an integral exercise of the liberalization and privatization drive.

These three political economy trends completed the development ensemble advanced by Vibha Pingle in her comparative study of the role of state in industrial development. Evans underscores the most significant component of this development ensemble which is the autonomous role of state

1. Richard Heeks (1996), *India's Software Industry: State Policy, Liberalization and Industrial Development*, New Delhi: Sage Publications, p. 69.
2. Sridharan, E. (2004), "The Growth and Sectoral Composition of India's Middle Class: Its Impact on Politics of Economic Liberalization", *Indian Review*, vol. 3, no. 4, p. 425.

actors in taking policy decision and advancing performance-based incentives to the private entrepreneurs. In such a decision-making framework 'qualitative regulation' or 'regulation ensuring qualitative production' assumes an important place. In other words, the developmental role of state becomes meaningful only when the government is able to strike the right balance between liberalization and regulation. Any disturbance in this equilibrium may cause political opposition. The policy backtrack in the late-1980s was a result of this imbalance. When import liberalization was stretched beyond its limits, there were political pressures to restrict imports. But, overall a combined package of benefits and restrictions provided a strong boost to the software industry during its initial stages of development.

The initiatives taken by the government in the 1980s thus provided groundwork for the future growth of the software industry. The emergence of a technocratic-entrepreneurial state with a coalition of politicians, bureaucrats and technocrats as policy-makers gave an impetus for private investment especially in sectors that exhibited a strong potential for the future growth of the economy. Other than a short period of policy backtracks in the late-1980s, liberalization of software policies followed a more or less consistent path since then.

The next stage of software development necessitated policies supporting export-oriented firms more directly. The underlying idea was to grow faster by integrating with the international market. This was in line with the adoption of structural adjustment programme in response to the economic crisis of 1991 leading to the advancement of open door policies. The economy was made open to private investment from both domestic entrepreneurs as well as multinational companies. The policies marked a complete shift from import-substitution industrialization to export-led growth. In this direction, a thorough attempt was made to internationalize the software industry.

One of the most significant institutional developments in the software sector was the establishment of NASSCOM in 1988 as the industrial organization for the software and service companies. The alliance between NASSCOM and the DoE (now the Department of Information Technology within the Ministry of Communication and Information Technology) helped trigger the promotional agenda. Both the institutions consistently lobbied with the government for the creation of software technology parks in the 1990s. As observed, NASSCOM has also been highly instrumental and has worked in close collaboration with the government and international agencies to strengthen cyber laws to prevent software piracy. Its membership has broadened to include firms of different size and capacity, BPOs (business process outsourcing) and KPOs (knowledge process outsourcing). NASSCOM has served as a channel for demand aggregation and reconciliation on conflictual issues within the industry. It organizes conferences and workshops frequently inviting high officials and dignitaries from different ministries and departments to articulate the interests and demands of the industry as a whole. It maintains close liaisoning with concerned ministries, departments and stakeholders; and intimates the government of the challenges faced by the industry in the international as well as the domestic market. Recently, it raised serious concerns over the termination of tax benefits in the STPs.

The collaboration between NASSCOM and DoE provided a strong momentum to the export-oriented firms and has assisted in the process of global integration of the software industry. Three significant trends have been observed as far as the growth of IT sector since 1991 is concerned. These are as follows:

1. Rate of growth has consistently shown an upward trend.
2. This rapid growth has primarily resulted from the expansion of exports.
3. IT sector's growth has been driven largely by the private sector (Chandrashekhar 2003: 42-85).[3]

While encouragement for global integration led to exponential expansion of exports, it has resulted in new kinds of predicaments both internally and externally in the IT & software industry. The autonomy of the state was seriously

3. C.P. Chandrasekhar, "The Diffusion of Information Technology: The Indian Experience", *Social Scientist*, July-August 2003, vol. 31, nos. 7-8, pp. 42-85.

compromised in setting desired goals and objectives for the IT industry. Incentives and benefits were not complimented by considerable guarantees for a balanced growth of export and domestic segments. As the chief emphasis has been on exports, the domestic market continued to be neglected for a very long time.

The domestic market and industry provides immense opportunities for the IT sector. Recently, the government has taken efforts to facilitate the application of IT & software in meeting its developmental goals. Almost all departments and ministries have resorted to the use of information and communication technology to improve public services. The introduction of e-governance in the recent past for this purpose has been an innovative step. In this regard, the government launched the National e-governance plan in 2006 with the objective of 'ushering in e-governance on a national scale'[4] (DIT 2009-10: 2). It consists of 27 Mission Mode Projects (MMP), 9 with the Central government, 11 state governments and 7 integrated ones. However, it is observed that the benefits of e-governance have remained confined to the economically well-off sections of the society. As Mascarenhas points out that, 'Empowerment and transparency are unlikely to be achieved unless governments are committed to e-governance and are willing to adopt major restructuring...E-governance is not merely a case of providing resources for the purchase of hardware; its operability has to be tested in the context of citizen response (Mascarenhas 2010: 152).'[5] Second, from a private sector perspective, the public sector provides immense business opportunities for the IT firms. However, due to excessive bureaucratization the possibilities of tapping the opportunities appeared bleak. Therefore, a substantial portion of business in the public sector for the private industry remains largely untapped.

4. *Annual Report 2009-10*, Department of Information Technology, Ministry of Information and Communication Technology, Government of India, p. 2.
5. R.C. Mascarenhas (2010), *India's Silicon Plateau: Development of Information and Communication Technology in Bangalore*, New Delhi: Orient BlackSwan, p. 152.

Additionally, for almost an entire decade after 1991, the software services industry relied heavily on the onsite model whereby the services were to be provided at the client site. The offshoring or outsourcing of services remained a distant goal. The monopoly of DoT as a service provider created difficulties in getting cheap and high-speed data communication. However, the situation subsequently improved with the establishment of TRAI and the entry of private players in the telecom market. The onsite model that put additional financial burden of sending professionals to the client site (most of which were in US) was gradually replaced by the offshore model with improvement in telecommunication facility.

Alongside, some of the big companies like TCS, Infosys, Wipro and IBM also started undertaking large turnkey projects in addition to services that were provided at the lower end of the service chain. As Carol Upadhya observes that, "Large companies like Infosys also started to move up the value chain by offering turnkey projects, end-to-end business solutions and consultancy services rather than only low-value added services"[6] (Upadhya 2004: 142). The SMEs burgeoned with the STP facility. In contemporary times, they serve as major drivers of growth in the software industry. The segment includes several BPOs and KPOs. However, SMEs have been primarily involved in providing low-end services to the clients located mostly in United States. R&D expenditure in such firms is close to negligible. From this, it could be inferred that due to lack of R&D expenditure particularly in the area of product development, the smaller firms do not get enough space to serve higher ends of the spectrum. Second, we still do not have concrete policies, unlike China or South Korea, for providing special incentives for R&D in IT and software. On the other hand, the R&D innovations of the premier research institutes have either remained untapped or in other cases have not really matched with the requirements of the industry. Moreover, the synergy between such institutions and

6. Carol Upadhya, "A New Transnational Capital Class? Capital Flows, Business Networks and Entrepreneurs in the Indian Software Industry", *Economic and Political Weekly*, Nov. 27—Dec. 3, 2004, vol. 39, no. 48, p. 142.

the industry is lacking. In fact, the burgeoning of universities, professional colleges and research institutions is not tantamount with the production of quality research and technical education. The private industry feels that there is an asymmetry between the educational curriculum of the government and private educational and professional institutions and job requirements of the industry.

Challenges of globalization have been equally disturbing. Global integration entails dependence on the political environment of the host country. If the political environment of a country is conducive, it becomes simpler to do business. On the contrary if social and political groupings develop antagonistic feelings towards foreign companies, commercial engagements become difficult to continue. The software firms exporting to US have been vulnerable to recent disturbances that have arisen from politicization of the unemployment issue in the wake of outsourcing. More than 90% of the total IT business comes from US. The growing economic and political ties between New Delhi and Washington since 1991 provided a sound basis for business engagement in the frontier areas of science and technology for mutual benefit. Service trade has been one of the key areas of engagement between the two countries. But, recently there has been resistance against service outsourcing which is seen as the chief cause of unemployment in US. The social unrest has since then been used as a political resource to oppose the ruling party in both Presidential and Congress elections. Earlier, the Democrat government, going by its electoral promises to protect jobs at home resorted to protectionist policies putting several restrictions on outsourcing. On a similar note, the Republicans have retreated from their earlier position of supporting globalization. The political preference for protectionism in the recent Presidential elections is a case in hand. The Indian software industry being heavily dependent on outsourcing from US has been vulnerable to such politics.

While the spill-over effect of globalization on the software industry is already being felt, policy backtracks at home have put additional burden on export-oriented software firms. The termination of tax benefits given in STPs and the restrictive bureaucratized environment of the SEZs has put the industry on a back foot. These policy shifts mark a change in the orientation of state from global to local. Although, it may be too early to make such a point provided that globalization still remains a prior agenda with programmes like Make in India and Start-up India. But clearly there is a growing preference for re-orienting the industry towards the goal of local development. Another position that appears prominently with such policy formulations is about 'Going global, but thinking local!' It implies connecting with the globe to reap benefits for indigenous development. But globalization in this framework can only be perceived as a means to attain the goal of social development. Whether the concession withdrawals indicate a visible shift in orientation towards local from global or is it just a passing phase and a temporary response to the protectionist wave is still a matter a speculation. But, with globalization emerging both as a benediction and challenge, policy actions and reactions are but natural. But, our larger question here is: what do these policies suggest about state's economic role, the politics of state-capital alliance and its implications for the growth of the software industry. Following inferences can be drawn:

1. State's economic role has changed in response to the ups and downs of globalization. Earlier, the fresh start of an alliance with US motivated it to support industries like software and IT that were involved in global trading through STP and other related institutional schemes. Government support was thus crucial in the growth of the industry. Currently, in response to global recession and protectionism, the government prefers to re-orient the industry towards local business and its social welfare agenda.
2. The growth has been lop-sided. This is evinced by the concentration of IT services in the lower end of the value of chain. Although, upward mobility is visible amongst large companies, the SMEs lack both the zeal and incentive to move up the value chain and invest resources on R&D. Government's intervention to

support in-house R&D and upward mobility has been featherweight.

3. The alliance between state and NASSCOM has been crucial for the growth of the industry. But, NASSCOM was always confronted with a fragmented institutional state system. While it was always corroborated by DoE and Ministry of Information and Communication Technology in its globalization agenda, others like ministries of finance and commerce have altered in their support. This is clearly evident in their firm position on withdrawal of tax concessions in STP.

Turning to other side of the story which is about the restrictive work environment, the greatest internal challenge to the industry's development. The exclusion of the software sector from labour regulations has resulted in new forms of labour rights concerns. In such circumstances, the position of software and BPO employees appears vulnerable to the domination of firm managers and racial abuses by foreign clients. Secondly, the employees also do not find appropriate channels to ventilate their grievances due to complete absence of employee's associations. Although NASSCOM has recently started looking into the labour issue particularly gender-specific concerns of women employees within the industry (Report on 'Gender Inclusivity'[7]), more concrete steps may be required in future to address such concerns. The working conditions continue to remain constraining and restrictive. Thirdly, being one of the most globally integrated industries, it is most vulnerable to global downturns and recession and its ill-effects like job precarity. The recent economic turbulence resulted in job losses not only in the SMEs but also in some of the large software companies like TCS and IBM. Additionally, it left little scope for new intakes, including candidates who obtained degrees from prestigious educational institutions in the country like IIT and IIM.

7. The Report analyzes marginalization of women within the industry in terms of lesser opportunities upward mobility and the nature of work performed within the industry. It also recognizes the fact that their contribution towards the growth of IT-BPO industry is enormous although their position remains weak.

Therefore, the vulnerability of the software industry is a result of both internal and external disturbances. State policies, which initially provided the required incentives for software firms, were withdrawn. Moreover, little has been done to facilitate R&D for technological upgradation. This is in contrast with Korean and Chinese strategy where the respective governments not only extended financial and non-monetary incentives but also paid adequate attention to indigenous R&D and performance standards.

The tripartite alliance between the state, private sector and NASSCOM that provided a strong impetus to export firms in the 1990s and early part of 2000s is now in a state of disarray. As the industry becomes heterogeneous in character with firms of different size and investment capacities, it becomes difficult to deal with multifarious interests and articulate the demands of the industry in a coherent manner. There are big, well established software companies that have made a mark in the international market. On the other hand, there are a large number of SMEs whose business strategies appear to be differently placed from that of large companies. Because of low investment capacities they tend to serve at the lower side of the service spectrum and take little interest in R&D. There is lack of consistency in terms of the needs and requirements of the software firms. The SMEs have their own specific set of problems and challenges different from that of the large companies. For instance, being low investment segments of the industry they require greater financial and infrastructural support from the government. The prospective claimants of benefits under STP are SMEs; hence withdrawal of such benefits naturally affects them the most. The SMEs have emerged as major drivers of growth in the recent past. But remaining confined to low-end services they have not been able to contribute effectively towards qualitative growth of the industry as a whole. The chances of upgradation become hazier due to lack of possible assistance from the government agencies and NASSCOM.

While exports over the years have shown a consistent rise, confinement to low-skilled works remains a big challenge. It appears bigger in the wake of stiff competition from Asian countries like China, Philippines and Indonesia. The governments in these countries have modified their strategies and policies according to the requirements of the global market and at the same time maintained their autonomy vis-à-vis the private players. Attractive incentives were given to their engineers and professionals working in Silicon Valley to return home and invest in local infrastructure. In recent years, the Indian government has also taken the lead by organizing programmes like *Pravisiya Divas* for rewarding its successful businessmen settled abroad. The encouragement for reverse brain drain in IT & software will facilitate knowledge and technology transfer that will give a boost to the industry. The present government under the leadership of Narendra Modi has taken concrete steps in this regard. Modi's recent visits to US and Australia and appeals to NRIs in these countries are relevant pointers. Plus grand investment programmes like Make in India, Start-up India and Digital India will also open new windows of opportunity for prospective players.

To conclude, uncontrolled but lop-sided growth of the software industry in the export market has reached its pinnacle. While liberalization during the early stages helped the industry grow at its take-off stage, globalization has given rise to new forms of predicaments in contemporary times. Markets for IT & software have become concentrated and the emerging political dynamics in the Western world that has led to a protectionist upsurge has made the position of the Indian software & IT industry vulnerable. Moreover, withdrawal of incentives previously extended by the government appears to be an additional hurdle. The troubled waters call for a revision of existing policies and regulatory mechanisms that would ensure quality control and provide greater scope for technological application in local arenas.

❐

Bibliography

Primary Sources

Annual Report 1992-93, Department of Electronics, Government of India

Annual Report 1996-97, Department of Electronics, Government of India

Annual Report 1997-98, Department of Electronics, Government of India

Annual Report 2002-03, Ministry of Communications and Information Technology, Government of India

Annual Report 2007-08, Department of Information Technology, Ministry of Communications and Information Technology, Government of India

Annual Report 2005-06, Ministry of Communications & Information Technology, Government of India

Annual Report 2006-07, Ministry of Communications and Information Technology, Government of India

Annual Report 2001-02, Ministry of Communications & Information Technology, Government of India

Annual Report 2009-10, Department of Information Technology, Ministry of Information and Communication Technology, Government of India

"A Report of the Review Committee on Electronics" (March, 1980). *Electronics Information and Planning*, vol. 7, no. 6

"Budget Speech: 1980-81", *Ministry of Finance,* Government of India

"Budget Speech: 1981-82", *Ministry of Finance,* Government of India

"Budget Speech, *Budget for 1998-99 (Part A)*", Ministry of Finance, Government of India

Economic Survey 1998-99, Ministry of Finance, Government of India, New Delhi

Economic Survey 1999-2000, Ministry of Finance, Government of India, New Delhi

Economic Survey 1992-93, Ministry of Finance, Government of India, New Delhi

Fourth Five-Year Plan: 1969-74, Planning Commission, Government of India

Inaugural Speech to the "National Convention on Small Industry", New Delhi, 17 September, 1986 in *Rajiv Gandhi's Selected Speeches and Writings*, vol. 2, May 1989, pp. 102-06

Lok Sabha Debate, 1985, p. 146.

Lok Sabha Debates, 15 December 1999, vol. 3, no. 13, New Delhi: Lok Sabha Secretariat, pp. 71-73

Rajiv Gandhi's Selected Speeches and Writings: 1986, vol. 2, May 1989, p. 116.

Report of the Review Committee on Electronics Part-I 1980, 1981, Government of India, New Delhi

"Sondhi and Menon Committee Report on Electronics: Government Decisions" (May 1981). *Electronics Information and Planning*, vol. 8, no. 8

Strategic Review 2001, New Delhi: NASSCOM

Strategic Review 2002, New Delhi: NASSCOM

Strategic Review 2004, New Delhi: NASSCOM

Strategic Review 2003, New Delhi: NASSCOM

Strategic Review 2009, New Delhi: NASSCOM

Strategic Review 2010, New Delhi: NASSCOM

Secondary Sources

Books

Ahluwalia, Isher Judge (1985). *Industrial Growth in India: Stagnation Since the Mid-60s*, New Delhi: Oxford University Press.

Amsden, Alice (1989). *Asia's Next Giant: South Korea and Late Industrialization*, New York: Oxford University Press.

Amsden, Alice (2001). *Rise of the Rest: Challenges to the West from the Late Industrializing Nations*, New York: Oxford University Press.

AnnaLee Saxenian (2004). "The Silicon Valley Connection: Transnational Networks and Regional Development in

Taiwan, China and India" in Anthony P. D'Costa and E. Sridharan (eds.) *India in the Global Software Industry: Innovation, Firm Strategies and Development*, New York: Palgrave Macmillan.

AnnaLee Saxenian, "Government and Guanxi: The Chinese Software Industry in Transition", DRC Working Papers, March 2003, no. 19, *Global Software in Emerging Markets*, Centre for New and Emerging Markets, London Business School.

Anthony P. D'Costa (2004). "The Indian Software Industry in the Global Division of Labor", in Anthony P. D'Costa and E. Sridharan, eds., *India in the Global Software Industry: Innovation, Firm Strategies, and Development*, New York: Palgrave Macmillan.

Athreya, Suma S. (2008). "Human Capital, Labour Scarcity and Development of the Software Services Sector in Ashwani Saith and M. Vijaybaskar's. eds., *ICTs and Indian Economic Development: Economy, Work and Regulation,* New Delhi: Sage Publications.

Bardhan, Pranab (2013). *The Political Economy of Development in India*, New Delhi: Oxford University Press.

Bhagwati, Jagdish (1993). *India in Transition*, New Delhi: Oxford University Press.

——— (1988). *Protectionism*, Cambridge: MIT Press.

Chibber, Vivek (2003). *State-Building and Late Industrialization in India*, New Jersey: Princeton University Press.

Evans, Peter (1995). *Embedded Autonomy: State and Industrial Transformation,* New Jersey: Princeton University Press.

Evans, Peter, Dietrich Rueschemeyer and Theda Skocpol (1985). *Bringing the State Back In*, ed., Cambridge: Cambridge University Press.

Frankel, Francine (1978). *India's Political Economy: 1947-77*, New Delhi: Oxford University Press.

——— (2006). *India's Political Economy: 1947-2006*, New Delhi: Oxford University Press.

Friedman, Milton and Rose Friedman (1980). *Free to Choose*, Mariner Books.

Gerschenkron, Alexander (1962). *Economic Backwardness in Historical Perspective*, Harvard University Press.

Haggard, Stephan (1990). *Pathways from the Periphery: The Politics of Growth in the Newly Industrializing Nations*, Princeton: Princeton University Press.

Hashim, S.R. and N.S. Siddharthan (2008). *High-tech Industries, Employment and Global Competitiveness*, London: Routledge.

Heeks, Richard (1996). *India's Software Industry: State Policy, Liberalization and Industrial Development*, New Delhi: Sage Publications.

Joseph, K.J. (1992). "The Growth and Performance of the Electronics Industry in India and South Korea: A Comparative Analysis in Arun Ghosh's, et al. (eds.), *Indian Industrialization: Structure and Policy Issues*, Oxford: Oxford University Press.

Joseph, K.J. and Vinoj Amraham (2008). "Moving Up or Lagging Behind? An Index of Technological Competence in India's ICT Sector" in Ashwani Saith and M. Vijaybaskar, eds., *ICTs and Indian Economic Development: Economy, Work and Regulation,* New Delhi: Sage Publications.

Joseph Grieco (1984). *Between Dependency and Autonomy: India's Experience with International Computer Industry,* Berkeley and Los Angels: University of California Press.

Kohli, Atul (1992). *Democracy and Discontent: India's Growing Crisis of Governability*, Cambridge: Cambridge University Press.

——— (1994). *Korea Business*, World Trade Press.

Kumar, Nagesh (2005). "Indian Software Industry: National and International Perspectives", in Ashwani Saith and M. Vijaybaskar, ed., *ICTs and Indian Economic Development: Economy, Work and Regulation,* New Delhi: Sage Publications.

Lok Sabha Debate, Eighteenth Session (Thirteenth Lok Sabha), vol. 20, no. 3, New Delhi: Lok Sabha Secretariat.

Marathe, S.S. (1989). *Regulation and Development: India's Policy Experience of Controls over Industry*, New Delhi: Sage Publications.

Mascerenhas, R.C. (2010). *India's Silicon Plateau: Development of Information and Communication Technology in Bangalore,* New Delhi: Orient BlackSwan.

Midgal, Joel (2001). *State in Society: Studying How States and Societies Transform and Constitute One Another*, Cambridge: Cambridge University Press.

Milner, Helen V. (1988). *Resisting Protectionism: Global Industries and the Politics of International Trade*, New Jersey: Princeton University Press.

Murthy, N.R. Narayan (2009). *A Better India A Better World,* Penguin Books.

Nayyar, Baldev Raj (1989). *India's Mixed Economy: The Role of Ideology and Interest in Development*, Bombay Popular Prakashan.

——— (2005). *The Geopolitics of Globalization: The Consequences for Development,* New Delhi: Oxford University Press.

Nayyar, Deepak (2002). *Governing Globalization: Issues and Institutions*, New Delhi: Oxford University Press.

Nilekani, Nandan (2011), "The Potential of the Unique Identity Number in India" in R.K. Shyamasundar and M.A. Pai's, ed., *Homi Bhabha and the Computer Revolution*, New Delhi: Oxford University.

Pallan, Ronen and Jason Abbott (1999). *State Strategies in Global Political Economy*, New York: Pinter Publications.

Pingle, Vibha (2000). *Rethinking the Developmental State: India's Industry in Comparative Perspective*, New Delhi: Oxford University Press.

Sengupta, Bhabani (1989), *Rajiv Gandhi: A Political Study*, New Delhi: Konark Publication Private Ltd.

Sharma, Dinesh (2009). *The Long Revolution: The Birth and Growth of India's IT Industry*, Noida: HarperCollins.

Shyamasundar, R.K. and M.A. Pai (2011). *Homi Bhabha and the Computer Revolution*, New Delhi: Oxford University Press.

Stanley Nollen and N.S. Siddharthan (2008). "Software and Hardware Firms in India and China: How they differ?" in S.R. Hashim and N.S. Siddharthan's *High-tech Industries, Employment, and Global Competitiveness*, New Delhi and London: Routledge.

Subhramanium, C.R. (1992). *India and Computer: A Study of Planned Development*, New Delhi: Oxford University Press.

Susan L. Shrirk (1993), *The Political Logic of Economic Reform in China*, Berkeley: University of California Press.

Upadhya, Carol and A.R. Vasavi (2008), "Outposts of the Global Information Economy: Work and Workers in India's Outsourcing Industry", in Carol Upadhya and A.R. Vasavi, eds., *In an Outpost of the Global Economy: Work and Workers in India's Information Technology Industry,* New Delhi: Routledge.

Verma, Vidhu "Globalization and the State in India", Kameshwar Chowdhary's, ed., *Globalization, Governance Reforms and Development in India,* New Delhi: Sage Publications.

Vogel, Steven K. (1996). *Free Markets, More Rules: Regulatory Reform in Advanced Industrial Countries,* Ithaca and London: Cornell University Press.

Wade, Robert (1990). *Governing the Market: The Economic Theory and the Role of Government in East Asian Industrialization,* New Jersey: Princeton University Press.

World Bank Report 2005, "A Better Investment Climate for Everyone", The World Bank & Oxford University Press.

Journals and Newspaper Clippings

Avgerou, Chrisanthi, "Discourses on ICT and Development", *Information Technology and International Development*, Fall 2010, vol. 6, no. 3.

Business Standard, 24 June 2009.

Chakraborty, Chandana and Dilip Gupta, "Indian Software Industry: Growth Patterns, Constraints and Government Initiatives", University of Sydney, 2002.

Chandrashekhar, C.P., The Diffusion of Information Technology: The Indian Experience, *Social Scientist*, vol. 31, nos. 7-8, July-August 2003.

Chithelen, Ignatius, "Outsourcing to India: Causes, Reaction and Prospects", *Economic and Political Weekly*, 6 March 2004, vol. 39, no. 10.

Economic Times, 27 April 2011, New Delhi.

Ernest, Dieter, "Catching-up, crisis and industrial upgrading: evolutionary aspects of technological learning in Korea's electronics industry", *Asia Pacific Journal of Management*, vol. 15, 1998.

Financial Express, 24 June 2009.

Khanna, Tarun and Krishna G. Palepu, "Globalization and Convergence in Corporate Governance: Evidence From Infosys and the Indian Software Industry", *Journal of International Business Studies*, vol. 35, no. 6, November 2004, pp. 484-507.

Kharbanda and Suman, "Chinese initiative in the software industry: quest to leap", *Current Science*, 25 December 2002, vol. 83, no. 12.

Kim, P.R., "R&D and Firm Sizes in the Information and Telecommunications Industry of Korea". *Small Business Economics*, vol. 15, no. 3, November 2000.

Kohli, Atul, "Politics of Economic Growth: 1985-2005", *Economic and Political Weekly*, April 1, 2006, vol. XLI, no. 13.

Luis Suarez Villa and Pyo-Hwan Han, "The Rise of Korea's Electronic Industry: Technological Change, Growth and Territorial Distribution", *Economic Geography*, 1990, vol. 66, no. 3, pp. 273-92.

Mahalingam, Sudha, "Computer Industry in India: Strategies for Late-Comer Entry", *Economic and Political Weekly*, vol. 24, no. 42, 21 October 1989.

Martin Neil Baily and Robert Z. Lawrence, "What Happened to the Great U.S. Job Machine?" Brooking Papers on Economic Activity, vol. 2004, no. 2.

Mukherji, Rahul, "Interests, Wireless Technology, and Institutional Change: From Government Monopoly to Regulated Competition in Indian Telecommunications", *The Journal of Asian Studies*, 2 May 2009, vol. 68, no. 2.

Murali Patibandla, Deepak Kapur and Bent Petersen, "Import Substitution with Free Trade: Case of India's Software Industry", *Economic and Political Weekly*, (April 8-14, 2000) vol. 35, no. 15.

Parthasarathy, Balaji (May 3, 2004). "Globalizing Information Technology: The Domestic Policy Context of India's Software Production and Exports", *Iterations: An Interdisciplinary Journal of Software History 3*.

——— (3 May 2004), "Globalizing Information Technology: the Domestic Policy Context for India's Software Production and Exports" and *Strategic Review 2004*, New Delhi.

Puri, Balraj, "Era of Indira Gandhi", *Economic and Political Weekly*, January 26, 1985, vol. 20, no. 4.

Rakesh Basant and Uma Rani, "Labour Market Deepening in India's IT: An Exploratory Analysis", *Economic and Political Weekly*, vol. 39, no. 50, December 11-17, 2004.

Ramachandraiah, C., "Information Technology and Social Development", *Economic and Political Weekly*, vol. 38, no. 12/13, (March 22-April 4, 2003).

Sarnot, S.L. "Status and Perspectives of the Electronics Component Industry in India", *Electronics Information and Planning*, (June, 1979), vol. 6, no. 9.

Schware, Robert (1987), "Software Industry Development in the Third World: Policy Guidelines, Institutional Options and Constraints," *World Development*, vol. 15, no. 11.

Shin, Roy W. and Alfred Ho, "The Role of Science and Technology in Creating Korea's Electronics Industry", *Asian Affairs* (Winter 1997), vol. 23, no. 4.

Singh, Zail, "Electronics in the Indian Parliament", *Electronics Information and Planning*, vol. 18, no. 4, January 1981.

Sood, Aditya Dev, "How to Wire Rural India: Problems and Possibilities of Digital Development, *Economic and Political Weekly*, vol. 36, no. 43 (October 27-November 2, 2001).

Sridharan, E., "The Growth and Sectoral Composition of India's Middle Class: Its Impact on Politics of Economic Liberalization", *Indian Review*, vol. 3, no. 4, 2004.

The Hindu: Business Line, 7 February 2011.

The Times of India, 22 February 2009.

The Times of India, 27 August 2003.

Thomas Hellaman and Yoon Je Choo (1994), "The Government's Role in Japan and Korean Credit Markets: A New Institutional Perspective", *Seoul Journal of Economics.*

Upadhya, Carol. "A New Transnational Capital Class? Capital Flows, Business Networks and Entrepreneurs in the Indian Software Industry", *Economic and Political Weekly* (Nov. 27-Dec. 3, 2004), vol. 39, no. 48.

Vijaybhaskar, M. and V. Gayatri, "ICT and Indian Development: Processes, Prognoses, Policies", *Economic and Political Weekly*, vol. 38, no. 24, June 14-20, 2003.

WTEC Report on the Korean Electronics Industry, www.wtec.org By a Special Correspondent (December 1, 1984), "Computer Policy: Technology Goals Forgotten", *Economic and Political Weekly*, vol. XIX, no. 12.

Zemin, Jiang. "Development of IT Industry in China in the New Age", J. Shanghai Jiaotong University (Science), 2009, vol. 14, no. 1.

Websites

http://www.mit.gov.in/content/acts-policies, The official website of Ministry of Information and Communication Technology, Government of India.

http://it-taskforce.nic.in/index.html, the official website of National Task Force on Information Technology and Software Development, Government of India.

http://www.azimpremjifoundation.org/home.html, website of Aziz Premji Foundation.

http://www.stpi.in/ (the official website of STPI).

http://www.microsoft.com/billgates/speeches/2000/10-18 digitaldividends.asp, Bill Gate's Speech in a Seminar on Digital Divide.

http://apit.ap.gov.in/index.php/e-gov/e-gov-projects, Official website of Information Technology and Communications Department, Government of Andhra Pradesh.

http://www.apinvest.co.in/inside/ict_policy_2010_15.pdf, *Press Release on ICT Policy 2010-2015*, Information Technology and Communications Department, Government of Andhra Pradesh.

http://tier.cs.berkeley.edu/docs/Renee-ppp-ictd2007.pdf, Reene Kurian and Isha Ray, "Public-Private Partnerships and Information Technology for Development in India", *Proceedings of the 2nd IEEE/ACM International Conference ICTD 2007.*

http://www.bangaloreitbt.in/informationtechnology.html, *IT Policy*, Official website of Department of IT, BT and S&T, Government of Karnataka.

http://www.iitk.ac.in/ (IIT Kanpur official website).

www.naascom.in (NASSCOM official website).

http://www.moneycontrol.com/news/business/nasscom-seeks-two-year-extensionstpi-scheme_444504.html (NASSCOM).

China Daily, 27 June 2009, http://www.chinadaily.com.cn/bizchina/2009-06/27/content_8329730.htm

China Economic Net, http://en.ce.cn/Insight/201104/02/t20110402_22343698.shtml

http://www.nsf.gov/statistics/nsf07319/content.cfm?pub_id=1874&id=7, "Asia's Rising Science and Technology Strength: Comparative Indicators for Asia, the European Union, and the United States", National Science Foundation, National Centre for Science and Engineering Statistics.